THEATRES & AUDITORIUMS

HAROLD BURRIS-MEYER & EDWARD C. COLE

THEATRES
&
AUDITORIUMS

PROGRESSIVE ARCHITECTURE LIBRARY

REINHOLD
330 WEST 42ND STREET, NEW YORK, U.S.A.

Printed in U.S.A. by The Haddon Craftsmen, Inc.

table of contents

foreword

This book was undertaken in 1938 when we finished work on SCENERY FOR THE THEATRE. The long period of gestation is not entirely attributable to the war. To derive plan from the analysis of theatrical function, requires first the reduction of function to terms of time and physical dimension. Data of this sort were almost completely lacking. There were no accurate studies of audience activity or time studies of even the most routine aspects of producing or presenting a show. It has been necessary to establish by experiment many items which have a determining effect on theatre structure and to study specifications of many theatres here and abroad in connection with the efficiency and effectiveness with which productions are mounted in them.

This book treats auditoriums almost exclusively as parts of theatres. This treatment is warranted on the ground that an auditorium almost never succeeds in remaining only an auditorium. Sooner or later somebody uses it for a theatre. Its efficiency as a theatre is very often the measure of its usefulness, for the purely auditorium function will seldom pay for or support a building.

We have avoided setting up detailed and precise specifications for a good theatre. We have however endeavored to set forth the methods by which specifications may be developed, and have listed essential considerations, to the end that no important aspect of planning any element of the theatre shall be slighted.

We have been encouraged in this work by the everready counsel and assistance of the people of theatre, of our clients, of architects, and the people of many crafts and professions concerned with theatre building and operation, and by Jeff Livingstone who is the kind of an editor every author wants to work with. We acknowledge in particular the constant affection, encouragement and patience of our wives, Alice Cole and Anita Burris-Meyer.

Individuals and organizations who furnished illustrations or data and permitted us to use them, whose help is hereby gratefully acknowledged include: Robert E. Costello, Jr., who has capably set forth in pen and ink sketches the basic structural elements of the theatre, but whose spelling of *procenium* must not be accepted as a *prescedent*; American School and University; American Seating Company; Architectural Record; W. E. Backus; John Beaumont; Warner Bentley; Clinton T. Bissell; Fanny Browne; Jean Buhler; Curtis Canfield; Century Lighting, Inc.; The City Record of the City of New York; J. R. Clancy, Inc.; Peggy Clark; Celine Cobb; The Celotex Corporation; Cheryl Crawford; G. S. Eyssell; Rudolf Frankel, F.R.I.B.A.; Lewis S. Goodfriend; Alberta Gordon; Samuel Gottscho; B. H. Griffin; Frank Gruys; Elizabeth Harris; Cyril M.

Harris; George C. Izenour; John D. Jones; Stephen G. Kelley; Enid Klauber; Kliegl Brothers; Herbert Kliegl; Vern O. Knudsen; Helge Kokeritz; Edward Kook; Donald Kurtis; Jens Frederick Larson; J. D. Logsdon; Frank Lopez; Fred Lynch; Stanley R. McCandless; Vincent Mallory; The Malmö Municipal Theatre; Peggy Meyers; Jo Mielziner; The National Board of Fire Underwriters; Otto Niederer; George Nixon; Donald Oenslager; Stamo Papadaki; W. L. Pereira; Lawrence B. Perkins; George H. Quimby; Harry Robin; Eero Saarinen; Hale J. Sabine; Edward Serlin; Roger L. Simons; Harvey Smith; The Stevens Theatre; Edward D. Stone; C. E. Tompkins; Joseph Vasconcellos; Ralph Walker; Fred Weaver; The Yale Department of Drama; Panos Yeannakis.

1: existing conditions

Definition

The desire of people to witness performances by other people appears to be so deeply rooted in the human spirit as to be instinctive. Theatre is the gathering together of a group of people to witness a planned performance. It is one of the major modes of diversion of modern civilization. It is materially non-productive, its values being entirely spiritual and cultural.

The building of theatres, from the fifth century B.C. to the present, has been the provision of the essential physical equipment for the gratification of the playgoing urge. The planning and building of modern theatres, and the modernization of old ones, is the use of current materials, methods, and practices to keep that equipment up to date.

Types of theatrical entertainment have varied in the last twenty-five centuries from Dionysian revel to cinema. Some productions of almost every epoch have the timeless and universal significance necessary to draw audiences today. Audiences have varied no less widely than the productions. They have supported the court masque and the productions of the brothers Minsky. Their demands vary as do the material equipment, economic aspects, modes, manners, customs, and spiritual concepts of human living. Most American theatres open now in mid-twentieth century were designed in, or to the standards of, an earlier period.

Basic Requirements

The audience comes to see the show and to hear the show. It wants a maximum of comfort, a minimum of distraction, and complete safety.

The producer wants facilities for preparing the show, good conditions of performance, efficient production organization and machinery; in short, a fair showing at low cost. (Cost to a producer must be taken as all-inclusive; non-commercial producers must think of labor as part of their costs, even when it is volunteer and does not show on the books.)

Theatre artists (playwrights, composers, directors, actors, musicians and designers) want adequate facilities for the achievement of their theatrical projects.

This chapter undertakes to list types of production, describe existing theatre structures, and indicate wherein and why structures impose unwarranted limitations on production.

	Subject Matter	Visual Components	Auditory Components
Pageant	Incidents from history or local folk lore having historical or religious appeal assembled into a plow boy's epic. Story over-simplified, direct, romanticized, salutes a glorious past, promises paradise as a just reward for something or other. No controversial matter included.	Realistic dramatic episodes acted or mimed. Period costumes. Mass movement. Ballet, folk dances. Marches. Permanent decorative backgrounds with movable scenic pieces. Scenery simple, suggestive rather than closely representational. Local geographic features included. Stage machinery in operation. Elaborate lighting. Steam and water curtains. Pyrotechnics. Display of technical virtuosity. Individual performer counts for little.	Music: symphonic, organ, choral. Synthesized descriptive score. Speech: narrator's, principals'. Speech dubbed on pantomime scenes. Incidental sounds, descriptive effects. All sound amplified. Level often too high for comfort. Reproduction often less natural than in motion pictures.
Grand Opera	Classic tragedy, folk lore, sagas, mythological tales, superheated passion, men vs. gods. As currently produced subject and story are of little importance.	Elaborate conventionalized pantomime by principals. Elaborate costumes, symbolic color. Occasional mass movement by chorus and ballet. Monumental settings (Valhalla, the bottom of the Rhine). Elaborate lighting. Technical tricks: appearances, magic fire, etc.	The world's best music sung by the most accomplished artists, accompanied by thoroughly competent orchestra and chorus. Soloists sing everything at relatively high intensity to achieve audibility and dominate orchestra.
Presentation	A simple theme or concept (a popular song, a holiday, a fad) made the basis for striking show. No story or plot continuity. Intellectual and emotional level set by crowd for which show is devised.	Solo performers, singing and dancing choruses, ballet. Flashy revelatory costumes. Large, simple, colorful backgrounds, little representational scenery. Movement of scenic elements and stage machinery (revolving stage, elevator, etc.). Spectacular lighting. Projected backgrounds. Effects using gauzes, translucencies, complementary colors, ultraviolet light. Follow spots on solo performers.	Music, (vocal, choral, instrumental, organ, orchestral): popular classics, current song hits adapted and arranged to fit the show. Little or no original composition. High standard of excellence for performers. Nevertheless, quantity dominates quality. Styled to the taste of the crowd. All music amplified. Dynamic range better than opera.
Vaudeville-Revue	Vaudeville: Assorted songs, dances, dramatic episodes, blackouts, trained animals, acrobats, bell-ringers, jugglers, magicians, ventriloquists, mind-readers, musicians, clowns; in fact any feat or phenomenon of man or beasts (not excluding elephants) which can be gotten onto a stage and which is calculated to have sufficient audience appeal through uniqueness, novelty, skill, virtuosity, renown or notoriety. Revue: same material assembled about a central theme or idea, produced for a run, trouped as a unit.	Performers principal visual element. Costumes bright. Scenic background unimportant except as it contributes necessary paraphernalia or adds flash to act. Lighting conventional: follow spots on principals: no illusion of time or place. All scenic elements combine to center attention on performer. Revue: Design unity sometimes runs through whole production. Much more elaborate and effective setting than in vaudeville.	Speech and music. Not subtle, high in intensity, aimed at the gallery. Popular and classical songs, instrumental and orchestral numbers. Revue has musical unity and balance.

Routine	Audience	Comment
One or two a day, generally long. Sunday shows where permitted. Realistic episodes connected by spoken narrative. Dance, march, choral, orchestral interludes. Single intermission. Closely integrated carefully timed performance. High production costs.	Same as country fair. Pageant is the only type of live show many ever see. Best mannered audience in the show business. Subject matter principal attraction: production next. Ball park system of seating. Considerable advance sale. Admission low.	Always good for a season when there is an event or institution which can generate enough interest to draw an audience. More truly the people's theatre than any other dramatic form.
8 a week in repertory. Show, 2 to 5 acts or two short operas on one bill. Long performance. Long intermissions to shift scenes usually set full stage. Despite repertory organization, rehearsals slighted to save costs which are excessive. Performance often slipshod in all save rendition of songs. Names in cast count.	Gallery and standing room: Music lovers. Boxes: The guests of patrons. Sometimes patrons. Orchestra: Average theatre goers with a special liking for music, averaging about 62 years of age. Large potential audiences alienated by shabby productions and high prices. Boxholders' manners worst in show business. Admission high.	Democratization of opera under way in America. Dramatization of plot started by Herbert Graf. Mass attendance at conventional repertoire questionable, since the subject matter of most operas is so far removed from American cultural heritage. Present efforts to revitalize opera handicapped by stuffy tradition and record of dullness.
Continuous: five-a-day, seven days a week. 20 to 40 minutes alternating with feature motion picture. New show each week using same company. 5 to 8 numbers alternating shallow and deep. No pause between numbers. Smooth well-timed performance. Established weekly routine tends to set pattern of the show and force acceptance of the quick rather than the best effect. High operating cost. Efficient production and permanent company keep production costs reasonable.	John Q. Public (urban) seeking surcease from routine which includes ledger or stamping press and flat in Flushing. His mental and physical state and intellectual capacity prescribe that the show shall be big, beautiful, non-controversial, and as pure as the radio, that sudden disturbing influences such as Moussorgsky be excluded and that the theatre exude the rich luxuriousness of a rajah's palace. The admission is low, the house is big, so he can attend en masse.	Form very popular in 1920s. Exists now only in large cities. May recover lost ground as neighborhood houses and television supply the demand for straight movies and operators of motion picture palaces need additional attraction.
Vaudeville: Two-a-day to five-a-day (continuous cycle: noon to midnight). 8 to 15 acts per performance. Each act 10 to 15 minutes long. Acts arranged in ascending entertainment value with preferred spot next to closing. Acts alternate full stage and shallow to facilitate changes. Changes fast, covered by music from pit orchestra. Revue: Eight a week, otherwise similar to vaudeville. Production costs vary widely from peanuts up.	Vaudeville: The late George V, Judy O'Grady and a large coterie of people who prefer vaudeville to any other type of theatrical performance. Vaudeville addicts had attendance habits more thoroughly ingrained than any other audience. Admission between legitimate and presentation which has in part succeeded it. Revue: Audience and admission same as for musical comedy.	Vaudeville is too ancient a form and has survived too many vicissitudes to justify fear that its present eclipse is permanent. Simple motion picture routine and low film costs have induced managers to abandon it. Ominously falling motion picture attendance now apparent, may bring it back. Revue: Similar in genre to vaudeville. Overworking of the principals constitutes a severe handicap and makes for a dull final half-hour.

(Continued)

	Subject Matter	Visual Components	Auditory Components
Operetta-Musical Comedy	Line of demarcation between types not clear. Reasonably simple story. Framework garnished with music and dancing. Book generally satirizes some current situation of general interest. Boy meets girl in fanciful rather than realistic surroundings. Dramatic type: generally farce.	Actor's business realistic or appropriate to script: conventionalized for musical numbers and dancing. Elaborate costumes harmoniously keyed to color scheme of the production. Scenery usually functional, decorative, stylized rather than realistic. Machinery for quick change and for effect. Lighting arbitrary and for novelty and visibility rather than for conformity with dramatic necessities. New production forms and techniques readily adopted. Pleasant eye entertainment.	Auditory component given appropriate importance relative to visual as dictated by necessity for achieving maximum total effect. Semi-classical and popular music (sweet, hot, and blue), sung by principals, occasionally with chorus and usually with pit orchestra accompaniment. Subject matter and personality of singer often more important than musical excellence. Noisy entr'acte overture, and covering pieces played by pit orchestra (about 20 pieces). Spoken dialogue between songs. Ear entertainment.
Legitimate Drama	Plays. Live shows employing all dramaturgical, artistic, and technical devices to persuade the audience to suspend disbelief and credit the characters and the story as presented.	The actor. Human scale used for all elements of production. Business realistic or in conformity with any other stylistic idiom. Costume appropriate to the character, situation, and production style. Visual elements of the production coordinated to achieve maximum dramatic impact. Lighting in conformity with style of production; provides visibility sometimes greater than that in nature.	Human voice in speech. Incidental sound to indicate locale, advance plot, create and sustain atmosphere and mood. Overture and entr'acte music from orchestra (by no means universal). Vocal, instrumental or reproduced music as required within the play.
Motion Pictures	Original screen plays. Adaptations from plays, short stories, novels, musicals, comic strips, and radio programs to the celluloid medium changed in conformity with intellectual and artistic limitations of the producers to what they think is palatable to an audience. Boy meets girl, etc., ad infinitum. Current events and animated cartoons.	Rectangular screen on which are projected moving images in black and white or in color of anything which can be photographed. The 18 x 24 face that launched (or sank) a thousand ships. Infinite variety (giants to dwarfs, planets to micro-organisms, moving glacier to humming bird's wing).	Reproduced sound of anything that can be got onto a sound track and off through a loudspeaker. Useful dynamic range: about 35 db; frequency: 60 to 8,000 at best. Result, realism seldom achieved with equipment now in use.
Burlesque, Dance, Concert, Puppets, Cabaret	Of the forms not covered in the table, burlesque and puppets are so simple in routine as to impose very few demands upon the structure. They can be presented in any theatre which can house legitimate drama and in most motion picture houses except those with no stage whatever or with a reverse	floor slope. Dance would show best in a theatre designed expressly for it. It is not, however, a popular enough form to warrant the structure and must therefore be performed in theatres intended for other uses. Concert halls can be steadily used as such only in the largest cities. Dance recitals and	

Routine	Audience	Comment
Eight-a-week. Six evenings. Matinees Wednesday or Thursday and Saturday. Combination production. Running time about two and a half hours. Conventionally two, at most three acts. Few but elaborate sets. Stage machinery used in view of audience for novelty. All changes except act change covered by music or singles in one. Star often more important than show. Production costs high.	Operetta: The whole family, particularly in the case of Gilbert and Sullivan. Musical comedy: downstairs, the tired business man, the hostess and her party, the deb and her boy friend. Upstairs: The clerk and his date, the suburbanite and his wife, Tilly and the girls (with chocolates at matinees). The holiday spirit is to be found in the audience at the musical show more than in any other audience except at circuses. Admission high: only slightly below opera.	Operetta very durable, good for revival as long as grand opera. Popularity of chamber opera with components similar to those of operetta, increasing. Musical comedy perishable but source of songs with lasting popularity. Both forms good all-season entertainment.
Same as operetta and musical comedy. Considerable variation in structure from no intermission (HOTEL UNIVERSE) to 52 scenes (GÖTZ VON BERLICHINGEN). Performance length varies from one hour (THE EMPEROR JONES), usually played with a curtain raiser, to three evenings (MOURNING BECOMES ELECTRA). Production combines generally most skillful planning and direction and most painstaking rehearsals of any popular entertainment form resulting generally in most finished performance and best obtainable interpretation of playwright's script.	People with sufficient culture to appreciate a conventionalized and aesthetic form of entertainment. As the general cultural level rises, audiences for legitimate drama increase. Small house and high production costs keep admission scale above that of motion pictures.	Legitimate drama is best dramatic medium for revealing character or constructing plot. It is the freest and most flexible form in the theatre, and therefore the try-out ground for new ideas, concepts and techniques. The legitimate theatre is always reported to be on the verge of total and final collapse, and probably will be for another twenty-five centuries or so.
As many shows per day as can be run profitably. Picture Palace: Feature, shorts (travel, cartoon, one-reel dramatic sketch, etc.), news, trailers. Total show time two hours. Ten a.m. to midnight seven days a week. Five-minute intermission between shows covered by recorded music or the mighty organ. Neighborhood: 1:30 to midnight or three a day. Show changed twice or three times weekly. Second feature takes place of news and shorts. Intimate: Single feature plus news. News Reel: One-hour show, news, shorts, and cartoons.	The American people. Frequency of individual attendance ranges from habitual addiction to occasional patronage of selected programs. Little attention given to announced starting times; hence, continuous flow of audience with some concentration in early afternoon, late afternoon, early evening and late evening. Admission low.	Since 1920 the most popular type of theatrical production. Manifestation in theatre of American mass production, embodying duplication, ease of distribution, standardization, low unit cost. Simple mechanized presentation makes the type easily adaptable to widely varying circumstances, from motion picture palace (originally a presentation house), to drive-in theatre (in structure only a terraced parking lot with picnic facilities). Basically simple conditions of presentation have been adequately refined by engineers and architects.

puppet shows can take place in a living room if it is big enough. The cabaret show is essentially a tabloid revue: minimum scenery, maximum flesh, bright costumes and lights, high intensity sound. While demanding for best results a highly specialized plant, it is usually to be found in a structure originally built for some other use. Basically it needs provision for lights, dressing rooms, intimate contact between performers and audience: raised stage floor, semi-circular apron extending into the house. Comfortable eating arrangements and a good chef are non-architectural requisites of a successful cabaret.

Multiple Uses of the Theatre

Theatres can also be and are used for church services, town meetings, and assemblages of all sorts. The motion picture palace was yesterday's presentation house and may well be the vaudeville or opera house of tomorrow. The theatre which houses opera, concert, and ballet is economically sounder than a theatre limited to any single type of show. The theatre planned for motion pictures will have to accommodate a live show sometimes. The legitimate theatre will have to show motion pictures if only as a part of a legitimate production. It is proverbial that in a capitalistic society the new owner of a building tries to make money with it in a way different from that of the previous owner who lost money. To limit architecturally the uses of the theatre is to reduce its potential income and shorten its useful life. To provide for multiple uses of the theatre, planning must be based on an analysis of attendance and performance of each type of production to be housed.

Changing Demands on Theatre Buildings

Theatrical forms, particularly in live shows, vary so widely that it is impossible to predict trends with accuracy for even a decade. Influences now apparent as they apply to the theatre building seem to be:

1. Liberation of the performance from the proscenium arch. Exponents call attention to the distracting influence of ornate, badly lighted proscenium arches and the separation of audience and performance.
2. Architectural contact between stage and auditorium by means of steps, ramps, large aprons, etc. Devices for providing such contact can be made flexible. If permanent they limit the use of the theatre.
3. Arena performance in which the audience surrounds a central acting area.
4. Abstractionism in scenery. In the belief that each member of the audience can supply for himself imaginatively the best surroundings of the dramatic action, attempts have been made either to eliminate scenery altogether, to strip it of limiting detail, or to reduce scenery to the elements of pure design.
5. Multiplication of scenery. Episodic plays mirror the increasingly peripatetic nature of human living which demands frequent change of locale. Unlike the foregoing trends, this one demands not less but more scenery, and with it greater stage facilities for changing scenes.
6. Reactionary trends. Currently noticeable are two separate and allied tendencies, both revolting from the recent strong realism of drama and theatre. The one calls for a return of poetry and romance to the theatre. The other demands a recognition of the fact that theatre is theatre, that it is not real, cannot be real, and to be most effective must be frankly artificial, and theatrically conventional, calling a stage a stage. These tendencies are opposed to the foregoing because they demand stage and theatrical facilities of an established kind: painted scenery, wings, borders and backdrops, in fact such scenery as can most easily be handled on our somewhat archaic present day stages.

Which of these trends, opposed as they are one to another, will dominate the future theatre? In the opinion of the authors: *none*. The theatre as an art form is broad enough to encompass and nurture them all. The theatre as an architectural form must be capable of housing them all. Well designed theatres have successfully housed all the changing forms of production in the past.

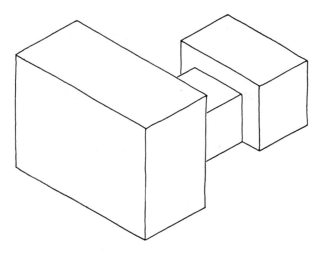

The basic form of the theatre is derived from an analysis of its function. The function has three parts: to accommodate the performance, to accommodate the audience, and to bring the two together. The performance is accommodated in the stage block (left), the audience is accommodated in the house block (center) and the front house block (right).

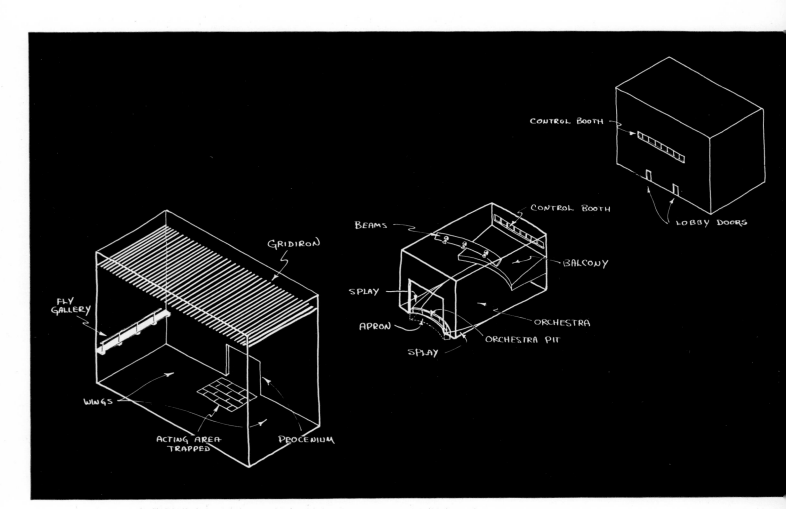

This exploded view of the three block divisions of the theatre shows principal structural elements.

The production types listed in the foregoing table make specific demands upon theatres. These demands are often inadequately, inefficiently or uneconomically met, as the analysis of existing theatre types which follows will indicate. This situation often makes it necessary to emasculate productions in order to get them into available theatres, and denies to a large portion of the public the kind of theatrical productions it could and would support.

Opera House

The opera house is the oldest, and was, until the advent of the motion picture palace, the largest theatre in the community. Its shortcomings are primarily due to antiquity. The traditional horse shoe plan and many balconies entail bad sight lines. Public rooms are adequate, ventilation an afterthought, acoustics accidental, gallery seats crowded. The stage is large enough to accommodate more than one production in repertory. Stage equipment is antique and inefficient.

The opera house was a good theatre in the era of gas lights and wing-and-border sets. Changed standards of audience comfort, and changed production techniques have outmoded both house and stage. Modern opera houses are, in most cases, patterned so closely on their antique equivalents that despite improved chairs and machinery they are unsuited to the demands of modern operatic production and are highly inefficient.

Inefficient structures resulting in high operating costs have been a contributing factor to the disappearance of resident opera companies in America. Conversely, productions whose budgets are burdened with excessive technical charges suffer from lack of rehearsals, and substandard visual production (scenery, costumes, lighting, stage direction) to the point that the music alone must carry the show and attract the audiences. The serious opera audience is almost entirely limited to music lovers. Theatre lovers stay away by the thousands.

The ironical result is that the Metropolitan Opera Company runs a very short season and loses money, travelling opera companies play in antiquated opera houses or in motion picture presentation houses, and old opera houses now serve for motion pictures or touring legitimate productions.

Commercial Legitimate Theatre

The commercial legitimate theatre offers more discomfort per dollar of admission than any other theatre. From about 30% of the seats it is impossible to see the whole show. Seats are cramped, the atmosphere is stifling in the house, foul in the jammed public rooms. Acoustic conditions are generally bad, varying with the size of the audience.

The stage is as small and ill equipped as it can be and still find a play willing to use it. It is unsuited to economical handling of more than single set shows. Multi-set shows often call for extreme ingenuity to get them into the stage house and shift them when they are there. Lighting equipment and all stage machinery except simple rigging must be brought in with the show. Dressing rooms are stacked about with no thought of the actor's comfort.

The commercial theatre was built as a speculative real estate enterprise during boom times. It was planned to squeeze the maximum number of income-producing seats into the minimum ground space. The builder was not a showman. Audience comfort and production efficiency were not a major concern to him as long as there were more shows seeking theatres than there were theatres to house them. Furthermore, he got his return from the box office gross, not the net.

Theatre inefficiency breeds high production cost which necessitates high ticket prices. This keeps people at home beside the radio. Half of the legitimate theatres have disappeared in the last twenty years. Many theatres on the road have been torn down; the touring show often has to play the Masonic Temple, the high school auditorium, the municipal arena or the motion picture palace, all less suitable than the old theatres. Where no theatre remains, thousands of customers do without playgoing and the theatre loses considerable potential income.

There are more performances of plays in high school auditoriums in a year than there are in any other single type of theatre. Such auditoriums vary widely in size and equipment. Their structural faults are so general and varied, irrespective of construction date, as to make one believe that the American educational system has been the victim of a gigantic swindle. Audience comfort is less than in the standard commercial theatre. Seats are hard and cramped, floors are often flat. Sight lines are usually very bad. Booming echoes lurk in nests of architectural gingerbread. The school ventilation system is often shut off at night when the play takes place. Access from the street is often difficult (three flights up). Corridors are neither designed nor furnished to serve as substitute for non-existent public rooms. Lavatories are likely to be in another wing of the building and locked.

The stage, called the platform, merits the title. It lacks wing space, depth, flying facilities, and has a hardwood floor. If there are shops, access to them is difficult. A single box set with no upstage windows is all that can be gotten on the stage.

Designers of high school auditoriums have apparently worked under the illusions that: 1. professional (commercial) theatres are good theatres; 2. amateurs can do with poorer facilities than professionals need.

The high school theatre usually costs as much to build as does a good theatre of the same seating capacity—often more. But this is not the only respect in which a badly planned theatre proves costly to the community. The educational program is vitiated; half a theatre is as bad pedagogically as half a play. Plays produced under limitations are shabby, invite a patronizing attitude on the part of the audience, do not draw enough paying customers. The local community amateur producing group cannot use the theatre. Traveling professional companies cannot rent the theatre, and often therefore cannot play the town.

University and college theatres suffer from the same limitations as those which apply to high school theatres save that there are more exceptions to the rule. Many are very bad indeed. Buildings designed principally for theatrical productions have been and are being built at an increasing number of colleges: some of them are good. Unfortunately, however, newness is no measure of excellence and almost all fall short of optimum specifications in a number of important respects.

Non-Commercial Theatre: High School

Non-Commercial Theatre: College and University

Arts are best taught under circumstances appropriate to artistic production and understanding. Despite this fact, theatrical plants in colleges have usually been designed first for non-theatrical purposes: the student assembly, concerts, lectures, commencement exercises. When theatrical productions have been envisioned as a primary purpose, specifications have often been drawn by persons either unfamiliar with the processes of production, or, and worse, obsessed with a single style of production, as a result of which, productions in that style can be adequately mounted but all others suffer. Donors of buildings often impose limitations on theatre plans by insisting on the incorporation of some pet features. Persons responsible for campus layout may prescribe limiting dimensions or architectural style to assure consistency in campus appearance. Imposition of limitations in response to non-theatrical considerations violates the principle of designing an educational institution for educational purposes.

**Non-Commercial Theatre:
Community**

The community group begins by presenting plays in any rentable space big enough to allow partitioning off one end for stage and placing folding chairs borrowed from the local undertaker in the remaining space. It progresses to the so-called stage of a social club, town hall, or high school. It prospers and builds or remodels an existing structure and proudly calls it a theatre. Theatres that were not built new as such, have been converted from all manner of buildings: churches, barns, schools, factories, fire-houses, a laundry, a morgue, a speak-easy (remember?). One community theatre is subsidized by its city government. One community theatre was built by its city government particularly to house the community players. Federal agencies assisted in the construction of at least two theatres. One community theatre produces plays in the local high school auditorium, which was designed to specifications drawn by the community theatre. Private philanthropies have helped several organizations to build their theatres.

Insofar as the community theatre has control over the planning of its plant, there is an effort to provide for maximum audience comfort and production efficiency within the limits of the building budget. Conditions are, however, generally primitive, due partly to limited funds and partly to the fact that amateurs, being familiar only with restricted producing conditions, don't know how to plan a theatre when they have the funds available.

**Motion Picture Palace and
Presentation Theatre**

The difference between the motion picture palace and the presentation house is that the latter puts on a stage show while the former does not. The palace usually has at least a rudimentary stage and changes categories on occasion. The most recent structures in these categories set the standard for audience comfort in all respects save horizontal sight lines. Though acoustics be bad, intelligibility is assured through sound reenforcement. Stages are usually too shallow for effective use of projected scenery and too narrow for live storage of large rolling units. Stage equipment and permanently installed lighting equipment are usually adequate for the demands of presentation programs.

Luxury is one of the principal commodities on sale at the box office. Production facilities have been consciously somewhat limited in favor of high seating capacity.

High operating costs make the life of the motion picture palace or presentation house precarious. Luxurious, easily accessible neighborhood houses can take away its business. At least one palace, a consistent money maker itself, is kept dark because the chain owning it shows a higher district net profit with the palace closed than with it open. And while the palace or presentation house can and occasionally does mount productions for which it was not designed (road shows, opera), it does so only inefficiently.

Intimate Motion Picture Theatre

The intimate motion picture house is a small theatre generally devoted to the running of exceptional pictures with intelligentsia appeal or news reels and shorts. The most recent news reel theatres are the best of the type. They offer unsurpassed facilities for audience comfort even to coffee and cigarettes. They are efficient. Many use entrance turnstiles to simplify audience handling. A number have very good sight lines.

Neighborhood Motion Picture Theatre

The largest and fastest growing single type of indoor motion picture theatre is the neighborhood movie house which is found principally in suburbs and small communities. It is structurally nothing more than a hall with a sloped floor, a screen and a projection booth, and a ticket office. Many structures of this type were built in the days of the silent motion picture.

New neighborhood houses seating 800 to 1200 are structurally as simple as their predecessors but are planned to assure high quality performance and audience comfort. Like the intimate motion picture house they are usually useless for anything but projected shows.

Motion picture houses of all types often provide more audience comfort and operating efficiency than opera house or commercial legitimate or musical houses because: 1. The exhibitor in most instances stages his own presentation shows and, if an independent, selects pictures himself. If the theatre is part of a chain, the same conditions are maintained save that most productions originally come from the same studio. The houses are owner-built and owner-operated, so that the owner profits directly from efficiency of operation. He is concerned with the net, not the gross income as is the owner of the legitimate theatre. 2. Moreover he sells luxury. He deliberately plans to make his theatre a pleasanter place than the homes from which most of the members of the audience come.

The results of this situation are history. One can go to a motion picture theatre cheaply and relax or to a legitimate theatre, expensively and suffer. It takes a very good legitimate production to be worth the double difference. The motion picture theatre gets the business. Under present conditions it deserves it.

Summer Theatre

The summer theatre occupies random accommodations usually adapted from other uses. There are exceptions, notably the summer theatre at Cain Park, Cleveland Heights, Ohio, which uses a large and well-equipped outdoor theatre especially designed for summer theatre productions; the Roanoke Pageant using an outdoor plant designed for that production; Jones Beach, Robin Hood Dell, and the St. Louis Municipal Opera; all housed in reasonably adequate outdoor plants. Aquacades and other similar summer spectacles generally use plants designed for those productions only. Some summer theatres such as the Ogunquit Playhouse, the Berkshire Musical Festival Theatre, and the Deertrees Theatre use plants designed specifically as summer theatres. These instances are exceptions, however. Summer companies playing in the town hall at Cohasset, Mass., in the motion picture house at Maplewood, N. J., and in the barn at Suffern, N. Y., are much more typical. In most cases the summer theatre has to make money if it is to continue in operation. It keeps down expenses by severely limiting production costs other than stars' salaries. The average provision for audience comfort in the summer theatre is inadequate. The parking lot is usually present but notable for poison ivy and mud. The stage and its equipment are usually makeshift and inadequate.

Theatre Facilities in Buildings Primarily for Other Uses

Amateur theatricals are ubiquitous and because they are the incubators of future performing and producing talent, as well as a popular social activity, they deserve adequate facilities. A large percentage of amateur productions are presented in buildings which are intended for all kinds of social and recreational activity, in situations the economic and social nature of which precludes the possibility or even the necessity of a theatre. If an organization or community can afford only a rudimentary building as a general social and recreational center, then that building must be designed to serve all purposes for which it is intended. If the hall must be used for dancing, basketball, Girl Scouts, bingo, bridge, and the harvest supper, it is unreasonable to expect that it should have a sloping floor and fixed theatre seats. But too frequently in planning such a building those provisions for theatrical production which might be incorporated in it for the general benefit of its theatrical users are either omitted, slighted, or wrongly planned. Inclusion of well-planned minimal provisions for good seeing and hearing, for backstage preparation and installation, for dressing and make-up, and for lighting, increases the usefulness of a social hall or community center beyond the relative cost of the facilities thus provided.

Summary

The foregoing survey serves to show that current theatres with exceptions as noted fail to provide for audience comfort or operating efficiency, are seldom suited to more than one type of production, and in too many cases cannot earn their upkeep.

Portents

The public, the producers, and the theatre owners are dissatisfied with this state of affairs, as evidenced by the following:

1. New York City has adopted a building code which omits income limiting restrictions under which all current opera, commercial, and most motion picture houses in the city were built.

2. Educators have begun to recognize the need for theatres in educational institutions which shall be capable of mounting any production adequately, and for classrooms, laboratories, shops for the study and practice of the arts, crafts, and techniques of dramatic production.

3. Architectural competitions, projects, and exhibitions have featured theatre designs in increasing numbers during the past ten years.

4. College theatres are being built in increasing number each year; the construction of several of them was prevented by the war but plans are already being taken down and reviewed.

The Building Code of the City of New York offers such possibilities for the improved design of theatres that it merits further consideration.

All of the existing commercial theatres, for legitimate and musical production, and many for motion pictures, whether in or out of New York, were built according to the dictates of municipal building codes which are now outmoded and in some cities, especially New York, superseded. Those theatres were limited by law to little more than one source of revenue, the sale of theatre tickets, because rigid limitations were placed upon the use of the buildings or parts of the buildings. The revised building code of New York City, adopted January 1, 1938, allows the construction of theatres in buildings from which other incomes may be derived, especially from rentals of street-front stores, and offices and apartments over the lobbies and auditoriums. Building over the stage is rightly prohibited. It is now possible, in New York, to free the theatre from the burden of defraying all cost of land and building, before showing a profit, and to charge some of that cost to other parts of the building. This means that the old need of getting the maximum number of seats onto and above the minimum amount of land no longer exists. It is economically sound to provide comfortable seat spacing, wide aisles, commodious and hospitable lobbies and lounges, and large, well-arranged and well-equipped stages. It is possible to build buildings containing theatres in which the carrying charges of the theatres are low enough to allow shows other than smash hits to meet expenses, make a profit, and enjoy reasonable runs of production. It is even possible that the prices of seats may be reduced to the level at which, as the Federal Theatre in New York demonstrated, new thousands of patrons are attracted to the theatre.

So far it is apparent then that: 1. There is a need for good theatres. 2. There is a demand for them. 3. Legal restrictions to their erection have been removed. 4. New theatres are being designed and 5. Built. It would seem then that all is well and that time and financial backing will give this country what it needs in the theatre. Unfortunately this is not the case, for a new theatre is not necessarily a good theatre; in fact it can easily be and often is a very bad theatre.

This deplorable circumstance arises out of the highly specialized nature of the theatre plant. The plant is, in fact, to a large extent, a machine and those who do not actually operate it cannot be expected to know its structural requisites. In any case the architect is, to use vernacular, on the spot.

The plan of any modern building depends on a knowledge of the purposes for which it is to be built. An architect designs a factory only after consulting freely with his client regarding the processes of manufacture to be housed; he does not design a residence without first studying at length the composition, personalities, habits, and circumstances of the family; nor does he design a church without knowing thoroughly the services, rites, and ceremonies to be celebrated therein. He cannot succeed in designing a theatre unless he obtains from some source information regarding the uses of the building.

In the case of the factory, residence, and church, the architect can get the necessary particular information directly from his client. In the case of the theatre this is not possible. In most instances of

Building Codes

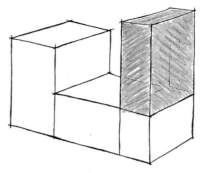

Prior to January 1, 1938, building for income-producing non-theatrical occupancy was limited to the space above the front house block.

Now building for such occupancy may be above and below both the house and the front house block. Relative income-producing cubage is indicated by shading.

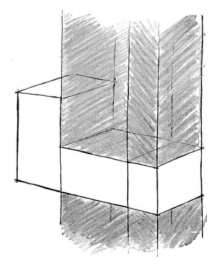

The Architect's Problem

theatre planning, the people who are in the position of client to the theatre architect do not know.

The Client's Problem

As has been pointed out, the commercial theatre owner is not a showman. Operating efficiency does not concern him since his income is based on gross receipts rather than net profit. He runs a boarding house for shows, not a theatre.

The aegis of theatre building in the field of education is variously located depending upon the type of institution. A board of trustees, a generous alumnus, president, general faculty, committee on policy, building committee, drama faculty, municipal school board, the state board of education, the legislature's committee on education, the legislature as a whole and the governor, may each exercise some degree of authority over the architect. To these may be added, if a federal contribution is received, officials and bureaus of the federal government up to and even including the latest equivalent of the administrator of public works. In this line-up there is a great scarcity of comprehension as to what goes on beyond the footlights of a theatre. This is fitting, proper, and condonable if those uncomprehending people refrain from making decisions which should be based solely and essentially upon knowledge of the theatre's arts, crafts, and methods.

The fact that the client often does not know enough about the theatre to be of any help to the architect does not prevent him from insisting on certain features toward which he has a predisposition: a fly loft only 30′ high to keep the outside appearance of the building consistent with something or other; a green room where wing space ought to be; an organ console fixed in position on stage; organ pipes in the fly loft.

The architect, unable to get information from his client or worse, saddled with requirements which are patently wrong, is flung on his own resources. Architects who have had a chance to familiarize themselves with the particular group of conditions and specified requirements which govern the planning of a theatre are very few. Compared with the planning of residential, commercial, or industrial buildings, the planning of a theatre or even of a building containing auditorium and stage is a rare commission to the average practicing architect. The architect must live by work other than the designing of theatres; it is little wonder that he gives his attention to residential, commercial, and industrial building problems, and leaves a study of theatres until he is actually commissioned to plan one.

If, as and when this occurs, however, he finds that there is singularly little organized information available and that existing publications are either out-moded, limited in scope, or qualitative rather than quantitative in precept. Such statements as "acoustics satisfactory" and "adequate stage" are of little help to an architect who is trying to discover what produces satisfactory acoustics and how big the stage must be for his particular set of circumstances. An analysis of the books and articles on theatre planning by some twenty writers, who by virtue of their experience in the theatre should be qualified to speak with authority on certain elements of theatre structure, shows many contradictory statements, much vagueness, and too little indication that the recommendations made have been preceded by a painstaking functional analysis of theatre operation.

The architect then decides that his best source of information is the practicing theatre, personified by its working members: stage carpenters, designers, actors, technicians, and stage equipment manufacturers, and he journeys to New York for conferences. From these he collects as many opinions and recommendations as there are people with whom he talks, all of them circumscribed by the sphere of action in which the individual conferee moves, and seldom confined to that sphere alone. The actor is always ready to say what is wrong with stage lighting methods. Stage hands have been known to praise old-fashioned methods with which they are familiar but to disparage new equipment and methods which are strange to them. Stage equipment manufacturers favor the status quo because innovation and invention mean costly new tools and processes for the manufacture of equipment. Some look upon each new theatre as an opportunity to sell the greatest possible quantity of their most expensive equipment.

Structure limits function. Mistakes in architecture are either permanent or expensive to rectify. They often last longer than their perpetrators, and they haunt all later users of the building in two ways: the presence of the faults, and the absence of the good features which might have been in their stead. To list at this point mistakes noted in existing theatres would be lengthy and serve no useful purpose. Suffice it to say here that the mistakes are chiefly the result of lack of information, misinformation, or wrong thinking as regards the function of a theatre, and that some of them are so stupid as to tax credulity. To attempt to place the blame for mistakes is pointless, when, as we have seen, so few laymen have any comprehension of theatre practice, and the planning of theatres is in their hands. To become familiar with theatre practice and to learn how it determines the size, shape, arrangement, and equipment of theatres seems to be a reasonable way to prevent similar mistakes in future theatres.

2: audience traffic

The showman's first contact with any member of his audience occurs when that individual comes in sight of the theatre. From that moment until the patron is on the highway or the subway headed for home, his every movement is the showman's concern. The easier and pleasanter the patron's progress from home to theatre seat and back again, the better the showman's chances of making and holding a repeat customer.

This chapter deals with audience traffic to, through, and away from the theatre, together with the architectural implications thereof. Architectural planning for clear, straight paths of movement must be preceded by a study of the phenomenon of theatre-going. The figures in the tables which follow are obtained by analyses made in New York and in various other communities on the eastern seaboard.

The Audience Goes to the Theatre

Table I

Type of Production	Theatre	Audience Transit Time	Audience Assembly Time
Pageant Spectacle	Considerable latitude in type. Large seating capacity only requisite. Stadium or sports arena	Weeks (Oberammergau) Days (Lost Colony) Hours (Aquacade)	1 hour. Audience is on time.
Concert	Any auditorium with a platform	Average 30 minutes	40 minutes from advertised curtain time until half hour after show begins
Opera	Opera house when available		
Dance	Demands vary from as simple as concert to as complex as opera		
Legitimate and Musical	Commercial, School, College, University, Profession School, Community. Lacking these: Barn, Opera House or tent	Less than an hour except for summer theatre. Average 30 min.	20 minutes beginning approx. 7 min. before advertised curtain time
Presentation Vaudeville	Presentation House Commercial	Slightly shorter than legitimate	Continuous show. Now alternates with pictures
Motion Pictures	Motion Picture Palace	15 minutes	Continuous
	Neighborhood	10 minutes	"
	News	maximum	"
Burlesque	Old Commercial	15 minutes	Same as legitimate

Whoever plans a theatre will do well to make similar analyses for his own community rather than to trust implicitly these figures which are averages, and cannot encompass special cases. The planner is warned, however, that the figures here stated are a much better guide

Transportation Methods According to the Location of the Theatre

	Metro-politan Urban	Metro-politan Suburban	General Urban	General Suburban	Rural	Institutional (School and College)
Public Transit System and/or Pedestrian	Majority	Large Minority	Large Minority	Large Minority	Small Minority	Large Minority
Owner-driven motor	Small Minority	Large Minority	Large Minority	Majority	Majority	Majority
Hired Motor or Chauffeured	Large Minority	Small Minority	Small Minority	Small Minority	Small Minority	Small Minority

Table II

than a guess, an estimate, or an unsupported prediction in any locality.

Motor Transportation

The average car (owner-driven, taxi, chauffeured) carries three theatre patrons. To the theatre patronized by owner-drivers, patrons come irrespective of weather if there is a convenient parking space. The party dismounts at the marquee and the car is then parked. Where parking must be done on the streets the driver habitually parks first and the whole party walks to the theatre. Such patrons often stay away in inclement weather. Most theatre goers are in the car-owning class. Most of them would drive to the theatre in preference to using public transportation at additional expense and inconvenience if they could park. Many of them prefer the neighborhood movie or the radio to the metropolitan theatre for, though access to the metropolitan area is usually easy on parkways and super highways, traffic congestion and the absence of parking facilities in the

The arrival of many people by motor car is common to both an airport and a theatre. A modern solution to this modern problem is the extended covered unloading curb. Photo, CAA Technical Photographic Division.

immediate vicinity of the theatre make the trip an ordeal. From the foregoing tables it is apparent that facilities for easy handling of motor-borne traffic are of increasing importance to the theatre owner. There are two principal problems: loading facilities and parking.

Loading Facilities

The amount of curb space which is available for discharging passengers at the theatre is limited by the length of the theatre wall facing the street or through driveway. Simple calculation based on the foregoing figures and tables will show that only the metropolitan urban motion picture presentation houses can have adequate curb-loading facilities. Other theatres will have congestion even if the curb extends around all four sides of the theatre. Under fortunate circumstances such congestion might be only momentary but the showman is interested in the patron who is trying to discharge passengers at that moment. It follows, then, that no plan to facilitate the approach of traffic to the theatre is likely to be over-elaborate; that no length of curb at front, side, or even back, of the theatre is too long. It is also axiomatic that driveways around the theatre be one-way, and at least two lanes wide; that the sidewalk be at least 10 feet wide and that the marquee cover all the curb-loading area.

The problem of curb-loading for metropolitan urban theatres cannot usually be solved by private driveways extending around the house because of high land costs. Therefore there is considerable advantage in having a theatre which occupies an entire block, as is the case with the Metropolitan Opera House where marquees cover

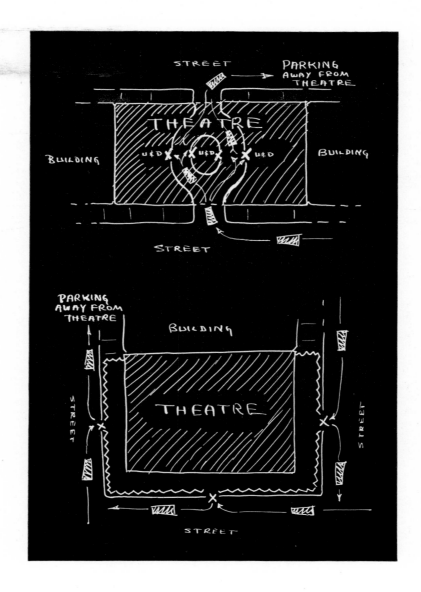

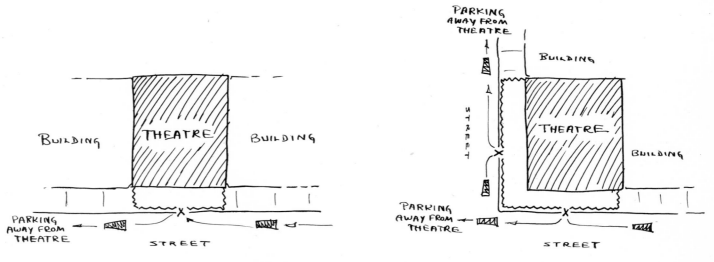

Loading facilities are affected by the site of the theatre.

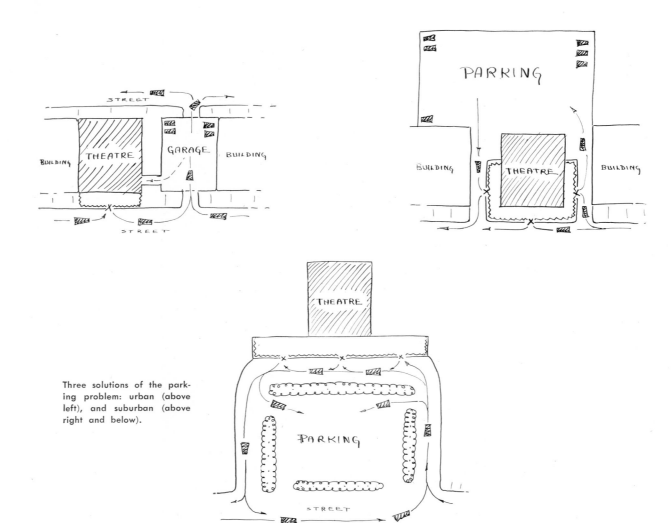

Three solutions of the parking problem: urban (above left), and suburban (above right and below).

substantial portions of three sides of the theatre. Where as many as two sides face the street, it is possible to provide for discharge of passengers and loading underneath the theatre, as is the case with Severance Hall in Cleveland. Several projected theatres provide for loading under the theatre.

Parking

Suburban theatres with their own parking lots large enough to handle one-third as many cars as there are seats in the house, often find the capacity of the parking lot is taxed. It is probable that legitimate theatres and urban motion picture theatres would attract larger and more dependable audiences if easily accessible parking facilities existed. Since land costs, except in suburban and rural areas, are usually too high to make it feasible for the showman to plan parking facilities for the theatre alone he must look upon his parking problem as one which is part of the whole community problem, particularly that of enterprises near the theatre. Before the war parking for the Radio City theatres was no problem except at matinees and occasional times of congestion such as New Year's Eve. The Rockefeller Center Garage, taxed to capacity in the daytime, could handle cars coming to Radio City theatres in the evening. If parking space is provided near the theatre, it may well earn its keep from daytime, non-theatrical patronage.

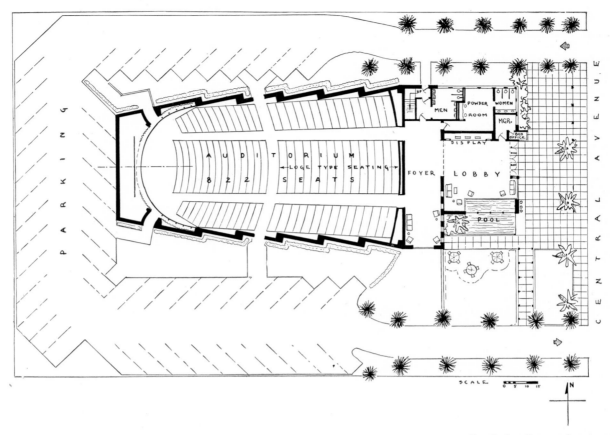

The Encino Theatre, Los Angeles. A convenient arrangement for parking around a theatre but only a partial solution of the problem because the 51 cars accommodated will only transport approximately ¼ the orchestra seating capacity. W. L. Pereira, Architect.

Site

Curb-loading and parking facilities constitute an extremely important consideration in the original siting of the theatre, in planning architectural revision of the plant, in policy concerning acquisition of abutting property and in collaboration with enterprises in the neighborhood and the municipality. In Garden City, Long Island, parking lots are situated behind the buildings which face the street in the business zone. Such an arrangement has obvious advantages for the showman. He may find it to his advantage to build a theatre

Marquee to Seat

Statistically the playgoers' progress averages as follows:	Opera and Concert	Legitimate and Musical	Pictures and Presentation	
% of audience which waits to meet friends in the foyer	6%	10%	Negligible	
% of audience which buys tickets within 20 minutes of curtain time	8%	20%	100%	
Time spent in line for tickets purchased or reserved	2 to 15 minutes	2 to 5 minutes	Negligible	**Table III**
Time spent in line to ticket taker	1 minute	1 minute	0	
Overall time, curb to seat	4-12 min. depending upon location. 4 min. to box	6 min. to Orch. 8 min. to Mezz. 9 min. to Balcony	2-5 min. depending upon location.	
% of audience which checks its wraps	6%	2%	Negligible	

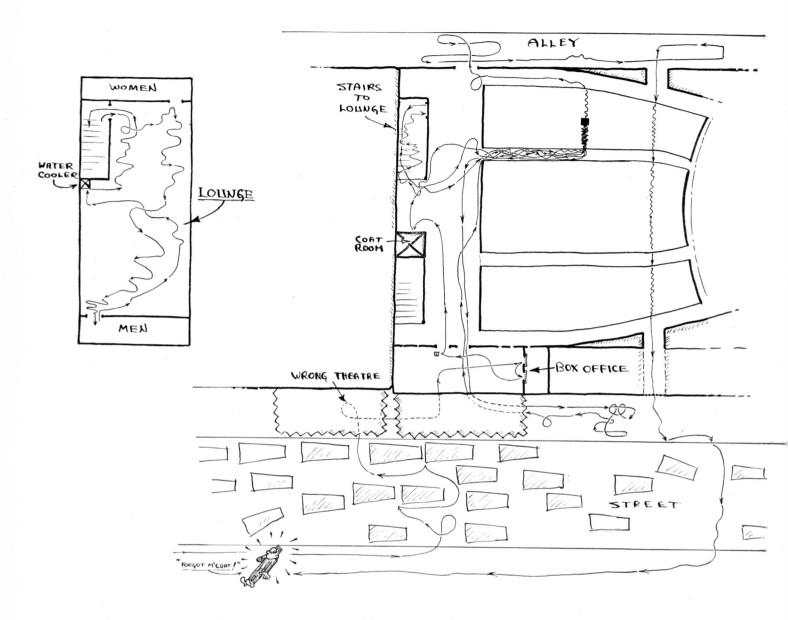

WOMEN

WATER COOLER

LOUNGE

MEN

ALLEY

STAIRS TO LOUNGE

COAT ROOM

WRONG THEATRE

BOX OFFICE

STREET

"FORGOT M'COAT!"

The playgoer's progress, New York, 1949. The wiggles in the path are occasioned by the patron's collision with other theatre-goers.

near a municipal parking lot; in fact it is now generally agreed among suburban motion picture exhibitors that they have more to gain by locating their theatres where access and parking are easy rather than on a congested main street.

The theatre in the college is often surrounded by spacious grounds which are a liability to theatre operation because patrons have to wade a long distance through the heavy dew to get to the theatre, or shake the snow out of their shoes once they are there. A theatre can look just as good if a marquee surrounds a substantial portion of it, a wide paved driveway encircles it, and a parking lot is adjacent, as if it is handicapped by the want of such facilities. Parking facilities associated with athletic stadia may serve theatre patrons.

Foyer

The first hiatus in the smooth flow of audience traffic is the waiting line for tickets. There is no occasion for this at a news reel theatre with a turnstile entrance. The line waiting at the advance sale window for a popular production is often long, and patrons may stand for hours. For the average legitimate house (capacity approximately 1200), one ticket window can usually handle seat purchases by that portion of the audience which buys immediately preceding curtain

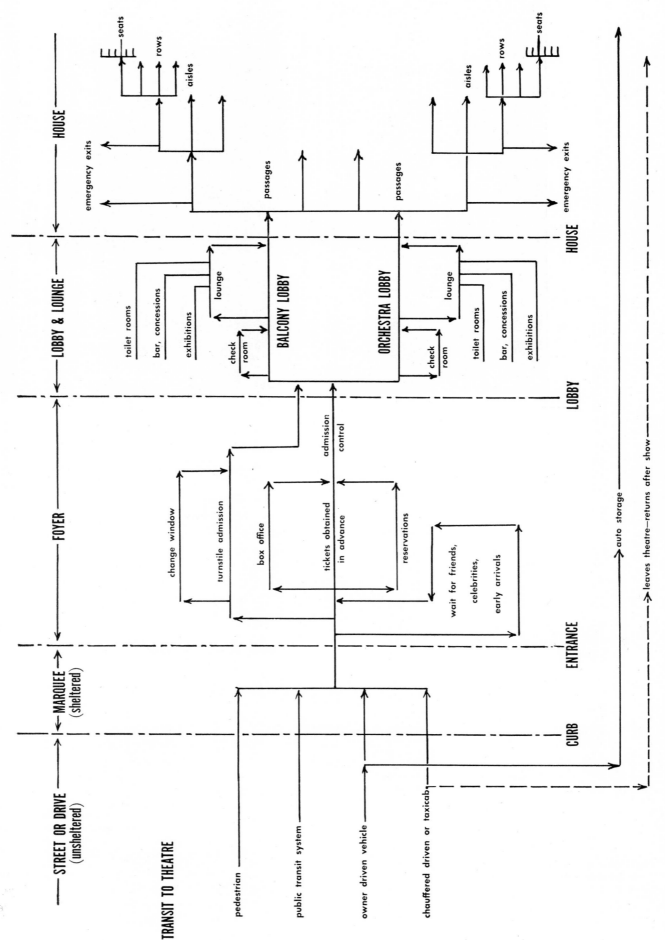

Composite audience flow chart.

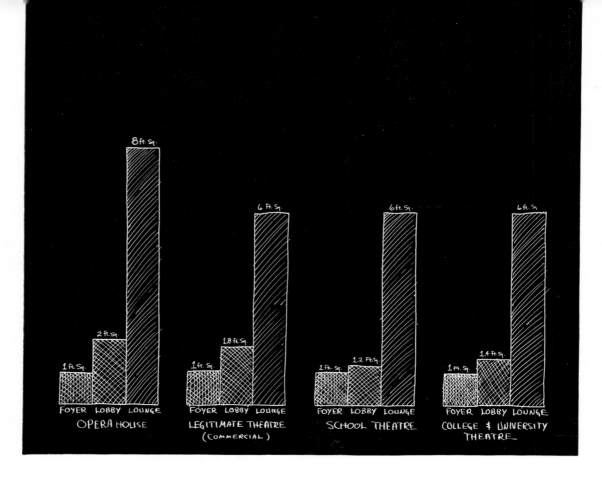

8 ft. sq.

6 ft. sq.   6 ft. sq.   6 ft. sq.

2 ft. sq.

1.8 ft. sq.

1 ft. sq.   1 ft. sq.   1 ft. sq.   1.2 ft. sq.   1 ft. sq.   1.4 ft. sq.

FOYER LOBBY LOUNGE   FOYER LOBBY LOUNGE   FOYER LOBBY LOUNGE   FOYER LOBBY LOUNGE
OPERA HOUSE   LEGITIMATE THEATRE (COMMERCIAL)   SCHOOL THEATRE   COLLEGE & UNIVERSITY THEATRE

time. The architect's concern with these hiatuses is in providing a comfortable foyer and enough ticket windows so located and arranged as to make possible as speedy a sale of tickets as the management may find efficient.

In addition to accommodating ticket queues, the foyer must provide space for members of the audience waiting to meet friends. While fulfilling these functions, the foyer must be so arranged that the patron who has his ticket can pass through without getting tangled in the queues or being obstructed by the waiting patrons.

A few theatres in which foyer space is observed to be adequate provide the following foyer dimensions which may be regarded as minimal if congestion is to be avoided:

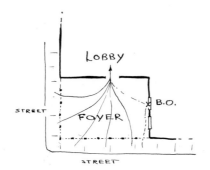

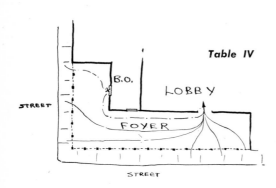

Table IV

Box office queues must be separate from traffic through foyer.

Foyer Area Per Seat

Opera House	1 ft. sq.
Commercial Theatre	1 " "
Non-commercial Theatre	
School	1 " "
College and University	1 " "
Community	1 " "
Motion Picture	
Palace and Presentation	½ ft. sq.
Intimate	negligible
Neighborhood	½ ft. sq.
Summer Theatre	Outdoor patio or terrace serving multiple functions usually adequate

No less important than the foyer capacity is its arrangement. Patrons waiting for friends habitually stand just inside the doors. Therefore doors are best placed on the long dimension of the foyer. Patrons having seats bought in advance must cross the foyer, therefore the direction of the queues at ticket windows must be so arranged as not to interfere with the straight path from foyer door to lobby

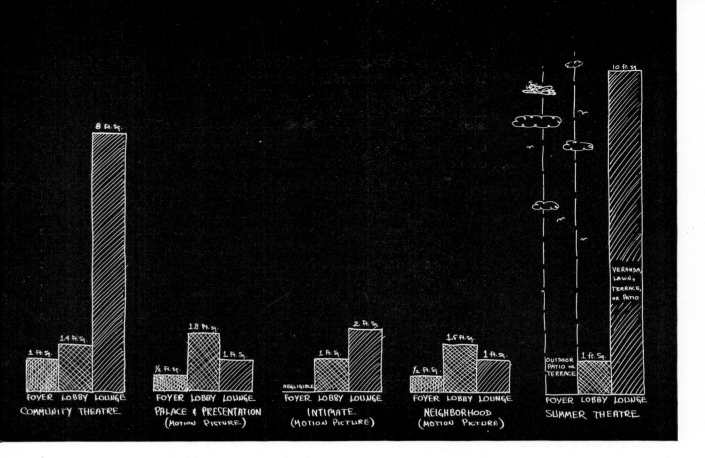

Relative areas of public rooms required for different theatre types.

door. These two requirements are sometimes well met by having the foyer doors to the street on two sides and establishing queues to ticket windows along the third side, or by building the foyer around the corner of the lobby and keeping the queue line and ticket windows on the side where lobby entrances are not located. It is obvious that there should be direct access to the foyer on all sides of the theatre where there is a marquee.

The ticket taker presides over the next traffic bottleneck. His entrance can easily be planned to facilitate through traffic but it must also be opposite a portion of the lobby affording short, straight paths to aisles, staircases, and elevators. No position has been discovered to date better than on the center line of the house. For legitimate production, a single entrance door can usually handle 1000 to 1500 persons. Since building codes require entrance-exit doors on the street at the rate of approximately one five-foot door to every 300 persons of audience, the bottleneck is not in the amount of entrance space but rather in the number of ticket takers. Auxiliary entrance doors, if used, should be adjacent to the first since the path of movement from street, through foyer, to lobby, will not thereby be forced to deviate. The lobby is principally a distribution area. Like the foyer its efficiency is measured not only by its size but by its arrangement. If the head usher standing inside the lobby door can direct each patron to his aisle or staircase by a route which will not involve the crossing of the route of any other patron, or even having tangential contact therewith, the lobby may be small but adequate.

The complicating factors in lobby design are access to the coatrooms and to the lounge. Obviously, the coatroom is most efficiently located where the entering line will pass it before dividing, as in the Hudson Theatre, New York. Where adequate checkroom facilities

Lobby

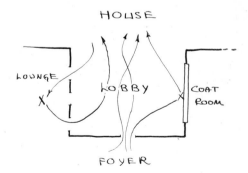

Pattern of traffic in lobby.

Checking Facilities

exist almost every member of the audience checks something. Theatre is one of a few forms of indoor entertainment at which patrons carry their outer garments with them. There is little logic in this and certainly neither comfort nor pleasure.

As far as lobby design is concerned there must be long enough runs of coatroom counter and sufficient floor area to make it possible to check wraps as rapidly as the audience moves.

Access to the lounge is from the lobby. Lobby planning involves locating lounge doors so that traffic to and from the lounge will logically follow a one-way path. The same rules which govern orchestra lobby planning apply to balcony lobbies. As in the case of the foyer, lobby area is, relatively, not as important as *lobby arrangement*. The theatre with a fixed hour performance must provide for peak lobby loads which never occur in continuous run houses. However, as has been pointed out, it is generally unwise to plan for one type of production only. Lobby areas which have been found to be adequate where arrangement is average to good, follow:

Lobby Area Per Seat

Opera House	**2 ft. sq.**
Commercial Theatre	**1.8 ft. sq.**
Non-commercial Theatre	
School	**1.2 ft. sq.**
College and University	**1.4 ft. sq.**
Community	**1.4 ft. sq.**
Motion Picture	
Palace and Presentation	**1.8 sq. ft.**
Intimate	**1 ft. sq.**
Neighborhood	**1.5 ft. sq.**
Summer Theatre	**1 ft. sq.**

For house capacities above 1500 incoming audience congestion may be relieved by the provision of separate foyers, box offices, ticket takers, lobbies, and passages for subdivisions of the house: viz. orchestra, dress circle, mezzanine, balcony, or left, center, and right. Very little congestion occurred in the seating of 8400 people for four performances daily of Billy Rose's New York World Fair Aquacade, thanks to the multiplicity of entrances and clear paths of movement inside the gates.

The best condition of traffic exists when there are passages from lobby to house directly in line with every aisle. When the plan renders this impossible, the crossover behind the seating area is part of the path followed by the audience between lobby and aisle. Since the crossover may have to carry at peak load the combined traffic of several aisles, its minimum width must be the combined width of the aisles it serves. In addition it furnishes standing room for those waiting to be shown to seats and for those who buy standing room. Ample crossover width is essential in motion picture houses where the crossover is generally used to accommodate four ranks of standing patrons. The motion picture house finds its peak crossover load at change of program. For this reason the normally planned crossover width must be increased to accommodate people waiting for seats. In legitimate houses, fire regulations usually forbid more than a single rank standing in the crossover. Since these people are close to the lobby, they are not in the way at the time of peak traffic. Crossover congestion in many theatres arises from assigning the lobby function to the

Table V

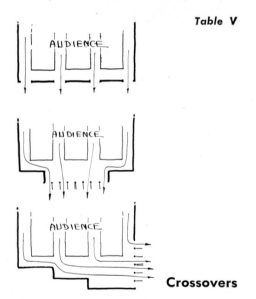

Crossovers

The width of crossover equals the sum of the widths of the aisles.

crossover and from terminating balcony stairs in the orchestra crossover. Such practices produce discomfort, and increase panic hazards.

The load for which building codes require the width of aisles to be planned occurs when a capacity audience leaves the theatre at one time in an emergency. From this safety requirement is also derived minimum seat spacing. The location of aisles in American theatres is governed by a code requirement, generally prevalent, which limits the number of seats between aisles to fourteen and the number of seats between an aisle and a wall to seven. Minimum seat spacing provided in the codes is too close for comfort, and, therefore, too close to be considered by the theatre planner. If seats are spaced farther apart than the code provides, the number of people served by a code-width aisle is thereby reduced and congestion minimized. Nevertheless, the safety-minimum-width aisle is seldom adequate for peak loads of audience entering or leaving through the lobby, but not using the emergency exits. To eliminate congestion when a capacity audience leaves the theatre by this means, aisles must be wider than code minimum. The width may be calculated on a rate of flow basis, as developed by the National Board of Fire Underwriters.

Some few codes allow as an alternate plan the so-called continental seating in which there may be any number of seats between aisles, provided seat spacing, aisles, and exits satisfy concomitant special requirements. For continental seating, it is necessary to make the side aisles wide enough to permit emptying the house within the time allowed under local fire ordinances, or to plan numerous side wall exits into corridors.

Minimum code requirements for safety, generally prevalent, do not produce comfort. Traffic and comfort must determine seat spacing. Under minimum code spacing, patrons cannot pass other seated patrons. This condition is barely remedied with a seat spacing of 36 inches, and is adequately overcome by a spacing of 45 inches. Since the depth of seat-back upholstery is a factor, the type of seat must be specified before spacing can be accurately planned.

Aisles

Continental Seating

The chamber music auditorium, an intimate theatre of the Malmö Municipal Theatre. Seats are wide and generously spaced consistent with continental seating. The floor slope affords all spectators a clear view to the apron. Photo, Jaerke.

Seating

Intermission Routine

	Opera and Concert	Legitimate and Musical	Optimum
% of audience which leaves seats during intermissions	75	50	100
Walking time: seat to lounge	4 min.	4 min.	2 min.
Time in lavatory line	1 min.	6 min.	0
Time spent in line at check room after show	3 min.	5 min.	0
Seat to curb time (without check room stop)	5 min.	6 min.	2 min.
Waiting time for cab or car	0 to 15 min.	0 to 15 min.	0 min.

Table VI

The theatre patron is often annoyed by the fact that the curtain is 7 to 15 minutes late. It is common practice to attempt to get it up 7 minutes after the advertised time. This delay theoretically provides the necessary time to seat patrons who are in the theatre at the advertised curtain time. In most commercial, legitimate and musical houses the time is insufficient, the curtain is further delayed, and people are standing in the aisles when the curtain goes up. Bad weather brings an increased number of cabs, further taxes the curb loading area and coatroom, and further delays the curtain. Bad audience manners, to some extent stimulated by the knowledge of congestion at curtain time, tend to delay the curtain further. The architect is concerned with facilities for getting people to their seats expeditiously. The theatre management cannot train the audience in punctuality if conditions conducive to congestion are built into the theatre.

Gregariousness, a desire for a smoke or refreshment, and uncomfortable seats drive many of the audience to lounge, lobby and foyer during intermissions. Those who remain seated do so because the public rooms are too congested. For those who leave their seats the difficulties of returning to them often exceed those of getting seated at the start of the show.

These facts viewed in conjunction with the foregoing tables establish conditions which militate against theatre going. They are to be contrasted with facilities for audience handling and comfort provided in presentation and news motion picture houses. There is this additional fact to consider: adequate, even luxurious, facilities for audience comfort in a presentation or news movie may be inadequate for a fixed performance where all facilities are used at the same time by the whole audience. To make it possible for the audience to keep its attention on the show, instead of fretting at bodily discomfort, unimpeded traffic to and from the lounge, and adequate lounge area must be provided.

In theatres so designed, particularly in Europe, the whole audience usually leaves its seats during intermission. As the audience proceeds from seat to aisle, to crossover, to lobby, to lounge, and back again, paths of movement must not cross; therefore, lounge entrance from lobby must be close to the crossover and easily distinguishable. If the exit from the lounge to the lobby is less plainly visible, and located farther away from the seat area than is the entrance, a natural circulatory traffic movement will develop, and persons entering and leaving the lounge will not collide in the lobby.

Intermission and Exit Traffic

Inadequate lobby and lounge facilities in a New York legitimate theatre force the audience onto the sidewalk during the intermission. Intermission is no fun. Photo, Wide World Photos, Inc.

Lounge

Traffic in the lounge itself is to bar, refreshment stand, and lavatories. Lavatories located left and right of, and close to the lounge entrance, split the traffic. A bar directly in front of the entrance and across the room, and telephone near the exit, help to spread out the traffic. Traffic eddies tend to form in corners, for which reason they can best be used for chairs, ashstands, etc. Large tables and groups of chairs in the center of the lounge help to keep traffic circulating to the left. Few theatres have adequate lounge space. The figures in Table VII may be taken as adequate but not luxurious.

Foyer, lobby, and lounge have separate functions. Astute planning may in numerous instances make it possible for the same area to serve, in part, more than one purpose but the space requirement for each function must be observed. There must be structural separation between foyer and lobby, but doors can be opened at intermission. Lobby and lounge can be structurally combined where paths of movement are so routed that both functions can be fulfilled simultaneously without crossing. Some lounge and lobby functions may be filled in school or college buildings by facilities having uses other than those demanded by the theatre. The theatre which because of season or climate can use a garden, lawn, or patio for lobby, lounge or both, need have no public room congestion. In any case, almost everybody wants to leave his seat during intermission. The total public area must therefore be adequate to accommodate the whole audience.

Lounge Area Per Seat

Opera House	8 ft. sq.
Commercial Theatre	6 ft. sq.
Non-commercial Theatre	
School	6 ft. sq.
College and University	6 ft. sq.
Community	8 ft. sq.
Motion Picture	
Palace and Presentation	1 ft. sq.
Intimate	2 ft. sq.
Neighborhood	1 ft. sq.
Summer Theatre	10 ft. sq. out of doors (veranda, lawn, garden, patio)

Table VII

Final Curtain

Aisles, passageways, lobby, foyers, marquee, and curb have peak loads at the end of the show. The theatre patron's return home is surrounded by conditions identical with those obtained in coming to the theatre save that they are met in reverse order, and (1) buses, street cars, and subway trains do not run as often, and (2) in inclement weather there may be a taxi shortage. Different also is the fact that arrival was spread over 20 to 30 minutes and departure is simultaneous for the whole audience. The use of auxiliary exits, ample marquees for shelter against weather, maximum loading curbs, and efficient parking lot management are essential, if the theatre goer's final impression is to be favorable.

The theatre planner must be diligent in separating those elements of theatre-going routine which are engendered by structural inadequacies (shivering under the marquee during intermission) from those which are germane to the process (waiting for friends in the foyer). If he is to build a useful theatre he must eliminate the former by providing facilities for the latter and thereby establish an effortless, comfortable, and pleasant routine of theatre attendance.

Public spaces within the Malmö Theatre afford ample accommodation for the entire audience during the intermission. Circulation is easy. There are art galleries at both ends of the lounge. Photo, C. G. Rosenberg.

3: the audience sees

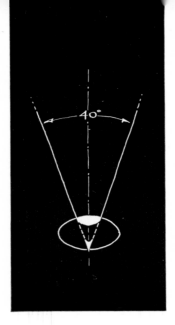

The horizontal angle of poly-chromatic vision (no eye movement) is approximately 40°.

The audience comes to the theatre to see the show. This is the primary consideration governing all planning on the audience side of the proscenium. The audience generally thinks of the show as that which takes place on the stage or the screen. The competent showman, however, sees to it that the audience feels itself part of the show from the moment it comes within sight of the theatre until it has turned the corner after leaving. He endeavors to make the impact of his showmanship felt every minute the audience is present. He must then provide, by means which the audience appreciates visually, for convenience, comfort, safety; for the audience's desire to see and be seen, the control of attention, the elimination of distraction, the creation and maintenance of mood.

As each member of the audience enters the auditorium he wants to see: the usher, the steps, the aisles, row and seat (including the hat rack), his wife's gloves (on the floor), the program, the show (at an angle and distance consistent with visual fidelity and credibility), the emergency exit, the regular exit. Many members of the audience will want to see and be seen by other playgoers. No member of the audience wants to see a silhouette of the occupant of the seat in front, the show distorted by angle to the side, above, or below, or insignificant because of distance, or an illuminated exit sign, or a twinkling galaxy of orchestra-stand lights when he is trying to pay attention to the show.

The showman wants the audience to see: walls and ceiling only as they contribute to the atmosphere of the theatre, objects of decoration which are significant as focal points in the decorative scheme and contribute to the feeling of luxury, the organ console and orchestra when they are part of the show. The showman wants to conceal from view all elements in structure or equipment which will detract from the desired atmosphere of the house or fatigue the audience, as: backstage areas sometimes visible through the wings, loud-speakers about the proscenium, stage lighting units (balcony pans, insufficiently masked booms at the sides of the proscenium), orchestra and organ console when their visual aspects are not essential to the show, or bright open light sources.

It is the job of the architect to satisfy completely the demands of audience and showman. To ignore or neglect any of the items listed, or to fall short of a satisfactory solution of the problems implicit in them will inevitably increase hazards and impair the theatre's function and earning power.

If the patron is to see satisfactorily, plan and section must conform to a number of limitations which are set forth in the following list. To design an auditorium is to determine a seating area within these limitations and to establish position (not shape) of walls and shape of floors therefrom.

1—The horizontal angle of polychromatic vision (no eye movement) is approximately 40°.

2—The horizontal angle to the center line at which objects onstage, upstage of the curtain line, cease to bear the intended relationship to other objects onstage and to the background is approximately 60°.

3—The horizontal angle to the projection sheet at which distortion on the screen becomes substantially intolerable is 60° measured to the far side of the projected image.

4—Judged by the audience's ability to recognize shapes, and confirmed by free audience choice of seats, the following is the order of desirability of locations:

a—front center (except when the screen is close to the front row);

b—middle center;

c—middle side;

d—front side;

e—rear center;

f—rear side.

5—Audiences will not choose locations beyond a line approximately 100° to the curtain at the side of the proscenium.

6—The vertical angle beyond which ability to recognize standard shapes falls off very rapidly is approximately 30°.

7—The recommended maximum angle of motion picture projection to the horizontal is 12°.

The horizontal angle to the center line at which objects onstage, upstage of the curtain line, cease to bear the intended relationship to other objects onstage and to the background is approximately 60°.

The horizontal angle to the projection sheet at which distortion on the screen becomes substantially intolerable is 60° measured to the far side of the projected image.

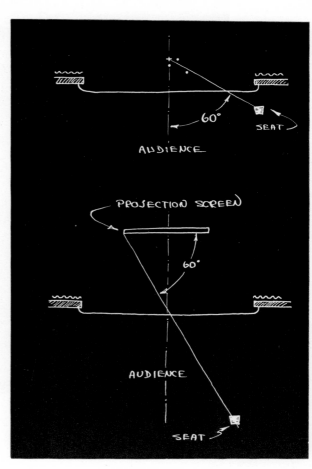

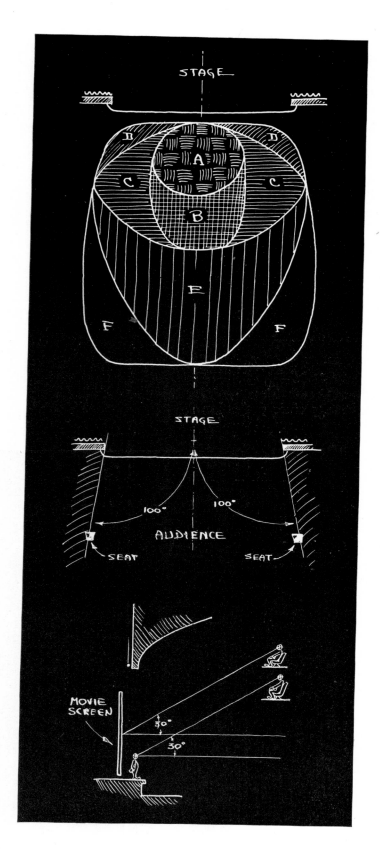

Judged by the audience's ability to recognize shapes, and confirmed by free audience choice of seats, the following is the order of desirability of locations:
a—front center (except when the screen is close to the front row);
b—middle center;
c—middle side;
d—front side;
e—rear center;
f—rear side.

Audiences will not choose locations beyond a line approximately 100° to the curtain at the side of the proscenium.

The vertical angle beyond which ability to recognize standard shapes falls off very rapidly is approximately 30°.

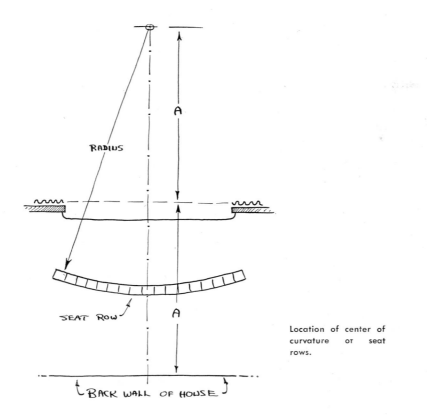

RADIUS

A

SEAT ROW

A

Location of center of curvature or seat rows.

BACK WALL OF HOUSE

Plan

If the foregoing limitations are applied in the horizontal plane for any given proscenium opening, they will limit an area of maximum value as seating space which is approximately elliptical. It is interesting to note that this shape for an auditorium plan was pioneered by the late Joseph Urban who had little of the present data to work with and may safely be assumed to have chosen the shape largely on esthetic grounds. A fan shape provides additional seating space at minimum sacrifice of sight lines, but nobody wants the seats in the extreme rear corners.

Seating

Occupants of all seats are visually related to the performance when the seats are oriented toward the stage. This necessitates curving the rows of seats. The center of curvature is located on the center line of the auditorium approximately the depth of the house behind the proscenium.

Stagger

To provide best visibility from any seat, no patron should sit exactly in front of any other patron unless more than one row distant. This requirement makes it necessary to stagger seats. Staggering is accomplished by the nonuniform placement of seats of varying widths in succeeding rows. Unless the walls of the theatre are parallel (which is acoustically hazardous), it is extremely unlikely that more than a very few rows can be made up of seats of uniform width. The lack of uniformity thereby introduced provides the means by which staggering can be accomplished. Seats are made with uniform standards and interchangeable backs and seats so that a wide variation

Seating in the Park Theatre, Stockholm (Björn Hedvall, Architect) is staggered to allow all spectators unobstructed vision. Seats are fully upholstered and have nearly flat backs. Continental seating eliminates longitudinal aisles.

Aisles

Depth of House

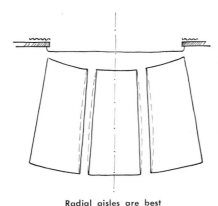

Radial aisles are best

of seat width is possible and a variation from seat to seat of an inch or two, cumulative enough to accomplish satisfactory stagger and make rows even, is not noticed by the patron.

Aisles are of questionable desirability except in the largest houses. They must, however, be employed in many localities because of building laws which make no provision for continuous-row or so-called continental seating in which all rows are widely spaced and serve as transverse aisles. Many a bad sight line has resulted from putting the maximum legal number, usually 14, seats into each row in every section. Obviously, for purposes of seeing, radial aisles are best, with curved aisles only slightly less efficient. Aisles perpendicular to the curtain line often have the accidental result of making side section seats undesirable. The box office would like a theatre with all seats in the center section. A center aisle wastes the most desirable seating area in the theatre and inevitably causes the objectionable condition of seats directly in front of each other near the aisle.

There are many formulas used to determine the depth of the house, or more accurately, to determine the relationship between depth of house, width of house, and width of screen or proscenium. They vary considerably and are all empirically derived on the basis of existing theatres, with too little reference to whether such theatres are good or not. Typical are the following: Optimum depth equals 4 times screen width. Maximum depth equals 6 times screen width. Depth equals 1.25 to 2.35 times house width when house width is 2.5 to 3.5 times screen width. Practically, there are only two significant considerations in planning the depth of the house:

1—Visual acuity. Normal human vision can perceive a minimum dimension or separation equal to 1 minute of visual arc. Translated into space measurement this means that at 10 feet a normal eye can perceive a dimension of .035 inch, at 50 feet, .175 inch, and at 100 feet, .35 inch. Details of actors' make-up and facial expression are not plainly recognizable at distances of more than 50 feet from the stage.

2—Capacity. The larger the house, the lower can be the price per seat or the greater the gross. If the box office is not to be considered, capacity may be limited by optimum seeing requirements, and the last rows kept within 50 feet of the stage. As various requirements operate to increase capacity, the distance of the rear seats from the stage must be increased and seeing conditions impaired in proportion. The theatre operator may compensate the occupants of these seats by charging less for them. For shows involving live human actors, 75 feet is generally accepted on grounds of visibility as maximum house depth.

In theatrical entertainment which has as its chief visual component human actors (live shows) the degree to which these performers must be seen to satisfy the audience and put the show across varies.

A—Details of facial expression and small gesture are important in legitimate drama, vaudeville and burlesque, intimate revue and cabaret.

B—Broad gesture by single individuals is important in grand opera, presentation, musical comedy, and the dance.

C—Gesture by individuals is unimportant and movement of individuals from place to place is the smallest significant movement in pageant.

It follows then that theatres planned for the types of entertainment listed under A must be limited in depth of auditorium so that visibility from the remotest seat still allows the occupant to perceive facial expressions (not over 75 feet).

Theatres planned for the types listed under B may have greater distance from the stage to the remotest seat, but this distance is set at a maximum beyond which the individual actor is diminished to insignificance (approx. 125 feet).

Spectators in the last rows at the Radio City Music Hall in New York, looking through a distance ranging from 160 feet to over 200 feet, depending on the location of the performers onstage, see a ballet reduced to the size of midgets, and an individual performer, even with the dramatic enhancement of a follow spot, is a very insignificant figure indeed.

Summary

Given the proscenium opening and capacity, laying out the orchestra and balcony or balconies in plan becomes a simple and straightforward process. Sight lines determine proscenium splay and house width. Visibility limits and capacity determines depth. Minimum distance from stage or screen to first row is determined in the section.

Section

The vertical angle of 30° at the spectator's position establishes the distance from the closest seat to the screen or to the highest significant object on the stage. The lowest seat in the orchestra must be located where the patron can just see the stage floor (except in the case of theatres built for motion pictures only). The highest seat in the balcony must be on a line which is not more than 30° to the horizontal at the front curtain at the stage floor if it is not to be beyond the limit of reasonable distortion. The standing patron at the back of the orchestra must be able to see the top of the screen, which is usually as high as any significant portion of a stage setting. Each spectator must see the whole stage or screen over the heads of those in front of him. Within these limits the floor slope of orchestra and balcony can be laid out: the first step in determining auditorium section.

Several methods have been offered heretofore for developing the floor slope. Doubtless others will be offered in the future. The authors present the following method as one which assures unobstructed vision from all seats. It may be noted that this system produces a floor slope considerably steeper than that in many existing theatres. It also produces better seeing conditions.

To determine floor slope, establish eye position of spectator in first row on center line by approximately 30° vertical angle above. For live shows, stage floor will be approximately 2″ below this level. For theatres designed solely for motion pictures, the location of the stage floor is not critical; the position of the bottom of the screen is.

A point 3′-8″ below, and 18″ in front of the eye position will be the floor level for the front row. Draw a sight line from the eye position to downstage edge of stage, and extend it back of the eye position for the front row, step off horizontal seat spacing (back to back), and draw vertical lines at the points thus established. Establish a point 5″ above the intersection of the extended sight line and the next vertical

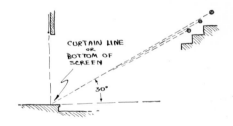

Maximum tolerable sightline angle.

The Gran Rex Theatre, Buenos Aires (Alberto Prebisch, Architect) has a generous floor slope, limited mezzanine, and a deep balcony. Note the increase in pitch from orchestra to mezzanine to balcony.

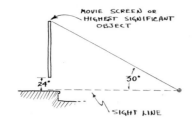

MOVIE SCREEN OR
HIGHEST SIGNIFICANT
OBJECT

24"

30°

SIGHT LINE

Maximum tolerable angle to top of picture screen.

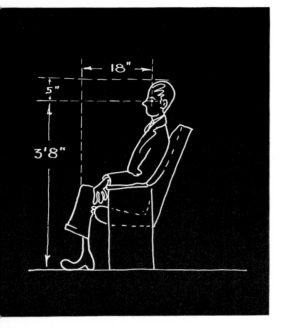

18"

5"

3'8"

Basic dimensions for plotting floor slope.

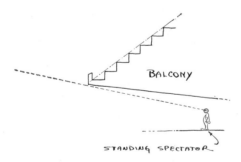

BALCONY

STANDING SPECTATOR

The sightline of the standing patron limits the balcony overhang.

Floor Dish

line. This is the eye position for the second row and the floor level at the front edge of the second row seat is 3'-8" below and 18" in front of the eye position. Repeat this process to the back of the house and draw in the floor slope. Where the slope exceeds 1½" per foot, platforms are required under the seats, and steps in the aisles.

The standing spectator's eye level behind the rear row of seats is assumed to be 5'-6" above the floor level of the last row. The sight line from this position to the top of the screen or highest probable curtain trim establishes the minimum height for ceiling under balcony.

Raising the stage will reduce the floor slope. If the stage floor is above the elevation of the first row eye position, the upstage portion of the floor will be invisible from the first row. It is generally preferable to leave the upstage floor out of sight by perhaps as much as 6 inches from the first row, to having an excessive floor slope, especially if more than one balcony is used.

When planning for motion pictures only, the lower sight line from the first row will come to the bottom of the projected picture, approximately 24" above the stage floor, or still higher if a reverse floor slope is planned.

In laying out the balcony, sight lines are laid out from rear to front because it is unsafe to change balcony slope. The focal point onstage is the point farthest downstage at which visibility is requisite, or, in the case of motion pictures only, the bottom of the screen. The maximum forward extensity of the balcony is then determined when the location of the spectator's eye position has been moved forward to a point beyond which the floor and supporting structure would intersect the upper sight line of the spectator standing at the rear of the orchestra.

As a rule, the pitch of balcony floors should not change since that would entail a change of riser height for aisle stairs and introduce attendant hazards. If vision from the rear row in the balcony is adequate, the rest of the balcony is satisfactory.

In theatres designed only to show motion pictures, the first row need not be located so that the patron can see the stage floor. It is satisfactory if he sees without obstruction the bottom of the screen which is seldom placed less than 2 feet above the stage floor. Raising the screen makes it possible to flatten the contour of the orchestra floor. The reversed floor slope developed by Ben Schlanger makes use of this relationship to get the maximum number of seats into the zone of least visual distortion, and to hold the height of motion picture theatres to a minimum. A result of the reversed floor slope is to place balcony seats in the zone of optimum seeing.

It is apparent that a theatre designed for maximum efficiency for motion pictures (reverse floor slope) is almost completely useless for any other sort of production except large screen television.

The planning of the floor slope is not completed when pitch of orchestra and balcony has been laid out on the center line. It depends also on the curve of the rows of seats. The whole row must be at the same elevation if the seats are to be level. The floor therefore is not a sloped plane, but a dished surface in which horizontal contours follow the seat row curve. The floor section at the center line, rotated horizontally about the center of curvature of the rows of seats, will determine the orchestra floor shape. The balcony is planned the same way save that the floor consists of treads and risers.

It has been established that conditions of seeing limit the depth of the house. Since capacity is a function of depth and width, increasing the width increases the capacity. However, since sight lines from the side seats limit the angular spread of the side walls, the width can only be increased by increasing the proscenium opening. The width of the proscenium opening is a function of the kind of productions contemplated for the theatre, according to the following table, and cannot be arbitrarily increased.

Proscenium Widths for Kinds of Theatrical Production in Feet

	Minimum	Usual	Reasonable Maximum
Drama	26	30 to 35	40
Vaudeville, Revue	30	35	45
Musical Comedy Operetta	30	40	50
Presentation Opera	40	60	80

In cases where it is unnecessary to build to minimum visibility standards, wall angles may be narrowed, floor angles increased, and balcony omitted, and visibility from the worst seats thereby improved to a point considerably better than what is just saleable. A very real problem, however, is to prevent precedent or personal prejudice from so influencing auditorium design as to cause the inclusion of large numbers of unsaleable seats. One manager insisted, after floor slope and stage height had been determined and the auditorium floor laid, that the stage floor be lowered some 10 inches below the height called for in the plan, in the interests of, as he put it, "intimacy." From the middle of the orchestra in that theatre it is hard to see below the level of the actor's navel.

Greek theatres were semicircular (horizontal sight line angle 90° to center line). This was all right in Greece where there was no proscenium. It is obviously not all right where a proscenium is used or where realistic box sets are employed. Yet, a misguided reverence for ancient practice still gives us some theatres with impossible sight lines.

Opera houses of the Renaissance had side boxes for the very good reason that the people in the boxes competed (often successfully) with the stage show for audience attention. This condition persists, but it is worth noting that the best example of such a theatre in America has not made a nickel for a decade. Nevertheless, theatres with at least vestigial side boxes are still built.

It is perhaps unnecessary to add that theatres planned in conformity with the principles here set forth may adhere in spirit to almost any superficial architectural style by the discreet planning of service and decorative elements which do not affect the basic shape of the theatre. In theatres which are being rebuilt, it is often possible to retain the desirable features and still provide a good theatre.

Seeing requisites determine the shape of the house and to some extent its size. They also determine the provisions for house illumination.

Requisites for lighting are mentioned earlier. There are three basic functions involved:
1. Visibility
2. Decoration
3. Mood

To fulfill these functions it is necessary to plan the lighting for each separately, combining instruments only if and when the requirements are satisfied. It is axiomatic in stage lighting that a different light is assigned to do each job. The McCandless method is the most economical of any which can accomplish a creditable result, and it does not duplicate functions of any instrument or group of instruments. This basic approach is as applicable to the house as to the stage, as examination of houses thus lighted will show.

It is as important to keep light away from areas where it is not needed as to get it where it is wanted, and a great deal harder. To the application of this principle we may trace much of the improvement in appearance and comfort that has come to interiors in the last two decades.

The best light by which to read the program will not produce a pleasing effect if it strikes the walls. The light which gives the house warmth and intimacy will require programs in Braille if that's all the light there is. The bunch light, chandelier, sconce, or other open light source may be a desirable decorative device, but if it is bright enough to see by, the audience won't see anything else, and will be seeing spots instead of the show when the curtain goes up.

Visibility

Light for visibility in the auditorium by which the patrons may find their seats, read their programs, and recognize their friends must be generally distributed with a minimum of shadows and preferably from concealed or low-brightness sources installed in the ceiling, the light passing through small holes or louvered openings. Even distribution at moderate intensity (15 foot-candles) is desirable. White light is best. Light thus controlled will not upset the balance of the house; in fact, the house may seem dim, though the patron sees and is seen. And the light source will not be seen unless the patron looks directly upward, and not many theatregoers do that often or gracefully.

Special visibility lights are requisite for safety. Building codes in many localities provide that in the interests of safety, aisle lights be provided near the floor on each or on alternate aisle seats. This number is clearly in excess of what is needed to give the requisite visibility, but a minimum safe number and arrangement of such lights is one for every three rows on alternate sides of the aisle, plus lights on both sides wherever there is a step or change in pitch of the floor and at intersections and ends of aisles and crossovers. Luminous guide lines and tread edges in the carpet, activated from ultraviolet sources, promote safety with minimum distraction.

All doors must have exit lights over them. Most fire regulations require that the lights be red. It is unfortunately true that red lights attract attention even when there isn't any fire. When they are close to the arc of vision of the spectator, they often constitute a source of visual distraction. Blue exit lights are perfectly visible when the spectator wants to see them, but do not obtrude into his consciousness when he is looking at something else. Therefore, blue exit lights are desirable.

Examples of downlights of the kinds recommended for visibility in the house; left to right "Series 388" fixture, Century Lighting, Inc.; "Series NL"; "Hi-Hat" fixture. General Lighting Co.

The Park Theatre, Stockholm. Adequate general illumination provides good visibility and a pleasing impression of the simple decoration of this motion picture theatre. Photo, Rodger L. Simons.

The Rigoletto Theatre, Stockholm. (Hagstrand and Lindberg, Architects.) This photograph shows various safety lights: lights recessed into the stair risers, illuminated row numbers and exit lights. Photo, Rodger L. Simons.

Decorative Lighting

Decorative lighting is a part of the decorative scheme. In itself and by means of that which it illuminates it establishes the character of the house. It does this by:

1. Illumination of walls, ceilings, and proscenium: balanced background lighting, intensity less than for audience area, color chosen to give desired quality to wall and ceiling color.
2. Highlighting of focal points in decorative scheme: niches containing objets d'art, wall hangings, etc.
3. Decorative lights: chandeliers, sconces.

The instruments for decorative lighting may be concealed direct sources, or indirect cove lights, to illuminate the walls and ceilings. Transverse ceiling louvers reduce the apparent depth of the house. Highlights, of course, require special instruments. Open light sources serve a decorative purpose (chandeliers sometimes serve an acoustic purpose) only when they can be seen by a considerable portion of the audience. If they are bright enough to supply illumination they are more annoying than attractive, and are therefore to be thought of as decorative objects rather than as lighting sources. They may contain concealed lighting sources for visibility, decoration, or mood.

Mood

It has never been absolutely established that the use of an appropriate color in house lights can do much to set the mood called for by the play in advance of the curtain, though theory inclines in that direction and almost every director will try to accomplish something by means of color if given the opportunity. Color control on house lights is always useful for spectacle, as is amply demonstrated in New York's Radio City Music Hall, and it is probable that that fact alone justifies provision therefor. To achieve it, two things are necessary—concealed lights in primary colors controlled as are the footlights, and a neutral tinted wall and ceiling surface to be illuminated by those lights.

Distractions

The music stand lights are often a source of a good deal of distraction and consequent annoyance to the audience, except perhaps at some performances of opera where the enjoyment is in inverse ratio to the visibility of what transpires on the stage. While it is easy to mask the music stand lights, it is impossible to stop reflection from scores and thus a relatively bright area will be in the audience line of vision whenever the musicians are visible. There are several ways to overcome this:

1. An orchestra lift.
2. A deep pit.
3. A louvered orchestra pit cover.
4. Scores with white notes on black paper.

Comment

There are two elements which tend to prevent the lighting of auditoriums from being as good as it should be:

1. The unwillingness of architects to plan lighting before wall and ceiling shapes are settled. This is a result of ignorance, and the consultant is called in more often to correct what has been incorrectly built than to insure the correct design of a theatre. The design, construction, installation, and consultant's fee for one of the most elaborate theatre lighting projects in America cost less than just the installation costs in many smaller theatres lighted without expert counsel, and badly done.

The Gran Rex Theatre, Buenos Aires. The arched, set-back ceiling panels produce a concentration of attention upon the proscenium and diminish somewhat the large scale of this theatre.

2. There is an inexplicable illusion among some architects and builders that light must come from "fixtures," despite the obvious fact that if you hang a light out where you can see it, when it is turned on you can't see much else.

While seeing is the first consideration in planning the position of proscenium, walls, floors, seating, and house lighting, all of these elements must also be planned with relation to the acoustics of the theatre.

4: the audience hears

The audience and the showman find it to their mutual advantage and satisfaction for the audience to hear only what it wants to hear, or the showman wants it to hear, and that, clearly. This chapter will concern itself with those parts of the theatre building which have a direct bearing on the audibility of the show.

Requirements

The audience wants to hear the actor, the singer, the orchestra, the instrumental soloist, the organ, the audible component of the sound motion picture, and any other sound which is part of the show. It does *not* want to hear the elevated, auto horns, fire sirens, wind or rain outside the theatre while the show is in progress, or scraping feet in the aisles and rows, rattling foot rests, squeaking seats, banging lobby doors, or whistling fans, roaring blowers, knocking radiators, or telephone bells, buzzers, snap switches, the noisy shifting of scenery, or any unplanned distortion of any sound which is a part of the show.

It is up to the architect to insure perfect audibility of the show, and by the same token to protect the audience against distracting sounds such as those listed above. He must: 1. eliminate from the audience area all unwanted sound (noise, that which is not part of the show); 2. assure audibility for all sound which is part of the show.

Noise Level

Unwanted sound is noise. Noise in the theatre masks portions of the show and limits subtlety. It is therefore desirable to keep the theatre as free as possible from outside noise, and noise originating inside the theatre.

The average noise level in existing metropolitan theatres with audience present is about 50 db[1]. In the same locations 40 db is an entirely feasible level involving little, if any, additional construction expense. The best theatres often have a level of about 30 db. The level of ordinary conversation (at 3 feet in open air) is about 65 db.

Sound Transmission

Noise is either airborne or solid-borne. Steel structural members transmit sound with considerable efficiency. Sound thus transmitted becomes air-borne when wall, floor, or ceiling areas or fixtures are vibrated by the structural members and act much as the sounding board of a musical instrument. Vibration from sump pumps, blowers, etc., hardly noticeable as noise in the air, becomes noise when struc-

[1] db=decibel, the handy unit of sound intensity; the log of the ratio of the sound power to a standard reference: 10^{-16} watts per square centimeter.

turally transmitted to the house. A concrete slab will usually transmit sound more efficiently than a brick wall.

1. List the sources of noise (this will include a noise survey of the site).
2. List the means of transmission by which such noise might be conveyed to the house.
3. Provide in specifications for elimination of noise at the source wherever possible, e.g., maximum allowable noise from machinery, vibration insulating mounts, etc.
4. Provide in design for minimum transmission of sound to the house: doors opening on alleys, roof insulation, no single door having direct access from outside to house or stage which must be used during performance, etc.
5. Provide in specifications for minimum sound transmission by materials in all places where sound exclusion is a factor: adequate minimum transmission factor by emergency exit doors, interior walls.

The specification (5) is arrived at by subtracting the desired house sound level from the level of the maximum outside noise. (30 db inside level, 90 db outside level—minimum allowable attenuation by door in frame 60 db.) Acoustic characteristics of most building materials are known and widely published. Most suppliers of building materials will have sound transmission tests made of their products if they have not been made. Most contractors who install machinery will plan their installation with reference to a maximum noise specification and guarantee to meet such a specification.

Note: All specifications dealing with sound should include a statement of the frequency range to be covered. Acoustic measurements are conventionally made at octave intervals from 128 to 4096 cycles per second. A 60 cycle hum can be most annoying, as can a 10,000 cycle squeal. The ear responds to frequencies from 16 to 16,000 cycles per second, and a subway rumble is felt at even lower frequencies. For building material specifications and noise level calculations then, materials must often be tested for transmission of higher and lower frequencies than has been conventional practice.

Procedure

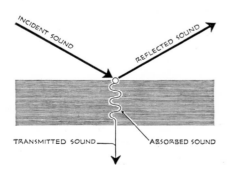

Action of sound on encountering a solid medium; in addition to being partially reflected, absorbed, or transmitted, sound is also refracted (changed in direction) by the more dense medium.

TABLE 1. Airborne noises originating outside the house and methods of exclusion.

Ingress	Method of Exclusion
Doors	Airtight fit. (This is requisite for efficient operation of ventilation system also.) Doors opening on alleys or halls are often less of a problem than if they open on the street. Preferably open only into spaces which can be kept reasonably quiet.
Windows	Do not belong in a theatre. Double where used and not capable of being opened.
Ceiling cuts	Exclude sound from loft by roof insulation, solid catwalks, tight doors.
Projection booth	Quiet machines. Sound absorbent walls and ceiling in booth. Glass in viewing ports.
Ventilation ducts	1. No metal connection between blower and steel structural members. 2. Ducts large enough not to rattle or whistle when blower operates at full speed (above normal operating speed). 3. Sound insulated ducts.

Source	Method of Prevention
Radiators	Heat the house entirely by circulated air, or wall or floor radiation. On stage, 1. Radiator return line graded to avoid condensate and resultant banging. NO VALVES TO HISS. 2. Circulate hot water rather than steam.
Stage Wagons Discs (Noise magnified because of reverberant stage floor)	1. Well made ball or roller bearing casters running on level tracks installed over stage floor. 2. Revolving stage on its own support structure (quieter than disc on stage floor). 3. Elevators are quiet unless they are of the screw jack type and run too fast.
Audience (Talk, shuffling)	1. Make rear crossover as sound absorbent as possible. 2. Lobby doors opposite aisles used for exit, NOT during show. 3. Divide rear crossover from house by a wall—a glass wall for motion picture houses. (This eliminates the rail for the waiting line.) 4. Carpet. 5. Silent seats.
Orchestra pit	Rubber feet on chair legs and stands.
Telephones	Locate only where one open door will not permit sound to reach house or stage. Light instead of bell on stage.
Snoring	Put on a good show.

TABLE 2. Airborne noise originating in the theatre and methods of prevention

Source	Method of Prevention
Train rumble (subway, elevated, surface)	Only satisfactory solution is to float floor and ceiling supports and, in case of excessive vibration, interior walls, as in radio broadcast studio design.
Vibration from non-theatre functions of building (gymnasium, bowling alley)	See above, or float the floor of the facility at which the vibration originates.
Motors, Machinery	Floating mounts.
Switches	Use mercury switches.
Plumbing	More than one wall between house and facility. Isolate from structural members.

TABLE 3. Solid-borne noises and methods of prevention.

To Hear the Show

Sight lines are apparent on blueprints. Anyone can take a ruler and see from the architect's designs whether or not it will be possible for the audience to see the show, and presumably anyone who builds a theatre will make a reasonably thorough sight-line analysis of the designs before approving them. No matter how much faith he has in his architect, he seldom cares to overlook any chances of error when he has a large investment to protect. Blueprints per se will not, on the other hand, show whether or not the audience will be able to hear.

Much of the data from which acoustic analyses are made are to be found in specifications for wall and ceiling surfaces, equipment, etc. The apparatus and engineering data for finding out from plans and specifications whether the theatre is acoustically good or not are not ready to the hand of the layman.

Acoustic studies must be conducted coincidentally with the design if the design is to avoid the risk of considerable alteration, but this logical procedure is still lamentably far from common practice. The science of architectural acoustics is new. Architects generally have not been trained in it. Though this situation shows some signs of improving, most existing and new theatres suffer from one of the four common architectural approaches to the problem of making it possible for the audience to hear, each of them successful in getting a good theatre about once in a thousand tries.

The first is to trust to luck: after all, the Metropolitan Opera House was built on that plan. No one has hit the jackpot since, however.

The second is to use a rule of thumb; it varies with what rule and whose thumb, but a few people, with much experience in theatre building, have learned perforce a little about acoustic phenomena, and have used that knowledge, more often to explain why the theatre was not good than successfully to make it satisfactory. Most present theatres were built by some rule of somebody's thumb.

Knowing that theatres usually turn out bad acoustically, there is a third architectural approach to the problem: build it first and fix it later. This means padding the walls or hanging up a drapery to stop an echo. No acoustically good theatres have resulted from this approach.

The final architectural triumph, however, is supposed to banish the demon of bad acoustics. It is born of despair and the public address system. If all surfaces in a theatre are made very soft and sound absorbent, the audience can hear practically nothing. There are no echoes. Then, if a powerful public address system is installed, powerful enough to frighten children blocks away, the audience can hear everything, including (and this causes much bewilderment) the echoes supposedly banished by the padding. Some of the largest theatres in America were thus designed. In them a strong human voice unamplified can hardly be heard a hundred feet. It takes much amplification to make a mighty pipe organ audible. And in some thousands of seats, everything the audiences do hear, they hear twice.

Oddly enough, a number of acoustically bad theatres were built wrong not because of any of the architectural approaches mentioned, but as a result of a sincere and outwardly intelligent effort to make them good. The miscalculations have come about through: (1) making an auditorium which is acoustically good while the asbestos is down, but bad when the play is on, through lack of provision for acoustic characteristics of stage, fly loft, and scenery; (2) assuming that the seats will all be occupied all the time (in two existing theatres acoustic conditions are fair when the house is full, bad when it is half empty, and it is impossible to rehearse in the empty theatre with the curtain up); (3) assuming that building materials with the word "acoustic" in their names will contribute to good acoustics no matter where or how used.

The theatre offers an acoustic problem replete with complexities which arise out of the nature of the show and the habits of the

Action of Sound

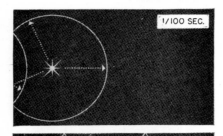

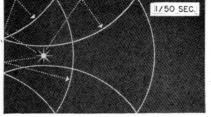

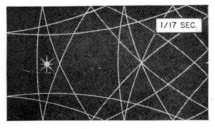

Distribution

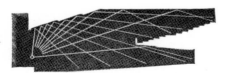

Progressive reflection of a single sound wave in an enclosed space.

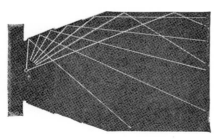

Section (above) and plan of an auditorium. Ceiling and side walls are designed to provide maximum reinforcement of direct sound particularly in the spectator portions most remote from the sound source. The stage at the left is merely suggested. Courtesy Celotex Corp.

audience. The architect and the engineer must work under a severe handicap unless they know show business.

The architect who knows show business well enough to design a theatre will often feel competent to prepare plans and specifications which will result in adequate exclusion and elimination of noise. The more specialized task of getting the sound of the show to the audience usually calls for the services of a physicist or engineer trained in acoustics to undertake the requisite calculations and tests.

In the theatre useful sound emanates from actors, orchestral instruments, organ, and loudspeakers; located on the stage, in the pit, and above and at the sides of the proscenium. The architect's job is to get it to the paying customers no matter where they sit without distortion or appreciable loss of intensity. Getting the sound to *all* the customers is a problem of *distribution*. Getting it there at almost equal intensity everywhere and having it die away rapidly at a predetermined interval after it has ceased to emanate from the source, so as not to interfere with the next sound as it comes along, is a problem to be solved by achieving a certain *reverberation time*.

Part of the sound pressure wave goes straight from the source to auditor. Part of it is reflected from ceiling and walls. Part of it gets to the auditor after it has been reflected back and forth about the house many times. Part of it has been for a trip around the stage, or has been reflected from the scenery or cyclorama.

Ceilings are the principal distribution surfaces. When ceilings are laid out, they must be planned to reflect the sound back to the audience, either directly or via walls, but in such a manner that it will neither be concentrated in certain spots, nor reflect back and forth between parallel surfaces, nor get to the audience out of phase with the direct wave. Moreover, since sound travels only about 1150 feet per second in air, the length of the path of the first reflected wave must not exceed that of the direct wave by more than 50 feet (preferably less) or the audience will hear everything twice.

The position of the side walls is determined by sight lines. The depth of the house (curtain to back wall) is governed by visibility requisites. Sound distribution requirements govern the shapes of the side walls, ceiling, ceiling under the balcony, and rear wall. The fact that the angle of reflection of a sound wave is equal to the angle of incidence (neglecting diffraction phenomena at low frequencies) makes it possible to lay out tentative shapes on paper. But since even the most unorthodox appearing shapes sometimes result in good theatres and vice versa, tests are necessary to establish the workability of any design. Plan and section of the theatre may be tested for distribution in ripple tanks, three-dimensional models by spark photographs and by tracing reflections of a small beam of light. The technique of testing is fairly complex. It can only be pointed out here that rough approximations are possible with single gravity waves in water and mercury tanks and that, within some limitations, varying frequencies may be studied stroboscopically with capillary waves. Photographs and visual observation reveal: 1. desirable distribution; 2. undesirable standing waves (repeated reflections between two surfaces); 3. echoes (a number of reflected waves whose path of travel is long coming to the audience, or part of it, in phase); 4. dead spots, into which very little sound penetrates, as is sometimes the case under balconies

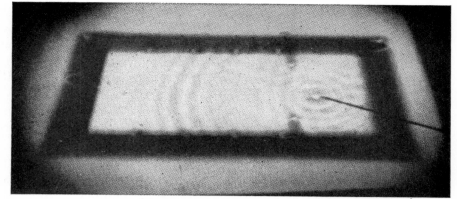

Photograph of a ripple tank test of a stage-auditorium model.

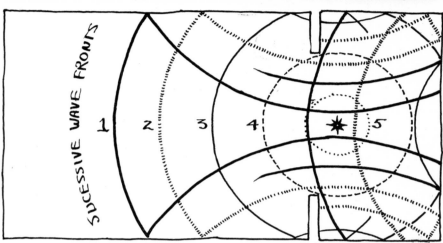

Diagrammatic representation of multiple sound reflections in a horizontal plane as revealed by the ripple tank test. This type of test indicates the acoustic properties of a specific architectural shape.

or where direct and reflected waves arrive out of phase and cancel out; 5. focal points such as the concentration of reflected waves on a small area of seats from a ceiling vault. When the wave pattern is rapidly broken up, and waves from all directions, of approximately equal size, cover the audience area, the distribution is probably satisfactory.

Spark photographs, actual pictures of the sound waves in air, have the advantage of greater clarity than most ripple tank pictures and are useful in the study of diffraction phenomena, and precise location of sources of trouble.

A small beam of light, reflected from surface to surface in a model, makes it possible to trace with reasonable exactness the path of the center of a sound wave.

There are pitfalls to be avoided when sound distribution tests of architectural shapes are made:

1. Sound sources are at numerous locations and tests must be repeated for from 6 to 12 locations on the stage with various teaser[1] trims as well as for all sound sources other than the stage.

2. Absorbent surfaces must be made non-reflecting (open or beached) in the model.

3. Stage and house must be tested together. They constitute a pair of coupled rooms. Plaster cycloramas *must* be designed as part of the acoustical planning of the *house* and tested with the house model. A cyclorama can be tipped toward the back of the stage far enough to put its focal point out of harm's way. Thus built it is also easier to light than if it is vertical.

[1] Masking piece or drapery which establishes effective height of proscenium opening.

4. Chandeliers, ceiling cuts for lights, and ventilation ducts *must* be included.

5. If reverberation calculations show any absorbent wall material to be desirable, its location must be determined by test so as not to interfere with sound distribution.

Finally, a ceiling under a balcony sloped up toward the back of the house, or a back wall which follows the curve of the seats, will almost invariably render good hearing impossible in at least part of the theatre.

Reverberation

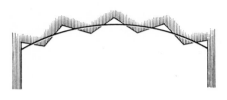

Methods of treating a curved rear wall of an auditorium to break up what would otherwise be a focusing reflected sound wave. (From LESS NOISE—BETTER HEARING, by Hale J. Sabine, published by The Celotex Corp.)

Reverberation is easy to calculate. But *what reverberation is desired* is another thing. The scale of desirable reverberation times runs from long for Widor's "Toccata" on the organ (it was composed to be played on the organ in St. Sulpice which is highly reverberant), to short, for speech which requires a high percentage of definition. In legitimate production, reverberation will vary from scene to scene depending upon the settings. The ideal theatre will have provision for controlling reverberation. At least one attempt to do this has been made, using wall panels which can be changed, but an analysis of the results is not at hand. Unless some means of controlling reverberation is provided, the best that can be achieved is a compromise between the optimum times for the various types of productions.

Reverberation optima have been the subject of much investigation. Recent studies directed toward the determination of optimum reverberation time for various house volumes show slightly longer times than those considered optimum five years ago. Moreover, as clients demand more and more precise acoustic conditions, optimum reverberation times tend to increase slightly. In a theatre planned for more than one type of production, if means are not provided for reverberation control, it is well to choose a reverberation time which is an average between optima for speech and orchestral music. The better the first reflections are controlled the closer orchestral optima should be approached.

For the calculations, the house and the part of the stage enclosed in a box set are considered. Tolerances, if any, are best taken on the long side. This is done for two reasons: 1. tolerance involves a margin of error. If the house is too dead, its correction is costly; if it is too live, correction is usually simple and cheap; 2. in calculation of reverberation time no account is taken of the stage house outside the set. The stage house has, however, some effect on the reverberation: when plein-air sets are used, the effective volume is greater than with a box set. In hung shows in which the flies are full, there is more absorption than with a box set. Both these conditions in practice call for slightly longer reverberation than would be requisite in the house with the proscenium closed.

Optimum reverberation time, it must be noted, varies with frequency. In large houses (over 200,000 cu. ft.) a slightly longer reverberation in the low frequencies than in the highs is generally considered requisite. Recent investigations seem to indicate the desirability of reverberation times more nearly equal throughout the audible range than was standard some years ago. If the reverberation time is made equal throughout the audible frequency range, the sound absorption characteristics of the audience will slightly unbalance it in favor of the lows.

Unfortunately the theatre does not play to the same sized audience

Optimum reverberation times as recommended in
ACOUSTICAL DESIGNING IN ARCHITECTURE by V. O.
Knudsen and C. M. Harris.

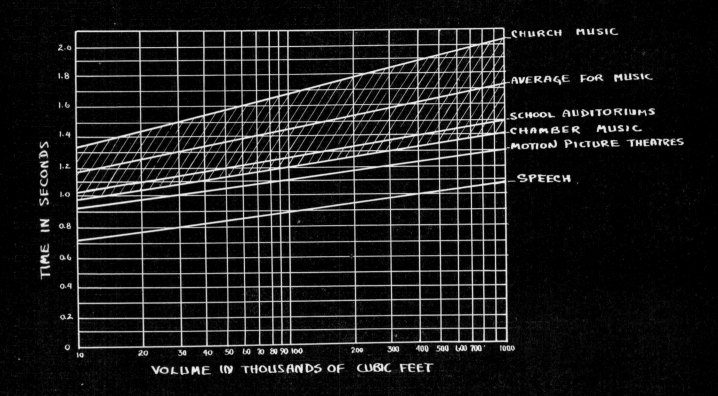

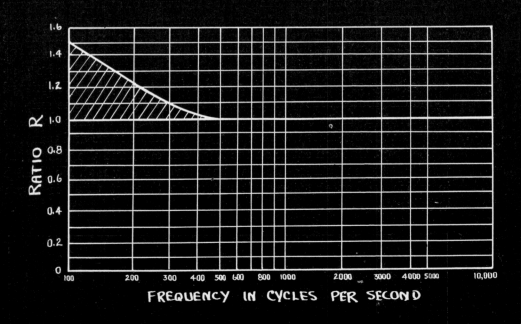

The values in the upper figure are all for 512 cycles.
When calculating reverberation for lower frequencies it
is necessary to modify the equation with a ratio R as
shown in the lower chart. For example $t_f = t_{512}\,R$.

at every performance. And the most neglected feature of acoustic planning is the provision of means of compensation for audiences of varying size. Yet it is possible to have the reverberation time the same with no one present as with a capacity house.

Each person in the audience absorbs a certain amount of sound. The unit of absorption is the sabine. If the acoustic specifications for the seats are so drawn that each seat empty absorbs as many sabines at the same frequencies as the seat plus a person sitting in it, the total absorption (and therefore the reverberation time) will be unchanged whatever the size of the audience. Seats and audience are therefore used to keep the reverberation time the same though the audience may vary in size. Before drawing seat specifications it is necessary to look into the question of what kind of people will constitute the audience and how they will dress. An audience of children will have fewer sabines than a matinee audience of women shoppers. Stiff shirts and bare shoulders are reflective as compared to soft shirts and afternoon dresses, a phenomenon which makes the traditional first night audience, at least acoustically, live.

When more absorption than that furnished by the seats or audience is necessary, it is well to get it next from carpet (which serves to eliminate the distraction of noise emanating from the audience), next from decorative hangings which can be changed in position and size, and last from permanent absorbent wall surface materials located so as not to interfere with sound distribution.

Procedure

The architect determines his house size from the necessary number of seats; its wall splay and depth from the requirements of good seeing; ceiling shapes from sound distribution and front stage lighting requirements; back wall and plaster cyclorama shapes by the necessity of preventing echoes and focal points. When model tests confirm the correctness of this much of the design, he may proceed.

His structure is conditioned by the necessity of avoiding resonance (it is generally believed that the organ caused the collapse of the roof in one theatre). His wall surface and heat insulating materials he specifies to give him: (1) the correct total reverberation time; (2) absorption where and to the extent he needs it. His ceiling he generally keeps as highly reflective as possible to insure undiminished sound distribution. He specifies seats which provide the same amount of absorption empty as do seat and occupant together when they are occupied. He insulates the theatre against outside noise and prevents inside noise. One can count on the fingers of one hand the theatres in which all these requirements have been scrupulously met. No theatre in which an honest attempt is not made to meet them is worth building.

The Princeton Playhouse (Thomas Stapleton, Architect). For this motion picture theatre Professor H. L. Cooke of Princeton University designed the ceiling to insure even distribution of reflected sound. Courtesy Princeton Alumni Weekly.

5: comfort and safety of the audience; front service rooms

The playgoer arrives under the marquee and proceeds to foyer, box office, lobby, house, lounge, and back to marquee again usually via lobby and foyer. It is good showmanship to conceive of the playgoer's progress through the theatre as a parade in which the playgoer will enjoy participating. Comfort and safety are primary considerations in planning those parts of the theatre through which the patron moves.

When the annual visit of the circus constituted the only show business in a community, the audience stood for crowding, hard seats, soiled clothes, dust, and perhaps a long trip home, and could spend the next day recuperating from the fatigue, excitement, and condiments. The audience could, would and did take it. The fact that people now buy seats in second balconies of theatres and in the bleacher sections of ball parks shows that hardy souls are still among us. However, there aren't enough people willing to look upon theatre going as a challenge to their fortitude to pay the bills for any but a very few exceptional theatres.

In the preceding chapters, causes of discomfort have been cited, and provision for comfort as it applied to traffic, sight, and hearing have been considered. This chapter considers provisions for comfort and safety from traffic, sight and hearing requisites, and of the functional design of the front service rooms not elsewhere considered.

Exterior

Comfort and safety become the concern of the showman when first the patron approaches the theatre. Architecturally, plenty of light on the street in front of the theatre, on driveways about it (5 fc.[1] minimum), clearly marked crosswalks, a lighted parking area (5 fc. min.) and lights under the marquee (10 fc. min.) and illuminated automobile traffic markers are requisite. An illuminated automobile call is indispensable where any substantial number of patrons use chauffeur-driven cars.

If illumination in front is not provided by the marquee it may be obtained from flood lights which illuminate the building, decorative lamp posts, bracket lights, or portico lights. Illumination under the marquee of minimum safety standard is poor showmanship. The higher the illumination, the more the audience makes its own show. Illumination of more than 25 fc. may be in order.

The marquee must be drained so that a curtain of water is not interposed between the automobile and the sidewalk.

A high degree of illumination is especially necessary wherever there are steps outside the marquee, or between marquee and foyer.

[1] 1 fc.=the illumination from 1 standard candle on a surface 1 ft. square at a distance of 1 ft. The unit measure of illumination.

The Hollywood Paramount Theatre. Illumination of the facade, the marquee signs, the theatre name and the entrance area under the marquee produce levels of illumination which render the theatre easily recognizable and the entrance area visually attractive and safe. Note the strong shadow at the curb and the even brightness of the sidewalk and vestibule. (W. L. Pereira, Architect.) Photo, Fred. R. Dapprich.

Gran Rex Theatre. An unbroken expanse of foyer doors affords maximum access to main and upper floor with a minimum of ground area. Structural simplicity is in contrast to elaborate interiors of North American motion picture houses. Photo, Alberto E. Terrot.

Outside illumination is no less important if the theatre is hidden away in a school building. It is not enough to make it possible for the audience to see after it has got into the building, the school building plant which contains the theatre must include theatre requisites in the planning of the whole building.

Changes of level from sidewalk through the vestibule, foyer and lobby into the house are best made by ramps. Stairs are forbidden by some building codes and permitted under careful restrictions by others. Isolated steps and steps at doors are to be avoided as hazardous. When steps occur they must be adequately lighted.

Doors Into Foyer

Fire regulations provide that all theatre doors must open out. Traditionally the doors to the foyer are hung in pairs, and are in most cases metal with large glass panels. For the sake of fulfilling their function there must be enough to handle the whole audience without congestion in a few minutes. For the purpose of making foyer doors architecturally impressive they are often much wider than is efficient. Thirty-two inches should be considered a maximum width for the single unit of a pair of double doors. The glass lights are principally for the purpose of giving daylight illumination to the foyer, one of the few places in the theatre where there is any use for it.

Where the theatre building is used for other purposes and access is via corridors, the entrance to the building itself must be so planned as to conform to minimum foyer standards.

Foyer

Foyer area and arrangement are determined by a study of the traffic loads (Chapter 2). In addition to traffic, the architect is concerned with doors and other entrances, floor, wall and ceiling materials, heat, ventilation, and light.

There is more traffic through the foyer than through any other part of the theatre. It is a room outside the theatre proper. The floor surfaces, therefore, must stand a lot of traffic, must not be stained or rendered hazardous by standing water, must be easily cleaned, must not be uncomfortable to stand on. Stone and tile are popular and good but are best covered by perforated rubber matting in wet weather as they tend to become slippery. The patron waiting for friends or in the ticket queue often has a dripping umbrella. Wall surfaces must resist defacing to at least shoulder height, and be easy to clean, and the junction between wall and floor must be watertight. These requisites rule out plaster walls and, except where foyer is so large as never to be crowded, wood paneling. Doors must all be silent and self-closing. If there is access from foyer to offices or other parts of the building, the doors are made as inconspicuous as possible to keep theatre patrons from using them.

Hard surfaced rooms tend to be excessively noisy; it is therefore desirable to surface the ceiling and, where appropriate from a decorative point of view, upper sections of the walls, with sound absorbent material. Such materials must be easy to clean. The higher the absorption coefficient, the more appropriate the material.

Since occupants of the foyer are dressed for the weather outside, provision for heating or cooling need not provide the difference between outside and inside conditions demanded by the interior of the theatre. There is no need for heating to achieve temperatures above 55° F., or cooling to more than 5° lower than the outside temperature. Humidity control is welcome to the same degree as that provided for the house. If air is blown into the foyer to accomplish any or all of the tasks of air conditioning (heating, cooling, ventilation, humidity control), it must *not* be re-circulated. Warm air may be forced into the foyer in winter as a buffer against outside cold air and cool air in summer as an attraction to passers-by.

The purposes and requisites for lighting in the foyer are the same as those which apply under the marquee. If any variation in illumination is undertaken, the bright spots must be at steps, areas in front of ticket windows, and area about the ticket taker's stand at the entrance to the lobby. Bright light sources within the normal visual angle are a source of annoyance and fatigue, which rules out sconces, standlights and usually chandeliers.

Standard equipment for foyers include the ticket taker's box (portable) which is only in place when it is in use, and rails to prevent the forming of double lines at ticket windows. If the foyer is so planned that lines of traffic do not intersect, the rails are dispensable. It goes without saying that the decorative treatment of the foyer must be such as to make it a pleasant place to be. A cold, dark, forbidding foyer discourages theatre-going.

Box Office

The most efficient box office is the change booth at the turnstile employed in some motion picture houses. Next in order of efficiency is the ticket cage at the entrance to the foyer which dispenses tickets automatically for unreserved seats. In both these types of box offices, the speed with which change can be made is the factor which determines the number of persons who can be handled. Automatic change dispensers are now practically universal in such box offices.

The problem of the theatre which has reserved seats is much more complex. Ticket purchasers often request specific locations. There is often considerable discussion, and change-making is not restricted to silver. The size, arrangement, and equipment of the booth constitute the most complex problem in booth design when reserved seats are to be handled. For all except the smallest or most specialized houses, the reserved seat policy must be envisioned.

The box office needs at least one window for current sale per approximately 1250 seats, and one window for reservations. The farther these windows are apart the easier the traffic problem will be. If the box office is at a corner, one window can be on one side and one on the other. The island box office can have lines on either side. The ticket bar as used in Europe has the advantage of handling more simultaneous transactions than any other type since the staff is not restricted to the number of windows. It has a further advantage in that it eliminates the elements of remoteness, formality, and regimentation which the window box office so often fosters. In large houses ticket sale may be divided between windows or sections of the ticket bar as follows: current show sale; reservations for current show; advance sale; each category further subdivided by price or location, or both.

Size and shape of box office are determined by (1) number of windows with their attendant equipment, change drawer, automatic change machine, (2) wall space for the ticket racks which include the day board for the current performance, the rack containing tickets for the rest of the current week, and racks containing tickets for subsequent weeks. Two day boards help to minimize ticket purchase time if one is used for the current and one for the next performance, especially on matinee days. Rack sizes vary with the size of the house but are seldom less than 20″×30″. For large houses orchestra and balcony tickets are sometimes efficiently handled at separate windows. If the day board is on the wall containing the ticket window, the ticket seller does not need to turn around during the transaction. Telephones, a desk and a safe complete the useful box office equipment. The safe must be large enough to contain all the racks without removing tickets from them, in addition to the usual cash box and ledger. Access to the box office is by a single door inside the theatre, often from an adjacent business office. Where the ticket bar is used, racks are on the wall behind the bar and the door in that wall leads into an office which serves all other box office purposes except ticket dispensing. The light in the box office is best concentrated on working areas with additional general illumination. School and college theatres are often handicapped because they were designed without box offices.

Confusion, inefficiency, and illwill engendered from lack of adequate architectural provision for the one point at which the theatre staff has business dealings with its customers can do much to discourage patronage. A typical condition is one in which the curtain is held while ticket sellers fumble through the box of tickets to try to accommodate the last-minute box office rush. The box office takes up very little space and cannot be neglected in any type of theatre.

For turnstile box office and the automatic dispensing motion picture theatre box office, specifications drawn by the manufacturers of the box office equipment may be followed.

Lest it be forgotten, the box office needs ventilation as much as any other part of the theatre, and heating to counteract blasts of frigid air from the foyer.

The requirements for lobby size and shape are derived from traffic studies. In the interests of safety, doors must usually occupy the whole wall between foyer and lobby. Their equipment and swing must fill specifications for foyer doors save that there is never any reason for glass lights in them. Doors between lobby and house may not be necessary unless the show is continuous. Between lobby and lounge no doors are necessary. Whether or not there are doors to the house, the lobby must be quiet, for which reason the floor must be completely carpeted, the walls sound absorbent or containing sound absorbent panels or covered with draperies, and the ceiling sound absorbent. Sound from the lobby must not leak into the house.

Lighting in the lobby must be warm enough to be flattering, bright enough to highlight jewels, so directed that it will not spill into the house. If lobby lights are dimmed during performance, there must still be enough illumination to read the ticket stub, see the stairs, find the coatroom or the lounge. For continuous run motion picture houses it is desirable to have the general illumination of the lobby of lower intensity than the foyer, to facilitate dark adaptation for the entering audience. These requirements can only be met by carefully planned combination of direct and indirect illumination, i.e., coves and louvered reflectors recessed in the ceiling, chandelier and ceiling containing a large indirect source of light or many small, flush, ceiling lights with frosted covers, lenses, or louvres. Illuminated signs indicating coat room, lounge entrance, and balcony stairs or elevator are desirable. Exit signs are requisite over all doors leading to the foyer.

Ceiling height may well depend upon other elements in the theatre

Lobby

The lobby (called in this instance Grand Foyer) of the Radio City Music Hall showing the free flow of audience traffic made possible by the grand staircase and the stairs down to the lounges. Entrances into the house are to the right of the picture. (Reinhard & Hofmeister, Architects.) Cosmo-Sileo Photo courtesy Radio City Music Hall.

Lobby of the Hollywood Paramount Theatre. An atmosphere of comfort without elaborate decoration, achieved along with the basic requisites of a good lobby. Photo, Fred R. Dapprich.

Orchestra Lobby of the Scala Theatre, Bucharest. Although severely simple in decoration, this lobby provides ample space for audience traffic, clearly delineated paths of movement, wide checking counter, and space off the direct paths of traffic for patrons checking wraps. (Rudolf Frankel, Architect.)

Balcony Lobby of the Scala Theatre.

structure and a high ceiling contributes to a feeling of luxury. If the stairs have a complete run along lobby walls, the ceiling may well be as high as that of the house. The aim of all decorative treatment must obviously be the promotion of the feeling of luxury.

The furnishings of the lobby are fairly obvious. They include mirrors. In them the theatregoer can be sure he is seen if only by himself. Mirrors have no value unless they are tall and obviously a part of the decorative scheme. A tinted mirror is to be preferred to the standard silver mirror; it is not so harsh and may be flattering to the modern Narcissus.

Wall tables for flowers and to hold the hat while the coat is being put on, benches to facilitate putting on rubbers, complete the necessary lobby furnishings save where lounge limitations and local law and custom demand ash receivers.

Furniture in the lobby must be located in space over and above the clear width required as passageways by building codes. Care must be taken that furniture does not impede audience traffic.

The best carpet is the cheapest in the long run. The original chenille carpet in the lobby of the Roxy Theatre in New York lasted more than a decade. No carpet could be subjected to heavier wear. Wilton is a good carpet but will not last as long as a good chenille. The design of the carpet may well be planned to lead the audience in the direction conducive to minimum traffic congestion, i.e., from foyer to checkroom, to stairs and crossover, from audience area to lounge entrance by circular path to the left, back to the house. When low intensity lighting is employed to accommodate the audience in a dark house, fluorescent lines in the carpet, energized by overhead UV lamps, have proved useful.

Stairs leading to balconies require carpeting for the same reason that the rest of the lobby is carpeted. Maximum comfortable riser height is 7½ inches, and minimum tread width 10½ inches. For added wear, for quiet and for comfort, carpets must be laid on padding.

Balcony lobby provisions for comfort and safety are derived by observing the same rules which apply in orchestra lobby planning.

Check Room

The check room counter should be wide enough for five attendants per 1000 seats in the house. With adequate check room facilities, the efficiency of checking is governed by the size of the staff, not by architectural limitations. Check rooms in balcony lobbies reduce orchestra lobby congestion. Racks built to accommodate coats, hats, sticks, umbrellas and parcels, used in some of the new dining rooms and check rooms of some modern hotels may well serve as models for theatre check room equipment. Self-service checking apparatus, using patented locking clothing holders, may be considered.

In conformity with the principle of keeping traffic moving to the right, the check room is best located at the right side of the lobby as the patron enters from the foyer. The fact that it is on the patron's left as he leaves the theatre is of little consequence because he faces no opposing traffic and he has already found out where the check room is.

Lounge

As the audience comes out of the house at intermission time, it finds the lounge most easily if it is located at the right, i.e., at the opposite side of the lobby from the check room. The lounge, as its name implies, is the place where the audience stretches, talks, and

Lounge of the Radio City Music Hall, New York. Although styles in decoration have changed since this theatre was built, the arrangement of space and furniture, the use of mirrors and the appeal to the creature comfort of the audience are as valid as they were in 1932. Photo, LIFE photographer Herbert Gehr. Copyright TIME Inc.

Lounge of the Palms Theatre, Phoenix, Arizona. Contrasting both decorative style and geography with the previous illustration, this lobby reflects concern for the same elements: comfort, luxury, informality. Interrelation of outdoors and indoors, as shown here, was a little-known concept in 1932. It has become popular since then and is particularly appropriate to the Southwest. (W. L. Pereira and Lesher & Mahoney, Architects.) Photo, Maynard L. Parker.

The lounge of the Kirby Memorial Theatre, Amherst College, serves the additional functions of rehearsal room and club room for the Amherst Masquers. Photo, courtesy Dept. of Dramatics, Amherst College.

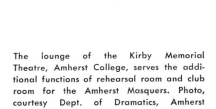

Lounge of the Municipal Theatre, Malmö, Sweden. Separation between foyer, lobby, and lounge has been eliminated from this theatre in favor of ample space for free circulation of the entire audience. This lounge area is on the balcony level, slightly delineated by steps down at either end. Photo, Jaerke.

refreshes itself during intermissions. Its hall marks are the deeply upholstered chair and the sand-filled receptacle for butts. In it are bar, telephones, water coolers, and entrances to lavatories.

Floor, walls, and ceiling of the lounge merit the same treatment as their counterparts in the lobby and for the same reasons. Lavatories may be located either at the right or left of the lounge entrance provided they are both visible without turning half way around as the patron enters the lounge; or they may be located one after the other as he starts a circuit of the room keeping to the right.

The lounge needs overstuffed chairs arranged as though in a living room, save that their normal groupings for conversational purposes need seldom provide for more than four. The occasional straight chair will serve to make the normal groupings flexible. Small but rugged tables to hold lamps, ash trays and drinks, and many ash receivers complete the requisite equipment. A piano is decorative and useful if the lounge serves as a room for gatherings other than the intermission audience. A fireplace is useful only if it can contain a real fire and does when the weather makes one appropriate.

Light intensity at lounge entrance, exit, lavatory entrances, and bar will naturally be higher than at other areas. For maximum effectiveness, it may well be planned so that as the patron walks through the lounge he passes through alternating areas of medium (10 fc.) and high (25 fc.) intensity. If direct light from ceiling to floor is a part of the scheme for the high intensity areas, sequins and jewelry will sparkle in them and a dramatic effect will be gained from the movement of groups of people.

It is gratifying to note that the vogue of amber lights in public rooms, which made the audience look like cadavers eight days drowned, is passing. White light is harsh and not very dramatic. Pale magenta is good for general illumination but must be supplemented by white or steel blue to highlight the audience as mentioned previously. Color is best achieved in shades and roundels or fluorescent tubes. The exposed bulb has no decorative value in most schemes.

A bar in the lounge is a source of income not lightly to be dismissed. In London, a play may run at no profit to the box office or even at a very slight loss, and the theatre may still operate on the profit from the bar. Aside from this, however, a bar undeniably adds to the spirit of carnival and helps to make theatre-going an event. The bar belongs in or near the lounge. Congestion, discomfort, and hazards introduced by soft drink vendors in the lobby or crossover are familiar to everyone.

The proportion of the audience which uses the lounge is, with little exception, limited only by the capacity of the lounge. Lounge area is inadequate in most theatres. It may well occupy all the space under the seating area of the house and the lobby and be supplemented by balcony lounges. In theatres located in warm, dry climates, the lounge may well be outdoors, in which case a large lobby is needed and the lavatories are located adjacent to it. The large indoor lounge constitutes, when properly planned, useful rental space for exhibitions, parties, lectures, and meetings at times when the audience is not in the theatre. The lounge is traditionally used for rehearsal.

Most building codes require and wisdom dictates exits from the lounge sufficient to evacuate its capacity crowd at the same rate at which the house may be emptied.

Bar of the Kleinhans Music Hall, Buffalo, New York. The long serving bar, the ample space in front of it, and the many small tables, easily accessible, all comply with the theatrical requirement that many people be served in a short time. (Eliel and Eero Saarinen, Designers; F. J. and W. A. Kidd, Architects.) Photo courtesy Kleinhans Music Hall Management, Inc.

Bottom: the bar at the Metropolitan Opera House. The pleasantest place in New York to spend an intermission. Photo, Louis Melancon.

Lavatories

It goes without saying that lavatories must have ante rooms: a smoking room for men, and a powder room equipped with at least one dressing table per 600 seats or fraction thereof in the house, for women. Five urinals, three wash basins and two toilets per 1000 seats are minima for the men's lavatory; five toilets and five wash basins per 1000 for the women's lavatory are minima. Where performances run over three hours, the lavatory traffic is increased fourfold, for which reason it is wise to exceed the lavatory equipment minima by a considerable margin.

Multiple Uses

Restricted building budgets sometimes lead clients and architects to slight or limit the public rooms, or attempt to combine their functions. People still have to get from here to there and still take up the same amount of room whether the builder likes it or not. A theatre wrongly designed in the first instance is seldom susceptible of much improvement. In planning front service rooms in the face of a restricted budget, the same precept applies as has been recommended for other parts of the theatre, i.e., plan a complete and adequate plant, build or finish only as much as the budget provides for, leaving provision for completion when funds are again available. Temporary expedients necessary to the operation of the uncompleted plant are seldom any more annoying than restrictions resulting from compromises, and have the virtue of being remediable.

Auxiliary Uses

When the theatre plant includes, or is a part of, an architectural unit which contains shops, restaurant, a broadcast station, or of a school or college, the public rooms of the theatre may well be planned to serve other than theatrical purposes at hours when no audience is present. Conversely, public rooms planned to serve non-theatrical purposes in hours when the theatre is dark may be made to serve the theatre. This condition is a critical one for the theatre in the school, located in a building which is used in part for non-theatrical purposes. If special front service rooms are not provided for the theatre in such a building, the lounge, lavatories, and hallways of the buildings must be arranged to serve the theatre.

House

If doors between lobby and crossover are used, they will normally stand open except while the play is in progress. The glass partition behind the last row of seats (found in some motion picture theatres) is no substitute for a wall and doors. A 4'6" high wall behind the seats is desirable, to prevent draft and to accommodate standing patrons.

Comfort in the house depends upon: 1. shape and upholstery of seats and the distance between rows; 2. temperature, humidity and freshness of air; 3. position and width of aisles; 4. house lighting; 5. decoration; 6. floor slope; 7. absence of distraction. Theatrical requirements other than audience comfort and safety prescribe adequate comfort specifications for some of these items.

The seat which is acoustically correct will be comfortably upholstered. No less important than the upholstery is the shape of the seat. For some unknown reason the curved back, bucket seat has been popular in America and is installed in many theatres. Sitting with the shoulders pinched forward becomes extremely uncomfortable by intermission time. Flat-backed chairs are therefore the only proper equipment for the theatre. A chair of this sort developed for the

Men's Lounge of the third mezzanine, Radio City Music Hall. Photo courtesy Radio City Music Hall.

The Little Gallery of the Esquire Theatre, Chicago, is suitable for art exhibits, matinee tea, and meetings of small groups. The stairs at the end lead to the Ladies' Lounge. Located over the main lobby and entered from the balcony lobby, it is off the main line of traffic without being inaccessible. (W. L. Pereira, Architect.) Photo, Hedrich-Blessing.

Chicago Civic Opera House has proved so satisfactory that it has become a widely used type. Despite the past record of the Province-town Theatre and the present success of the Hedgerow Theatre, hard seats won't encourage repeated patronage. The comfortable seat is no less important in the school or college theatre. Assemblies and commencements held in the theatre will benefit from comfortable seats.

Seats need to be spaced sufficiently far apart to permit passage of people without the occupant's rising. Cramming them close together for the purpose of slightly increased capacity is a very short-sighted policy. Closely spaced seats cause extreme discomfort, especially to tall people, and some inveterate theatregoers will not go into certain New York theatres no matter what the show. The marginal comfortable spacing, back to back, is 34″. Spacing to permit easy passage past seated patrons is 45″, back to back.

Seats with springs which raise them automatically or which slide back are considered hazardous by some theatre managers. This feature, however, simplifies cleaning and saves many barked shins. If employed it must be considered in the acoustic planning.

The building codes in most localities set minimum limits for aisle width and number of seats in a row. For economic reasons it is generally wise to use the maximum number of seats per row. Under no circumstances is a center aisle tolerable. Actors abhor center aisles for the very good reason that they split the audience and make the achieving of mass reaction difficult.

Exits

Local and state ordinances governing buildings for public assembly prescribe the number, size, and to some extent the location of exits. In the absence of specific requirements in the laws, the planner may refer to the recommendations of the National Board of Fire Underwriters.

Satisfaction of the code requirements for emergency exits, plus provision for the comfort and safety of the audience as set forth in this chapter will result in a house in which the audience will be psychologically and physically conditioned to enjoy the performance to the maximum.

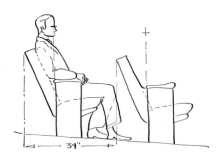

— MARGINAL —

This spacing affords comfortable seating. With a slide-back seat the seated person may remain seated when another person passes in front of him.

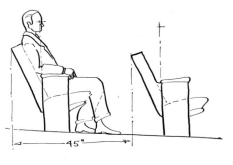

— ALLOWS EASY PASSAGE —

This spacing allows a person to pass in front of another person seated.

6: Power, heat, air conditioning, plumbing

The architectural and engineering practices and building code requirements which govern the installation of power, light, heat, ventilation, and plumbing in buildings are well standardized. This chapter will concern itself only with variations from standard practice made necessary by the peculiar demands of the theatre.

Power

The theatre differs from almost any other type of building in that its power requirement is 100% of outlet capacity, a considerable variation from the 10% requirement for residences, hotels, and office buildings. The reasons for this are obvious: it is not uncommon for every lamp and every motor in the theatre to be in use simultaneously. Failure, through overloading, must not occur during performance. It is wise at the outset to bring in enough power to handle the maximum load based on final installed requirements. Facilities for stage lighting must be included in the original building plans. Because of the increasing efficiency of light sources it is improbable that future unforeseen additions to lighting equipment will require more power than does the completely equipped theatre for which the power load is calculated.

Power Plant

Because of the intermittent use of the theatre, it is not economical for the theatre to generate its own power. If the theatre is part of a school which has its own power plant, the school plant must usually have capacity considerably in excess of that which is normal for an academic plant. A theatre imposes peak loads not only in the evening but often during the day, for which reason planning to divert power from darkened departments in the evening places undue restrictions on the daytime use of the theatre.

Auxiliary Power Supply

An emergency power supply from a source entirely separate from the regular one is required by law in most cities. This supply must be adequate to illuminate the house, all exit passages, and all exit lights. An auxiliary power supply capable of meeting the total load requirements of the theatre is desirable, though not required by law.

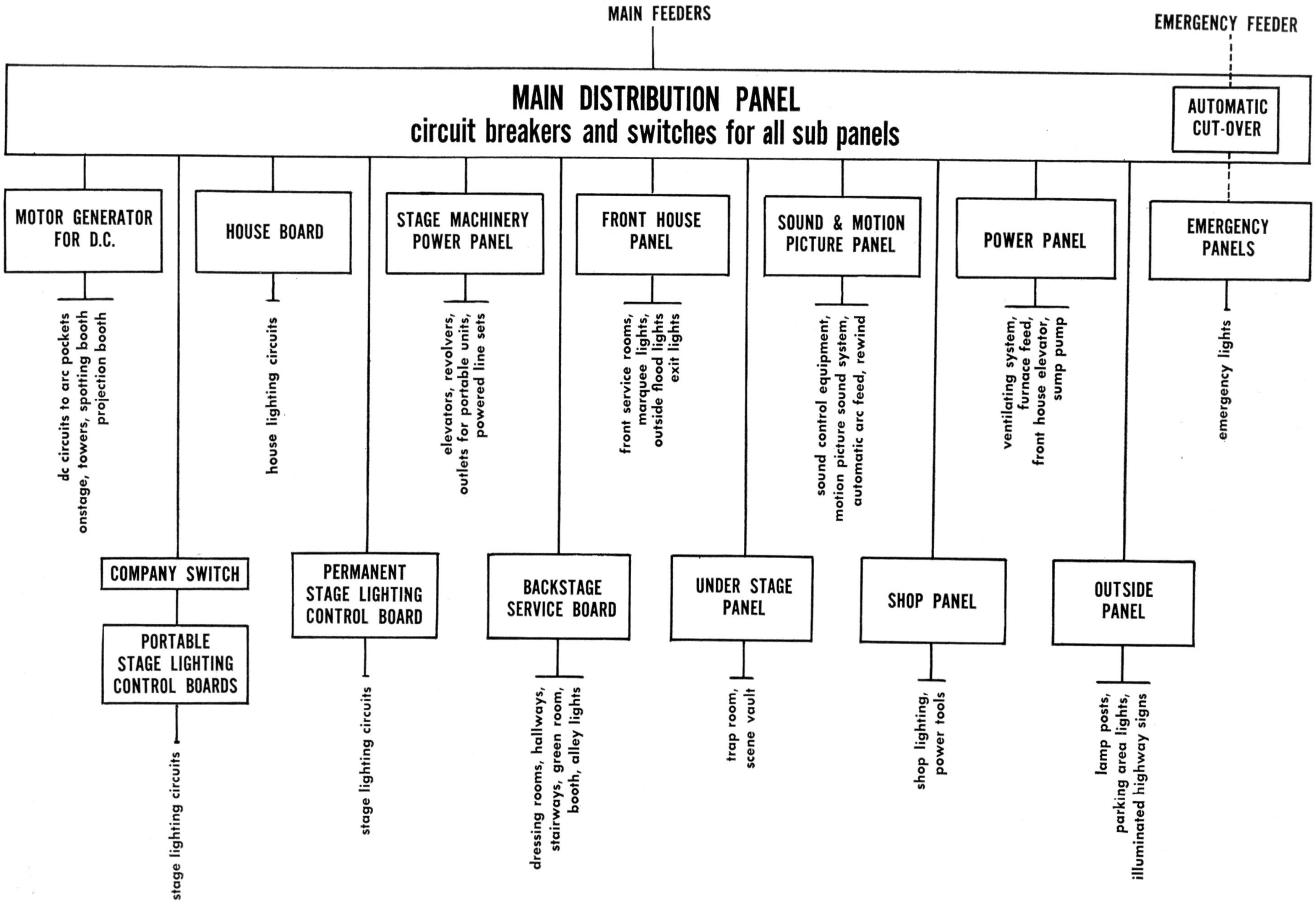

MAIN DISTRIBUTION PANEL
circuit breakers and switches for all sub panels

MAIN FEEDERS

EMERGENCY FEEDER

AUTOMATIC CUT-OVER

MOTOR GENERATOR FOR D.C.

dc circuits to arc pockets onstage, towers, spotting booth projection booth

COMPANY SWITCH

PORTABLE STAGE LIGHTING CONTROL BOARDS

stage lighting circuits

HOUSE BOARD

house lighting circuits

STAGE MACHINERY POWER PANEL

elevators, revolvers, outlets for portable units, powered line sets

PERMANENT STAGE LIGHTING CONTROL BOARD

stage lighting circuits

BACKSTAGE SERVICE BOARD

dressing rooms, hallways, stairways, green room, booth, alley lights

FRONT HOUSE PANEL

front service rooms, marquee lights, outside flood lights exit lights

UNDER STAGE PANEL

trap room, scene vault

SOUND & MOTION PICTURE PANEL

sound control equipment, motion picture sound system, automatic arc feed, rewind

SHOP PANEL

shop lighting, power tools

POWER PANEL

ventilating system, furnace feed, front house elevator, sump pump

OUTSIDE PANEL

lamp posts, parking area lights, illuminated highway signs

EMERGENCY PANELS

emergency lights

Schematic diagram of power distribution.

64

For stage use, both AC and DC are required. Either AC or DC may be employed where resistance plates are used as dimmers. AC is required where dimming is done by means of autotransformers or by electronic tubes. AC and DC are both necessary where control is by a thyratron-reactor circuit. DC is required for arc spotlights (on stage and out front). Motors for blowers, furnace feed, marquee moving sign, power tools in the shop, and other similar equipment are most efficient if they operate on AC. For elevators, motorized flying equipment, revolving stages, DC is often preferred though not essential. The amount of each kind of current is easily determined by totaling the requirements of each type of equipment. Standard voltage is 110 and single phase except where the demands of specific motors or lighting control equipment require three phase.

Current

It is wise to keep generating equipment—transformers, rectifiers, and motor generators—away from the operating areas in the theatre, in a separate building back of the stage house or in the corner of the basement under the stage farthest away from the proscenium. Such equipment is automatic, needs little attention, and needs to be kept out of the way. Some items cause interference or distortion in electronic equipment.

Location

If current enters the theatre in the form in which it is to be used, entry normally should be at the point which will require the shortest run of conduit from the main distribution and breaker panel to the stage loads.

This panel is located at the point of entry or origin of the current. It includes circuit breakers on all incoming feeders, except the solid ground on 4-wire AC installations, and provision for distributing each type of current to sub-panels at the next point of control. The sub-panels are:

Main Distribution Panel

1. House board located onstage from which all house lighting circuits branch.
2. Company switch.
3. Permanent stage lighting control.
4. Power panel for stage machinery.
5. Back stage service board from which are distributed circuits to dressing rooms, hallways, stairways, green room, stage doorman's booth, alley lights.
6. Under-stage panel for distribution to trap room, basement scene· vault, and other under-stage areas.
7. Front house panel carrying circuits for all front service rooms, marquee sign, and outside floodlight equipment.
8. Motion picture projection panel for all circuits feeding motion picture, sound, and other electronic equipment (not including stage lighting control).
9. Power panel from which come the individual circuits for ventilation equipment and furnace feed.
10. Shop panel from which are distributed circuits for shop lighting and power tools.
11. Outside panel feeding lamp-posts, parking area lights, and illuminated highway signs.
12. Exit light panel which supplies all exit lights which burn while the audience is in the theatre.

The main distribution panel is equipped with switches, circuit breakers and, in the case of small circuits, fuses. These are grouped according to sub-distribution points and each group contains distribution facilities for every type of current to go to the sub-panels. In other words, each type of current is distributed to sub-panels from the same main panel.

Variations within this distribution scheme will be treated after consideration of the individual sub-distribution points.

Company Switch

The company switch is traditionally located on the operating side of the stage. From it are tapped the main feeders for portable switchboards. When a portable switchboard is used, stage lights and lights on balcony facia are fed directly from the portable board.

House Board

Dimmers for house lights are standard equipment in all theatres. From the main panel the lines go to a sub-panel and thence to the house light switches and dimmers. Electrical or mechanical mastering facilitates even dimming of all or selected house lighting circuits.

In addition to the main switch and circuit breakers, small individual switches control orchestra pit lights, pinrail and scene dock work light, rehearsal lights and convenience outlets. All these switches must be silent.

Permanent Stage Lighting Control Boards

When the theatre has a permanent stage lighting control board feeders from the main distribution panel run directly to the control board or to the reactor room or circuit distribution panel depending on whether resistance, autotransformer, reactor or electronic control is employed. With the permanent switchboard located in orchestra pit or balcony, the house light distribution panel may be installed in the trap room or backstage adjacent to the stage circuit distribution panel.

Sub-Panels

Three conditions govern the location of all sub-panels: 1. they must be easily accessible to the persons responsible for their operation; 2. in the interest of efficient construction, they must be located in as direct a line as possible between the main distribution panel and the instruments served by their branch circuits; 3. no panels must be located at any point to which the audience has access.

The power panel for stage machinery is located beside or in the house board if the motors controlled are onstage or above it: in the trap room, if the motors are belowstage: or, if motors are located in both places, two panels individually fed from the main distribution panel are employed. In any case *control* is at the stage manager's position.

Backstage service board is located in the stage entrance corridor in or near the stage doorman's booth.

Understage panel is located at the foot of the backstage stairs leading to the basement.

Motion picture projection panel is located in the rear wall of the projection booth or the projectionists' office.

Power panel for ventilation and heating is located on a wall of the room which contains ventilation equipment or furnace feed.

Shop panel is located in the shop near the entrance at a point where there is no occasion for stacking scenery.

Outside panel is located in an office at the front of the theatre

Sub-panel assembly follows standard practice except that: (1) more than one kind of current may be controlled through switches in the same panel; (2) all switches in all panels, in all walls, which surround the stage, or any portion of the theatre occupied by the audience, must be silent. This restriction applies also to wall switches in individual circuits.

It is obvious that the arrangement here outlined is too elaborate for the small theatre, and inadequate for the presentation house. The routine of theatre operation, plus sound engineering practice, prescribe that the minimum power distribution facilities be a combination main distribution panel, a house board, a company switch, and a front house panel. The expansion of this system for very large houses can be developed from an analysis of the organization of such a theatre. When there is a permanent engineering or electrical maintenance staff attached to the theatre, sub-panel locations, with the exception of company board and motion picture distribution panel, are susceptible of considerable variation. In any case, however, the principle of grouping loads on sub-panels as here outlined must be adhered to if operation and maintenance are to be easy and effective.

Only by keeping branch circuits independent of each other can the varying load conditions in a theatre be successfully met. Typical results of variations from this practice are: in one theatre, the electronic organ would not play when the moving marquee sign was turned on, because the marquee sign caused the voltage in the AC line to drop to 92. In another theatre, the characters on the motion picture screen spoke something which sounded like monkey chatter because a transformer was too near. In another theatre, the grounded sump pump blew the fuses in the line which fed the motion picture projection arcs.

The only aspect of outside theatre lighting for which specifications do not naturally arise from the foregoing principles is the marquee billing and the theatre name sign. Whether or not these are used depends upon the location of the theatre. The urban theatre will want to dominate the block, and the rural theatre transfers its identification and billing from the marquee to the side of the highway. In either case, light is needed. Fluorescent tubes have considerable visibility per unit of power consumption. To determine the power for house identification and marquee billing, it is necessary to make a light survey of the locality and calculate therefrom the number of foot candles which will achieve the desired degree of visibility over the area to be employed. Theatre identification, marquee billing, under-marquee illumination and driveway lights—the last two discussed in previous chapters—constitute a large load.

Air conditioning is now belatedly recognized as a necessary feature without an approximation of which not even the meagerly equipped New York legitimate house can draw customers in hot weather. There are many systems and devices which allegedly provide air conditioning and do, in the sense that they do something to the air, but whether the processed air is thereby rendered any more conducive to comfort is, alas, another story. Briefly, the function of air conditioning is to provide comfort for the audience by providing the requisite amount

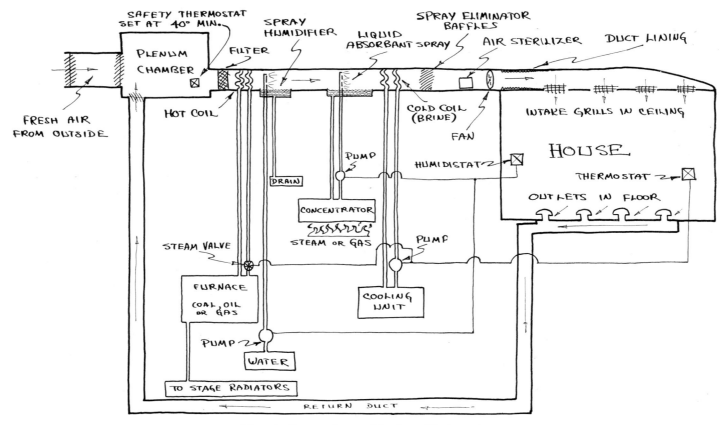

Schematic diagram of a complete air conditioning system.

of fresh sterile air (about 10 cfm per person), at the proper temperature (65° to 70°) and humidity (40% to 45%). Important subsidiary functions include protecting seat coverings, drops, and hangings from mildew. Metal surfaces and duct linings will rust through excess moisture in the air. Fabrics will be discolored and ultimately destroyed by dust if the air is not kept reasonably dust free.

Air Intake

The air conditioning cycle is as follows:

The air is drawn out of the house through grilles or mushrooms under the seats, preferably built into the seat legs to conserve foot room, through ducts to a plenum chamber. There it is mixed with fresh air drawn from outside the building. Dampers on fresh and return air ducts control the proportion of the mixture. The highest proportion of recirculated air is used in the winter when it is uneconomical to throw away heated air after going to the expense of heating it. When the air is well conditioned, as little as 20% fresh outside air will suffice to reestablish an adequate oxygen content. The wide range of heating requirements makes it necessary to induce varying amounts of outside air from the minimum to 100%, and to alter the proportion rapidly and easily during performance.

Dust Removal

From the plenum chamber the air is drawn through the filter, precipitator, or spray to have dust particles filtered, precipitated, or washed out. Filters are generally adequate for small theatres, or theatres in which there are usually not more than 8 performances per week. Large presentation houses which run 12 to 14 hours a day, 7 days a week may find electrostatic precipitation more economical and effective.

Since a system of forced ventilation is necessary in any case, and since heat is needed only when the ventilation system is also required, it is cheaper to heat the house by a radiator in the main air duct than by any other system. Therefore, the next unit in the air conditioning circuit is the heating coil, a steam coil fed from the boiler as in any other steam heating system.

An audience coming into a theatre will raise the house temperature approximately 1° per minute for the 15 minutes before curtain. This rate of change is too rapid for some control instruments to follow or for most systems to compensate. It is therefore necessary especially in cold weather to start with an empty house at about 65°, and thereafter concentrate on keeping the house cool (usually by feeding cold outside air only into the ventilating system) until the standard working temperature is reached. With an outside temperature below freezing in a well insulated house where about 60% of the air is recirculated, no heat may be needed until the third act. A theatre system must be capable of rapid adaptation to changed conditions in the house, and large excess capacity to minimize the change.

Heating dries the air, usually to a point below 40% which is generally considered minimum for comfort. Moisture is added by bleeding steam from the heating system into the air stream after it passes the hot coil. A humidistat supplies satisfactory control. Heating and humidifying are fairly simple processes, and may be all that are needed where the weather is never excessively hot and damp. Most of the theatres in the United States, however, need apparatus for cooling and dehumidifying the air if they are to operate from June to September.

Cooling is accomplished in most installations by piping a liquid refrigerant through a coil in the air duct. The refrigerant may be cooled by a cycle similar to that used in an ice plant, or home refrigerator. Such a system has the advantage of being self contained and capable of a wide range of temperature control.

A method of cooling popular in many legitimate houses in New York is to run through the cold coil water which has been sprayed over and melted from ice. This system is uneconomical if used for more than a few hours a day.

Similarly, city water or well water may be run through the cold coil if they are cheap enough and do not get warmer than 65°. City and well water should be quite popular as cooling agents since they require no complex and expensive equipment, sometimes only a little piping which the local plumber can install at small expense. Ironically several theatres use water to cool their expensive mechanical cooling plants which, if run directly through the cold coil, would cool the theatres adequately without the mechanical plants. Then operation would be simplified and made less expensive if they threw their mechanical coolers away and just used the water.

Cooling the air reduces its moisture content. This is fortunate, for the drier the air, the warmer it may be without causing discomfort. However, for most theatres, dehumidifying thus achieved is not sufficient. In fact, fashion designers have developed jackets to be worn with evening gowns to protect the wearers against the dank chill of allegedly air conditioned theatres.

Heating

Humidifying

Cooling

Dehumidifying

It is sometimes unpleasantly difficult for the body to adjust itself to a wide difference between the temperature inside and outside of the theatre, particularly in hot weather. In fact, it is now accepted as axiomatic that a 10° difference in hot weather is all that can be maintained without subjecting the audience to the danger of shock, particularly on leaving the theatre. However, comfort can be maintained in temperatures of 90° or even greater, by reducing the relative humidity to a point where perspiration is immediately evaporated, lowering the temperature of the skin. The dry heat of the desert is not uncomfortable—in the shade.

The most satisfactory system for achieving a desirable balance between temperature and humidity in hot weather is to employ chemical means of humidity control. Several substances notably triethylene glycol (also used for air sterilization) absorb moisture from the air readily, and are easily reconcentrated to keep the drying process constant. Any desired relative humidity may be maintained with systems using chemical dehumidifiers.

Sterilization

Air Sterilizer. Glycol Vaporizer of Air Purification Service, Inc. Vaporization is by means of heat and a glass wick. Photo, Crawford & Keating.

Air sterilization removes the threat of airborne infection in the theatre. It is essential in any modern theatre, and can easily be provided in old ones. The principle is the maintenance of a germicidal vapor (triethylene or propylene glycol about 50% concentrated) in the air. The quantity of glycol necessary is only one ounce per hour per 3000 cfm of air. Due to the fact that glycol decomposes at temperatures below its boiling point, vaporizing must be accomplished at a temperature held within a very few degrees. Glycol vapor is induced into the airstream by a small pressure drop. About 20 cfm passes through the vaporizer which is located in a plenum before the fan, or outside the duct ahead of the fan. Vaporizing equipment is electrically interlocked with the fan motor since it need only operate when the ventilating system is in use.

Fan

The fan or blower which keeps the air moving through the theatre and the conditioning apparatus must be silent as pointed out in Chapter 3, even when operating at maximum speed. It must be so placed that it is not supported on any of the steel which supports the walls of the house or from which the ceiling is hung or some of the sounds incident to its operation will be transmitted to the audience. Of the fans now on the market, those which are most efficient are the noisiest, thus efficiency must be sacrificed to silence in all but certain highly specialized instances.

Ducts

It is easy to lay out ducts which will take the air where you want it, but the requirements of the theatre are much greater than that. There must first be absolute silence, which almost always means sound insulation in the ducts at least near the fan, and an air speed considerably less than that which is satisfactory in homes or office buildings. House input grilles must be artistically appropriate, quiet, must assure appropriate distribution (no drafts), and must not direct currents of air along walls or ceiling where dust streaks will show.

Circulation

Hot air rises. Dust settles. If the air is used as the means of heating, and the path of the air in the house is from floor to ceiling the balcony will become overheated while the orchestra shivers due to the fact that the body heated air rises and the temperature throughout the house cannot be kept constant. Therefore the best cycle of air in the house is from ceiling to floor. Such a cycle will minimize dust, insure uniform efficient heating, and eliminate drafts.

The generally accepted amount of air needed in any room is 10 cubic feet per minute (cfm) per person. Experience shows this to be adequate for theatres if the air is fresh or well conditioned. The figure is a minimum, however, for American audiences, and a smaller amount of air or improperly conditioned air will bring complaints of stuffiness.

Public Rooms

For all theatres except those in which motion pictures are run continuously, it is not wise to recirculate air from the public rooms because of the difficulty of eliminating the great quantity of smoke which rises from the audience at intermission. Such rooms can be adequately conditioned under most circumstances by exhaust air from the house, where not much is needed during intermission.

The foyer is not air conditioned unless it is designed to serve more purposes than those assigned to it in Chapter 5. The air conditioning of offices is desirable but may depend on their use and whether or not the building budget is limited. As in all offices, air conditioning is desirable.

Production Shops

Dehumidification is desirable to dry paint in the paint shop, and to dry fabrics in the dye room. The stage heating installation (radiation) will usually take care of the house between performances when the asbestos is up. The stage is cooled and ventilated from and as part of the house during performance.

Dressing Rooms

Cooling and humidity control are quite desirable in the dressing rooms if the theatre operates in the summer. It is difficult to make up a perspiring face. Not all theatrical costumes are designed to be worn or to stay fresh at 90° in the shade. Conditioned air blown into the dressing room corridor, entering the rooms through door grilles, and exhausted to atmosphere will keep the cast comfortable and help the show.

Control

The control devices for the air conditioning system are the conventional thermostat and humidistat. They must be located in the house at the average audience elevation. If placed on the wall, they must be well insulated from it so that they will not be affected by the wall temperature or by a particular local humidity condition induced by the proximity of the wall. There must also be numerous automatic control devices in the air conditioning unit to control amount of steam injected into the air, steam valve leading to hot coil and flow of cooling liquid in the cold coil. Of particular importance is the thermostat placed just ahead of the heating coil which controls the shutters on the fresh air intake and closes them when the steam is off and the air gets down to 32° to prevent the freezing of any condensate.

Outside Sources

It is sometimes possible to have excellent air conditioning in a theatre without the installation of anything but ducts, by the simple expedient of buying the conditioned air from an adjacent hotel whose system has a greater capacity than is immediately necessary, or from a store which would otherwise shut its system down during the hours when the theatre needs conditioned air. The buying of conditioned air is perhaps most feasible where a number of theatres closely grouped can buy the surplus capacity of a department store installation.

Heating the Stage

The most efficient system for heating the stage house is by the conventional wall type radiator. The following restrictions limit the manner of its installation:

1. Radiators must be on the wall and at least six feet off the floor so that they do not use up floor space, and so that rubbish will not accumulate on the floor behind them.
2. To avoid using scenery stacking space radiators must be set in wall bays. Where the stage wall is not divided into bays, radiators must be as close to the wall as possible.
3. Feed and return pipes must not project into the stage space and may sometimes be partially countersunk into the masonry.
4. Battens must be placed in front of all radiators so that scenery stacked against the walls will not come into direct contact with the radiator.

Since lights, resistance dimmers, and leakage from the house heating system through the proscenium all contribute some heat to the stage, the capacity of the stage heating system need not be calculated to provide a stage temperature level of more than 65° in the coldest weather. The stage heating system, like that of the rest of the theatre, must be so planned as to eliminate the possibility of hissing valves or pounding pipes. The theatre with a noisy heating system has to shut off the heat at show time in order to get the show on.

In below freezing weather a down draft develops at the walls of the stage house caused by the cooling of the air at the walls with a resultant up draft near the center of the stage. This also produces a draft of cold air into the auditorium. When the act curtain is raised, it causes discomfort to actors and stage hands, and sometimes produces disturbing movement of hanging scenery and curtains. The heating and ventilating system must be designed to break up this phenomenon.

Wall radiators on stage.

Plumbing

The uses of the theatre impose special limitations on plumbing installations no less than on provision for power, heating, and ventilation. The admirable practice of putting pipes where they do not clutter up the stage and where they are not visible to the audience, often results in a trap room or scene dock so filled with piping as to render useless large sections of those two areas. If exposed piping must run through the scene dock, it must be on the wall or ceiling and the position of the wall and ceiling must be determined with respect to the plumbing installation so that the clear interior dimensions of the finished theatre will be those originally contemplated. This same principle applies, of course, to the planning of understage corridors, dressing room halls and other places where exposed piping runs. The trap area below stage must be kept clear of piping. Steam, water and drain pipe locations must be determined in advance of the final decision as to building arrangement if the systems they serve are to be efficient in installation and not interfere with the operation of the theatre.

Sprinkler System

The stage, scene docks, shop, sometimes the trap room and various other areas must be provided with sprinkler system as prescribed in building codes. A sprinkler installation, in addition to fulfilling its safety function, must be out of the way. Therefore, sprinkler heads must be protected by beams, or other structural members from accidental impact of moving scenery or machinery which might set them off. This feature is particularly critical on the stage; sprinkler pipes are best run parallel to and above the bottom level of the roof beams. The pipe will then not be hit when work is being done on the gridiron. Some codes prescribe stage sprinkler systems below the gridiron. In such cases, pipes must run parallel to the battens and between them so that an up-running batten will not strike a row of sprinkler pipes and cause all the heads in the group to discharge. In the trap room, sprinkler pipes located directly under the permanent supporting beams have some measure of protection and do not prevent the use of traps. As in the case of all other piping, clear heights must be calculated on the basis of the installed sprinkler system.

Building codes, underwriters' requirement, and local fire-fighting facilities govern the inclusion of hose lines in a theatre. A common regulation is that there must be two hose lines of specified length and diameter connected to pipes having equal diameter and specified pressure on each floor level backstage and on each floor in the house or lobby. A water tank atop the stage house is likewise commonly required.

A perforated water pipe across the proscenium opening with a hand operated valve near the stage floor adds fire-resistivity to an asbestos curtain.

Fire Hose, Standpipes, Water Tank, Water Curtain

The well-equipped theatre will have wash basins in all dressing rooms; lavatories containing wash basins, showers and toilets for actors and crews; lavatories with wash basins and toilets for front house organization, and lavatories for maintenance and janitorial staffs.

Lavatories, Showers, and Wash Basins

Slop sinks will be installed conveniently accessible to all locations where floors are to be mopped.

For water effects, rain, and the like in performance, water connections and drains must be available onstage, and there must be a drain in the trap room.

Sump pump and cooling coil and vacuum cleaning piping must be planned as part of the complete plumbing layout. Pumps and blowers must be silent.

For easy maintenance, it is often wise to plan to have all the piping in the theatre follow, so far as is feasible, the same path. All piping of the front of the house, and all piping to the dressing room wing or shops may well be hung in basement corridors on the same hangers. Color-coding of pipes is distinctly advantageous.

Miscellaneous

7: acting area, proscenium, orchestra

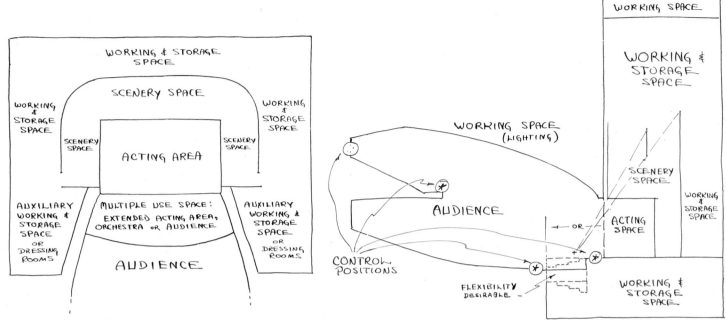

Diagram of the arrangement of backstage spaces. Plan. This diagram must not be interpreted in terms of size or shape.

Foregoing chapters have treated the means of making the front of the house and the house itself suitable to their function, the accommodation of an audience. It is now in order to consider those factors which determine the suitability of the stage to its function, the accommodation of the performance.

The stage is easily defined: it is that part of the theatre where the performance takes place. Its size, shape, arrangement, and equipment, therefore, must logically develop from the nature of the performance. The table of production types in Chapter 1 lists the visual and auditory components of all types of productions. Inasmuch as architectural acoustics and the electronic control of sound can provide for optimum audience perception of the auditory components, regardless of the form of the stage, development of the requirements for the stage may proceed from a consideration of the visual components and the routine of performance.

Stage Space

For all production types, the visual components divide into two categories: performers and scenic investiture. These indicate the functional divisions of the stage: (1) the space in which the performers work, which though actually three-dimensional, is usually referred to as the acting area; and, (2) the space wherein the scenic investiture is arranged, which will be called hereafter the scenery space. A corollary of the presence of scenic investiture is the need for its operation and storage. This indicates a third functional division of the stage: working and storage space.

The size and shape of the working and storage space depend upon the size, shape, and arrangement of the scenery space, and the size and shape of the scenery space depend upon the size, shape, and arrangement of the acting area. This chapter will develop the form and equipment of the acting area. Development of the form and equipment of the scenery space and of the working and storage space will follow in subsequent chapters.

The theatre situation is fundamentally one of relationship between the audience and the performers. Associated with the performers are the behind-the-scenes theatre artists who contribute script, score, direction, and scenic investiture to the support of the performance, and back of all theatre artists stands the showman, who plans and administers the theatre enterprise so that the ultimate relationship between audience and performer may take place.

In Chapter 1 the basic requirements of the audience, the theatre artist, and the showman were stated briefly and simply. For the purposes of this chapter it is necessary to amplify them. The audience wants to hear and see the show without distraction and in comfort and safety, as stated, but its ultimate objective in attending the show is to receive the utmost sensory stimulation toward the maximum intellectual and emotional experience. Maximum appreciation and enjoyment of, and in a very real sense participation in the theatre experience by each individual member of the audience depend upon the maximum enjoyment of it by the entire audience. Group reaction to a single performance stimulus is something less than total unless that stimulus be perceived at the same time, in the same measure, and with the same significance by the entire group.

The producer and the theatre artists have requirements consistent with these: they want the physical facilities which will allow their show to stimulate the audience to the maximum of intellectual and emotional appreciation. The skilled theatre artist applies knowledge of audience reaction to the preparation of every part of the performance. If, because of inadequacies of the theatre building the audience cannot perceive the performance as the artist has planned it, the artist fails through no fault of his own, and the audience is disappointed.

If the theatre does not permit total uniform stimulus and reaction, the performance can never reach its peak of effectiveness. The best efforts of theatre artists stand the best chance of appreciative reception by audiences if the audience-performance relationship fosters total uniform stimulus and reaction, hereinafter called total uniform effect.

Total Uniform Effect

Not only is it the height of theatrical artistry for the showman to achieve this condition of total uniform effect, but it is good business. The spectator who does not see or does not hear or does not comprehend a speech or action because of inadequate physical orientation toward the performance feels to some degree cheated of his admission fee, and less inclined to return to the theatre, than does the spectator who perceives all the components of the performance fully, and who feels that the performance is projected toward him and those close to him.

Expert showmen and artists use their productional knowledge and skills to the fullest within the limits of the physical plants at their disposal. It is the duty of the theatre planner to provide them with facilities which do not limit nor hinder their efforts.

The *size* of the acting area is a direct function of the number of performers who use it, their costumes, and the nature of their performance. A single performer, engaged in a static recitation, lecture, or soliloquy, without gestures and in plain modern dress, requires about 4 square feet. Elaborate period costume and sweeping arm gestures may enlarge the requirement to 18 square feet. Solo dancers

Acting Area

of the more energetic sort require a minimum floor area of about 300 square feet.

The shape and arrangement of the acting area are functions of the kind of action and amount of movement inherent in the production type, and of the audience-performance relationship which provides total uniform effect for the particular kind of action. If the action is of the concert or recitational kind, face-to-face relationship between audience and performer is necessary. If any part of the action, whether by individual performers or groups, requires the optimum condition for expressive communication between the performers and the audience, the shape and arrangement must permit the entire audience to see the performers face to face. Most of the expressive parts of the human anatomy are in front. If the performance involves communication, inter-reactions or opposition between performers, the shape and arrangement of the acting area must permit that action to take place on a line perpendicular to the general audience sight line to be uniformly perceived by the audience.

If the movement is to any considerable degree two-dimensional, as in ballet, optimum perception requires that the audience be elevated so that it may have a good view of the entire acting area, and thus become aware of the depth dimension of the movement. And if the entire action is truly two-dimensional, with no necessity for frontal expression by any of the performers, with no situations involving linear opposition between performers or groups of performers, and with no purely linear movement of performers, the acting area may be centrally located within a closed circle of audience. It should be noted, however, that because of the complete diversity of audience viewpoint in this situation, it is impossible for any but truly two-dimensional action, divorced from frontal expression, to produce a total uniform effect on the audience. In most of the group entertainment media employing this form at present (circus, athletic arena, stadium) the audience has expressed the truth of the perceptual relationship by placing a premium on the seats which are at right angles to the line of competitive movement, and by preferring the seats facing the band and the center ring of the circus.

Before considering the construction of a theatre for the current vogue of producing known as central staging, planners must measure the certain loss of total uniform effect against other possible advantages of the form.

Proscenium

The audience looks at the performance through the proscenium opening. Sometimes the action of the performance extends through it, toward, into, and around the audience.

The design of the proscenium is of two-fold importance: visually the design controls the attention of the audience and directs it toward the stage; physically, the proscenium conceals and discloses the stage and the acting area. Proscenium equipment is described in Chapter 11.

The typical proscenium in existing theatres is formed by a narrowing (splay) of the side walls of the auditorium toward a rectangular or round-topped opening in the wall between the auditorium and the stage, through which the audience sees the show. In older theatres the splayed walls contained audience boxes with very bad sight lines and various kinds of architectural ornament, most of it distracting. In presentation houses the space formed by the splay often contains

Auditorium and proscenium of the Kirby Memorial Theatre, Amherst College. The stage lighting control board is under the hood at the orchestra pit. (McKim, Mead and White, Architects.) Photo courtesy Dept. of Dramatics, Amherst College.

Conventional mid-twentieth century proscenium. Plan.

Proscenium, forestage, and sidestages in the Radio City Music Hall. The forestage is an elevator. Organ consoles are rolled automatically from the niches onto the sidestages. The stage lighting control is center, adjoining the forestage well. Photo, courtesy Radio City Music Hall.

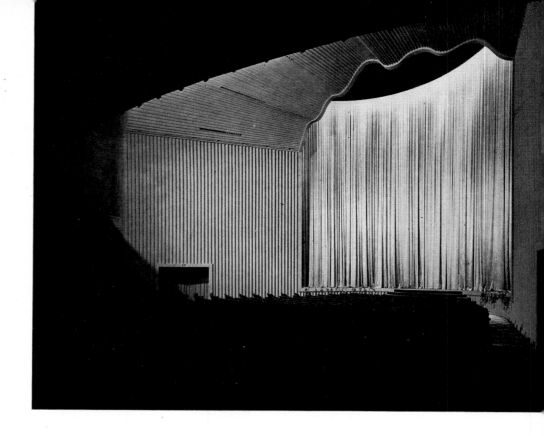

Proscenium of the Hollywood Paramount Theatre. Photo, Fred. R. Dapprich.

The Cine Plaza Theatre, Juarez, Mexico. The formal proscenium is unnecessary for the showing of motion pictures. Here curtains which form an unbroken decorative feature when down, are raised to disclose the picture projection area. (Rafael F. Calderon, Engineer.) Photo, courtesy J. R. Clancy, Inc.

organ pipes behind wall grilles. The acoustic function of these splayed walls is discussed in Chapter 4.

The typical form of proscenium is the early twentieth century terminus of an historically long development of the proscenium through many forms. Its functional foundation lies in the supposition that the entire performance is to take place in the space behind the curtain line or directly before the curtain line on the so-called apron. It sets rigid limits to the acting area and consequently limits the performance-audience relationship available to the showman.

Theatrical production refuses to be contained within a strictly limited space behind a rectangular opening. The existing proscenium form has been called the picture frame stage, and the peep show stage, and even during its incidence and rise to prevalence there were objections to its restrictive character. The theory of theatre admits and numerous modern plays contain instances where the contact between performance and audience must be more intimate than the formal frame permits. History of theatre shows twenty-four centuries in which the picture frame was either non-existent or modified by the use of acting areas in front of it, against the last century and a quarter during which the proscenium developed in prominence. Modern theatrical practice contains frequent instances of the performance's attempting to come through the frame, into, about, and around the audience.

Notable about recently constructed theatres and in schemes presented in architectural competitions are attempts to modify the fixed and inflexible proscenium. Part of this experimentation is due to a justified recognition that theatrical production demands more freedom of audience-performance relationship than the typical proscenium allows, and part is due to a current penchant for novelty, amounting even to a grim determination to be original. Critical appraisal of these efforts must be based upon sound understanding of the demands which theatrical production makes upon the proscenium. A proscenium which is variable according to requirements of several production types renders the theatre more useful to the showman.

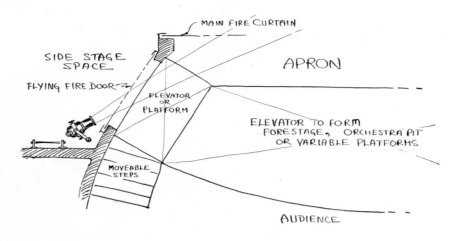

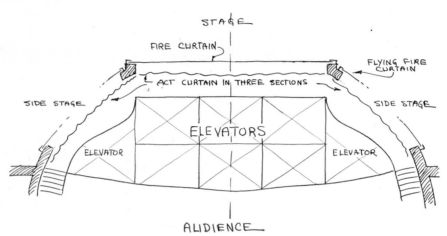

Examples of flexible and
variable arrangements of
proscenium and forestage.

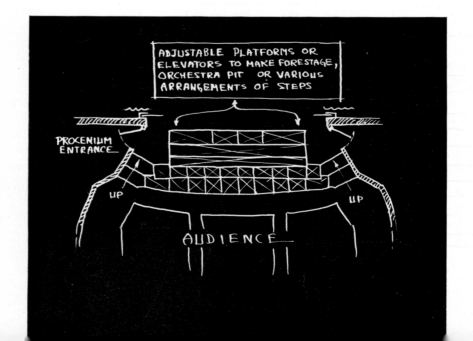

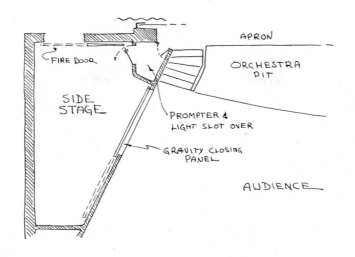

APRON

ORCHESTRA PIT

FIRE DOOR

SIDE STAGE

PROMPTER & LIGHT SLOT OVER

GRAVITY CLOSING PANEL

AUDIENCE

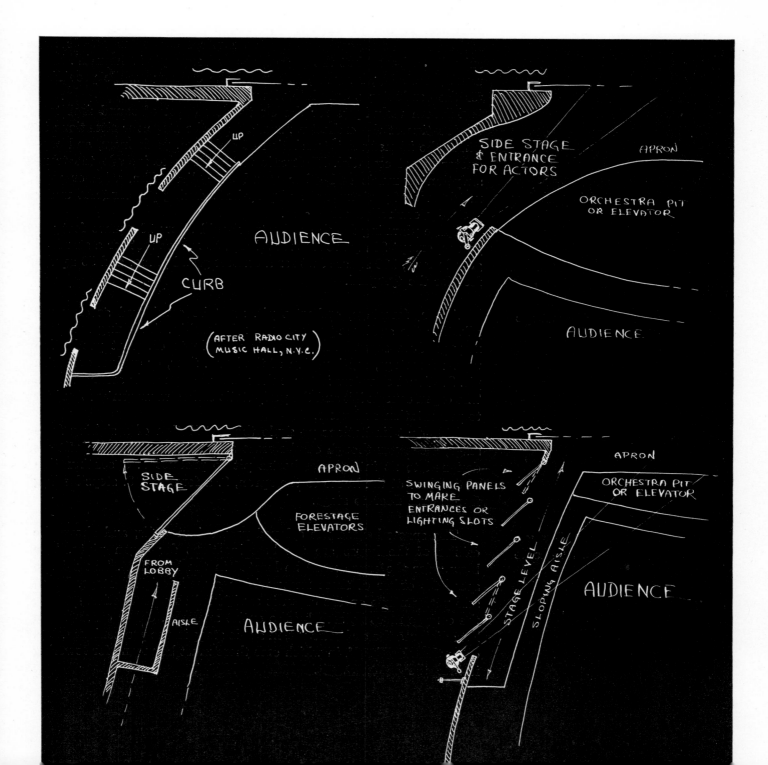

UP

UP

AUDIENCE

CURB

(AFTER RADIO CITY MUSIC HALL, N.Y.C.)

SIDE STAGE & ENTRANCE FOR ACTORS

APRON

ORCHESTRA PIT OR ELEVATOR

AUDIENCE

SIDE STAGE

APRON

FORESTAGE ELEVATORS

FROM LOBBY

AISLE

AUDIENCE

SWINGING PANELS TO MAKE ENTRANCES OR LIGHTING SLOTS

APRON

ORCHESTRA PIT OR ELEVATOR

STAGE LEVEL

SLOPING AISLE

AUDIENCE

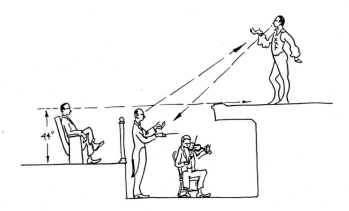

Required sightlines for orchestra pit.

Orchestra Pit

Music is an important auditory component of most production types, and an integral visual component in some. The developed location of the orchestra is in a pit between the acting area and the audience. If the production type requires exact cueing and close interrelation as in opera where the musical conductor directs not only the orchestra but the singers, the orchestra pit is essential. It is usually desirable, however, to conceal the orchestra while providing for the conductor a complete view of the acting area.

Modern techniques for the electronic control of sound facilitate the location of the orchestra remote from the stage for situations in which the immediate interrelation of orchestra, performers, and conductor is not essential. Electronic techniques also include the transcription of music and other sound onto discs, film, wire or tape in advance of performance and play-back during performance under precisely controlled conditions.

Space planning for the orchestra should allow 10 square feet per person, except 20 square feet for a harp, 50 square feet for a standard grand piano, 100 square feet for a concert grand piano, and 50 square feet for the tympani.

Sinking Forestage

Apron, forestage, orchestra pit, must be considered as elements affecting the audience-performance relationship. A sinking forestage may produce several arrangements suitable to different production types: forestage, continuation of the house floor, or sunken orchestra pit. Sectional elevators increase the number of possible arrangements. The organ console lift and the peripatetic orchestra wagon are familiar to presentation audiences.

If budget limitations preclude the installation of a sinking forestage, a cheaper though cumbersome substitute is a set of platforms designed to fit into the orchestra pit to produce 1. a continuation of the floor of the house to the apron, 2. a forestage, 3. steps leading from house floor to stage.

Organ Pipes, Blower, and Console

The spaces behind the splayed proscenium walls, and above the ceiling of the house are the best locations for organ pipes. The blower for the organ must be located in the basement. There is no space for either of these items within a well-designed stage. When solo performance on the organ is envisioned as a production feature, the console must be seen by the entire audience, either on an organ lift adjoining the orchestra pit, in a side stage in the proscenium splay, or on the stage itself, in which case there must be means for lowering it into the orchestra pit.

Orchestra pit elevator of the Purdue University Music Hall under construction. (Walter S. Scholler, Architect.) PURDUE PROGRESS Photo, courtesy J. R. Clancy, Inc.

Orchestra pit elevator of the Purdue University Music Hall showing lift mechanism. Photo, courtesy J. R. Clancy, Inc.

The Radio City Music Hall Symphony Orchestra on the elevator, raised to stage level. From this position the orchestra may be raised still higher and the car upon which it is riding may be rolled off the elevator onto the stage. Cosmo-Sileo Photo, courtesy Radio City Music Hall.

	General Characteristics	Acting Area Size	Shape
Pageant	Dramatic episodes, processions, marches, dances and crowd scenes. Masses of performers engaged in simple but expansive movements before very large audiences.	From 2000 to 5000 square feet, depending on the scale of the pageant.	Rectangular with aspect ratio between 1 to 3 and 2 to 3.
Grand Opera	Large numbers of performers on the acting area at one time; often more than one hundred in big scenes and finales. Movement is martial processions and group dances and the costumes are elaborate. Soloists perform downstage center, close to the footlights but within the bounds of the conventional proscenium, principals play twosome and group scenes in the area near the audience, and choruses and supernumeraries require space upstage. The ballet and the chorus of soldiers, pilgrims, peasants, or what not, sometimes fill the entire acting area. The performance is viewed objectively by the audience and does not benefit by intimate contact between performance and audience.	Minimum: 1000 square feet Usual: about 2500 square feet Reasonable maximum: 4000 square feet	Rhomboid with an aspect ratio between 1 to 2 and 2 to 3. Sides converge toward the back of the stage, following the sightlines from the extreme lateral positions.
Presentation	Presentation, though lacking the high style and quality of opera, embodies very similar visual components. Large numbers of people (sometimes as many as in opera, usually about half as many), are used in group movement, dances and processions for spectacular effect. The effects are in broad scale and essentially simple. Solo performers (singers, specialists, and masters of ceremonies), strive for a close relationship with the audience.	Minimum: 1000 square feet Usual: About 1200 square feet Reasonable Maximum: 2500 square feet	Rhomboid with aspect ratio about 1 to 3. Sides converge toward the back of the stage following the sightlines from the extreme lateral seats.

Arrangement	Proscenium	Orchestra	Comment
Long dimension of acting area perpendicular to general sightline. Audience entirely on one side, elevated to perceive two-dimensional movement. Large openings at ends and in side opposite audience for processions, group entrances, and exits. Some elevation of portion of acting area opposite audience, purely for compositional reasons.	None.	Space for 100 musicians between audience and acting area. Conductor must see performance.	Primarily an outdoor form, it is often staged in make-shift or adapted theatres, using athletic fields and stands or natural amphitheatres. A few permanent pageant theatres have been built.
Long dimension perpendicular to the general sightline. Audience elevated to perceive two-dimensional movement.	Width equal to the long dimension of the acting area.	Pit for 60 to 80 musicians. Conductor must have good view of action.	Movement in two dimensions in acting area is a significant visual component, predicating elevation of the seating area to make this movement visible.
Long axis perpendicular to the optimum sightline. Audience as close as possible to optimum sightline. Forestage acting area, acting areas extending sideways beyond the proscenium to connect with prosenium entrances or side-stages, and sinking forestages to enable chorus movement into the auditorium are possibilities for liberalizing the existing form and adding variety (the essence of presentation production) to the movement patterns.	Width equal to the long dimension of the acting area.	At all times an integral auditory component of the performance, sometimes integral visually. Elevating orchestra pit for from 50 to 100 musicians.	As more and more people depend upon television sets for their motion pictures, and as television returns to popularity the old galaxy of vaudeville stars and discovers many new ones, it is possible that motion picture palaces will be converted to the uses of presentation.

(Continued)

	General Characteristics	Acting Area Size	Shape
Vaudeville, Revue	Vaudeville and Revue emphasize the human scale. Although the vaudevillian keys his performance for the last row in the gallery, the form is characterized by intimate direct relationship between performer and audience: monologues straight to the front, confidential asides to the front row, and audience participation in illusions. Other acts (acrobatics, etc.) are played across the line of audience vision for maximum effect.	Minimum: 350 square feet Usual: About 450 square feet Reasonable Maximum: 700 square feet.	Rhomboid with aspect ratio about 1 to 3. Sides converge toward back of stage following the sightlines from the extreme lateral seats.
Musical Comedy Operetta	Musical Comedy and Operetta embody on a smaller scale the production elements of grand opera, plus a certain freedom and a quest for novelty which encourage the development of new performance devices. Close audience contact of soloists and specialists is borrowed from vaudeville and revue. Big scenes involve many dancers, singers, and showgirls, often with space-filling costume and movement. Fifty people on stage at one time is not unusual.	Minimum: 600 square feet Usual: About 1200 square feet Reasonable Maximum: 1800 square feet	Rhomboid with aspect ratio between 1 to 2 and 2 to 3. Sides converge toward the back of the stage following the sightlines from the extreme lateral seats.
Legitimate Drama	Of all production types, legitimate drama places the greatest emphasis upon the scale of the human actor. The importance of the individual actor requires that stage space and scenery do not dwarf him. Dominance of plot, locale, and characterization requires verisimilitude in the size and relationship of scenic objects. Too small an acting area crowds actors and furniture, hampers stage action, and detracts from the dramatic effect which is the sole aim of the performance. Too large an acting area diminishes the actor in scale and renders his performance ineffective by weakening the effect of his gestures and movement.	Minimum: 240 square feet Usual: About 525 square feet Reasonable Maximum: 800 square feet	Rhomboid with an aspect ratio about 1 to 2. Sides converge toward the back of the stage following the sightline from the extreme lateral seats.

Arrangement	Proscenium	Orchestra	Comment
Long axis of the acting area perpendicular to the optimum sightline. Audience grouped as close as possible to the optimum sightline. The forestage is an essential part of the acting area; steps, ramps, and runways into the house are useful.	Width equal to the long dimension of the acting area. Flexibility, as described under PRESENTATION is of some advantage in REVUE but of little value in VAUDE-VILLE.	Music and music cues closely integrated with both vaude-ville and revue performances. Pit space for from 15 to 30 musicians. Conductor must have good view of the ac-tion.	Most of the visual compo-nents of VAUDEVILLE and REVUE are such that they are perceived best in the con-ventional audience-perform-ance relationship. However, the development of dance as a popular entertainment form warrants some consid-eration being given to both the elevation of the audience to give a downward view-point on the two-dimensional movement, and the use of a part of the floor of the house as acting area. This latter feature occurs in the ar-rangement of cafes and night clubs.
Long axis of acting area per-pendicular to the optimum sightline. Mechanized mo-bility of structural parts to produce changes in acting area arrangement are desir-able. Forestages, sidestages, acting area elevators.	Usually as wide as the acting area, but should be adapt-able to changes in the ar-rangement of the acting area described immediately above.	Music an integral auditory component, sometimes inte-gral visually. Elevating or-chestra pit to accommodate from 20 to 40 musicians.	The assumption by ballet of a greater share in the per-formance of musical comedy indicates the need for a high general sightline from the audience.
The realistic style of dra-matic production confines the performance to an acting area entirely inside the pro-scenium. The apron is not used. Most historic styles and much modern dramatic theory demand more freedom of audience-performance rela-tionship than the realistic style and call for the pro-jection of the performance toward, into, and around the audience. For this projecting aprons, forestages, side-stages, runways, steps and ramps into the aisles are all to some degree useful. To meet the demands of differ-ent styles and stylists the act-ing area for drama must be capable of assuming many shapes. To confine it within the proscenium opening is adequate for the realistic style but inadequate for the others; to project it toward, into, or around the audience in any rigidly unalterable form is likewise adequate for one style but inadequate for others.	Width equal to long dimen-sion of the acting area. Mov-ing panels to vary width, openings in proscenium splay to form sidestages, moveable pylons or columns by which opening may be subdivided are all desirable. Flexibility and mobility are increasingly desirable. The application of motive power under remote control to the movement of structural parts, to produce different arrange-ments appears desirable but is costly. Manually alterable parts, particularly forestage proscenium panel and sec-tions of the stage floor, if not unwieldy, are reasonable substitutes.	Orchestral music is sometimes an integral visual part of the performance, but most gen-erally it is a purely auditory component. It is not gener-ally necessary for the or-chestra to be seen by the audience, but because cueing of music is so exacting, the conductor must see the action. It is reasonable to provide a pit for from 15 to 30 musicians, but the flexibility cited above must be provided, either by portable pit covers, steps, and platforms, or by mechanized orchestra lifts. There is opportunity for originality of arrangement.	

8: backstage operation

The process of preparing a theatrical production culminates in an operation called "taking-in the show" which means assembling all the elements of the show within the theatre and making them ready for the performance. An involved sequence of operations must be analyzed and the elements examined to determine how they best may be accommodated backstage in the working portions of the theatre building. This chapter proposes to state first the sequence of operations and then to consider how each of the elements of the show fits into the sequence, in order to derive the architectural requirements of each operation and element. Outline form is used as being more concise and more indicative than prose.

Operations Involved in Taking-in the Show

1. Architectural alteration of the theatre. Necessitated by
   a. archaism of the theatre.
   b. productional requirements: production very large; theatre too small, more often the case; production designs require it, as for Jumbo, The Eternal Road, The Great Waltz.

   The theatre planner must anticipate a variety of demands and provide a theatre which is large enough to meet reasonable maxima.

2. Adjustment of permanent equipment. The varying demands of theatrical productions require that all equipment of the stage including even the stage floor and the act curtain (fire curtain excepted by law) be either movable or removable.

3. Installation of new equipment. Special flying equipment, cycloramas, tormentors, light bridges, stage elevators, and even stage floors come under this heading.

   Original installation in a theatre of durable, dependable, and flexible stage equipment in sufficient quantity to meet carefully studied probable demand facilitates the "take-in" of every production which uses the theatre.

4. Installation and adjustment of lighting and sound equipment. In

present day commercial theatre practice no such equipment is in the theatre. The producer of each production must furnish all equipment required. Stage lighting technique and electronic sound control are the newest of the elements of theatrical production. Their recent rapid development postdates most existing theatres and advancement in instruments and techniques is still rapid. Few theatres, therefore, have adequate mounting and operating positions, branch circuits, outlets and control boards for stage lighting or speaker positions, conduits, mike lines, control apparatus or control booth for sound. Recently built college theatres approach a condition of adequacy in this regard although even in this case it is to be suspected that provisions for stage lighting and sound control are the last items included in, and the first items cut from, building budgets.

5. Installation of scenery. Scenery is brought to the stage in many pieces. These are fitted together, attached to stage equipment, assembled into sets, separated and stored in planned positions on the stage. The handling of scenery is routined and rehearsed by stage hands before the performance.

6. Properties fitted to sets. Properties are all objects which ornament the scenery and stand in the acting area: furniture, draperies, art objects, pictures, rugs, shrubs, flowers, etc., as well as all objects which are manipulated by the actors. Props are brought to the stage in trunks and crates, are unpacked, fitted to each set of scenery, and placed in planned storage positions. The handling of props is routined and rehearsed by property men.

7. Rehearsal of lighting, sound, and scenic effects by stage manager and stage hands.

8. Rehearsal of parts of the production in which actors are closely involved with lights, sound, or mechanical parts.

9. Costumes received, unpacked, inspected, fitted, altered, repaired, pressed, distributed to dressing rooms.

10. Dress parade. Actors wear costumes in sets and under lights. Move about to test costumes under performance conditions.

11. Dress rehearsals. Actors wear make-up and costumes and rehearse entire production. All conditions are as much like a performance as they can be.

12. Performances.

13. Take-out. When a show moves from one theatre to another or from one town to another time is of the essence. Therefore, the plan and equipment of the theatre must be conducive to speed and efficiency.

Production Elements

The elements of a theatrical production may be divided categorically into animate and inanimate, or people and things.

People: talent (actors, performers, singers, dancers, musicians); stage hands; stage managers; directors; designers.

Things: scenery, properties, lights, sound apparatus, costumes, musical instruments. Performing animals may best be considered in this category.

All of these elements exert specific demands upon the size, shape, arrangement, and equipment of the backstage portion of a theatre. The outlines below will take each important element into the theatre and through the process of a dress rehearsal or performance and out again, indicating at each point of each tour the significant requirements.

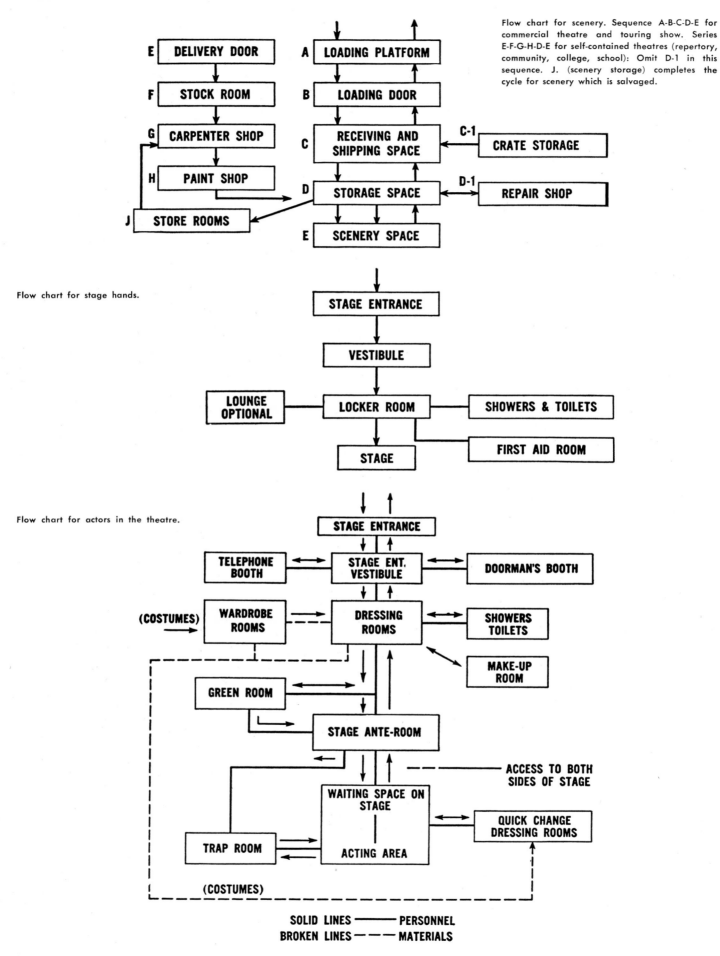

Flow chart for scenery. Sequence A-B-C-D-E for commercial theatre and touring show. Series E-F-G-H-D-E for self-contained theatres (repertory, community, college, school): Omit D-1 in this sequence. J. (scenery storage) completes the cycle for scenery which is salvaged.

E	DELIVERY DOOR
F	STOCK ROOM
G	CARPENTER SHOP
H	PAINT SHOP
J	STORE ROOMS

A	LOADING PLATFORM
B	LOADING DOOR
C	RECEIVING AND SHIPPING SPACE
	C-1 CRATE STORAGE
D	STORAGE SPACE
	D-1 REPAIR SHOP
E	SCENERY SPACE

Flow chart for stage hands.

STAGE ENTRANCE

VESTIBULE

LOUNGE OPTIONAL — LOCKER ROOM — SHOWERS & TOILETS

FIRST AID ROOM

STAGE

Flow chart for actors in the theatre.

STAGE ENTRANCE

TELEPHONE BOOTH — STAGE ENT. VESTIBULE — DOORMAN'S BOOTH

(COSTUMES) WARDROBE ROOMS — DRESSING ROOMS — SHOWERS TOILETS

MAKE-UP ROOM

GREEN ROOM

STAGE ANTE-ROOM

ACCESS TO BOTH SIDES OF STAGE

WAITING SPACE ON STAGE

ACTING AREA

QUICK CHANGE DRESSING ROOMS

TRAP ROOM

(COSTUMES)

SOLID LINES ——— PERSONNEL
BROKEN LINES — — — MATERIALS

talent: Actors, performers, dancers, singers, and musicians on stage

Enter the theatre	Stage entrance
Check in, get mail and messages, read calls and notices.	**Vestibule:** minimum 50 sq. ft. shape variable. Equipment: time clock or other in-out indicator, bulletin board, telephone booth with muffled bell. Location: central to all backstage departments. **Doorman's booth:** 30 sq. ft. shape variable. Equipment: counter, mail box, small desk, key rack. Location: adjacent stage vestibule to control all traffic to backstage part of building.
Dress for performance: take off street clothes, put on make-up, put on costume, inspection of costume.	**Dressing room:** minimum 50 sq. ft. per person. (See table.) School, college, community: group dressing rooms. Professional: stars, individuals, choruses. Opera: principal singers, choruses, ballets, supernumeraries. Equipment: clothes and costume hangers, 2 linear feet of rod per person, 2 linear feet of shoe rack per person, no doors on cabinets, curtains if anything, make-up table 30″ wide per person, 18″ deep, mirror 18″ wide per person, well diffused light, no shadows, 25 f.c. minimum on face before mirror, one wall outlet per two persons, full length mirrors: one in each star's dressing room, one per eight persons in each chorus room, one in corridor on way to stage. Call system, phone outlet, monitor loudspeaker. One lavatory in each small dressing room, one per four people in large dressing rooms. Location: near stage but not necessarily adjoining stage. (See Green room and Stage anteroom below.) **Make-up room:** minimum 100 sq. ft. Desirable in schools, colleges, and community theatres where actors are unskilled at make-up. Equipment: make-up tables or benches, chairs on two sides. 25 f.c. general light on faces. Location: adjoining dressing rooms. **Toilets:** use concentrated into short periods of time before show, and during intermissions. Peak load inevitable. Minimum one per six persons.
Wait for call to stage	**Green room:** minimum 300 sq. ft. Stage manager checks cast, assembles choruses. Directors talk to cast. Actors' social room.

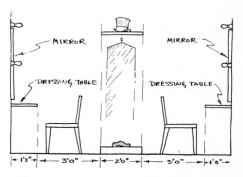

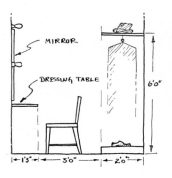

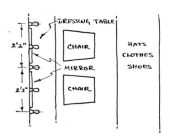

Minimum space allowances for dressing rooms.

Rockettes' dressing room. The serious student of theatre planning will find additional interesting material in the text. Photo, LIFE Photographer Herbert Gehr. Copyright TIME Inc.

Portable light tower for wing lighting set in first entrance right. Beyond is the stage manager's control panel showing, left to right, intercommunication control, contour curtain control and indicator and stage machinery controls and indicators. Photo, courtesy Radio City Music Hall.

	Equipment: lounge furniture, tables, smoking accessories, card table set, full length mirror. Call system outlet. Telephone outlet. Location: near stage, same level.
	Stage anteroom: alternate to Green room. Minimum 150 sq. ft.
	Equipment: chairs or benches.
	Location: adjoining stage near proscenium. Same use as Green room but stripped of lounge aspects. Strictly business. May be merely an enlarged passage between dressing rooms and stage.
Go to stage **Enter set and perform** **Leave set** (The next four actions are alternates)	**Passage:** minimum width 5 ft. Short and direct, *no stairs*, use ramps to change level.
(1) Wait for next entrance	**Waiting space on stage:** minimum 50 sq. ft., chairs. or **Stage anteroom** Actors are responsible for re-entrances. Must stay where they can hear show. Monitor loud-speaker desirable in Green room or Stage anteroom.
(2) Quick Change of costume and-or make-up before next entrance	**Quick change dressing room:** minimum 50 sq. ft. per actor. Space for dresser to help actor. Equipment: same as other dressing rooms. Location: immediately adjoining stage.
(3) Slow change of costume and-or make-up	**Regular dressing room** (see above).
(4) Wait for curtain calls	**Green room or Stage anteroom.**
Remove costume, clean up, and dress for street	**Showers:** one adjoining each star's dressing room, one for six actors otherwise. Peak load immediately following performance; body make-up may necessitate baths by entire company.
Confer with stage manager or director	
Entertain friends after show	**Green room:** kitchenette adjoining.
Check out and leave theatre	**Vestibule and stage entrance** (above).

Musicians who perform on stage follow substantially the same route as other talent. The following applies to musicians who play in the pit.

Musicians

| **Enter theatre,** check in, get mail messages, calls. | **Stage entrance, Vestibule, Doorman's booth,** as above. |

Prepare for performance: remove wraps, tune instruments, get out music, practice.	**Musicians' room:** minimum 300 sq. ft. Equipment: lockers or clothes racks, chairs, music cabinets, telephone and call system outlets. Location: basement level near pit and stage. Large instruments usually kept in pit. Visiting orchestra's instruments, stands, and music trunks may be received through prop loading door (see properties below), and large cases stored on stage.
Go to pit	**Passage:** direct. Large doors to allow carrying instruments. **Orchestra pit:** 10 sq. ft. per musician plus 100 sq. ft. for grand piano and 50 sq. ft. for tympani. Width from stage figured on a per man basis. Depth should keep musicians below audience sightline to stage but not lower. Conductor must see stage. Singers and orchestra must see conductor. Podium. Elevating orchestra pit floor 1. features orchestra as part of performance, 2. adds floor for chairs if brought to auditorium level, 3. makes forestage when desired. Portable steps or platforms may be set over orchestra pit.
Leave pit and leave theatre	Lavatories and toilets same as for actors. Dressing room with lavatory and shower for conductor.

Stage Hands

Enter theatre, check in	**Stage entrance and vestibule.**
Change from street clothes to work clothes	**Locker Room:** according to number of men. Equipment: individual lockers, chairs, benches. Call system outlet. Phone outlet. Location: may be in basement, near stage, serves as stage hands' lounge.
Go to stage	**Passage:** direct to either side of stage.
Work the show	**Passages:** easy access from stage to fly galleries, gridiron, light bridges, trap room, and auditorium ceiling. Clear passage across stage at back.
Wait between scene shifts	**Locker room** may serve as stage hands' lounge. Equipment: lounge furniture, card table set, smoking facilities, if allowed, adjoining toilets. There is little provision for comfort of stage hands in existing theatres. Traditionally they play pinochle in the trap room between shifts.
Clean up and dress for street	**Locker room** *Showers:* one to every four men. Peak load after performance inevitable. Stage work is dirty work.

Treatment of accidents	First aid room: minimum 50 sq. ft.	
	Equipment: surgical table, stools, chair, first aid cabinet, sink, hot water.	
	Seldom proper provision for first aid backstage. Stage work is hazardous on occasion. For co-educational organizations (amateur, school, college) dual locker rooms, showers, toilets, for crews. Common lounge.	

Stage Managers

Enter theatre, check in	Use stage hands' locker-room.
Manage the show	Stage manager's desk: on stage near proscenium on working side.
	Equipment: nerve center of backstage signal system: calls, phones, monitors, moving stage controls, etc.
Care of scripts, cue sheets, etc.	Office: minimum 50 sq. ft. Necessary only in permanent theatre organization: repertory or stock.

Directors and Designers

No specific routine, but they need backstage offices in permanent organization. Conference room near all offices is desirable. Empty dressing rooms may serve as pro tem offices.

PERSONNEL REQUIREMENTS FOR MAIN TYPES OF THEATRICAL ENTERTAINMENT

TYPE OF SHOW	ACTORS PRINCIPALS	EXTRAS	PLAN DRESSING ROOMS PRINCIPALS	EXTRAS	STAGE HANDS	MUSICIANS	STAGE MANAGERS	DIRECTORS	DESIGNERS
PAGEANT	10 TO 50	100 TO 2000	40	500	50	100	4 TO 10	3	3
GRAND OPERA	4 TO 10	20 TO 100	10	100	50	80	2 TO 4	3	3
PRESENTATION	4 TO 10	20 TO 100	10	50	30	30 TO 200	2 TO 4	3	3
VAUDEVILLE OR REVUE	4 TO 10	20 TO 50	10	50	20	10 TO 30	2	0 TO 3	0 TO 3
OPERETTA OR MUSICAL COMEDY	4 TO 10	20 TO 50	10	50	30	10 TO 30	2 TO 4	3	3
PLAYS ("LEGIT")	2 TO 20	0 TO 50	20	30	3 TO 30	0 TO 20	1 TO 4	1	3
MOTION PICTURE PALACE	NONE EXCEPT WHEN, AS, AND IF ONE OF THE ABOVE TYPES OF SHOW MOVES IN				2	0 TO 50	0	0	0
MOTION PICTURE NEIGHBORHOOD					0	0	0	0	0

Things	scenery		
	Brought to theatre	**Loading door:** 8′ wide, 12′ high at side or rear of stage. **Loading platform:** height above grade equal height of average van floor. Width to accommodate two vans. Avoid change of level inside. Use ramps outside to adjust to grade. Roof over.
	Stored pending set-up	**Receiving space:** minimum 200 sq. ft. 20 ft. high. Equipment: pipe frames at right angles to wall optional for stacking scenery, otherwise clear wall and floor space. Receiving space is lacking or scanty in existing theatres. Result: when delivered, scenery is stacked on stage, necessitating much rehandling during set-up. Scenery left outside theatre, sometimes damaged by weather.
	Set-up	**Stage equipment** for flying, rolling, sinking scenery.
	Rehearsed and operated during show	**Note:** the considerations determining the size, shape, arrangement, and equipment of the stage are treated in detail in the three following chapters.
	Repaired	**Repair shop:** minimum 100 sq. ft. Equipment: work bench, tools for working wood, tin, iron (cold), sewing, painting, electrical work. This shop will also serve property and electrical departments. This is in no sense to be considered a shop for the production of scenery, properties, or electrical equipment; it is merely the necessary repair shop in the event that scenery, properties, and lights are produced elsewhere.
	Dismantled	Receiving space.
	Shipped out	Loading door.
Properties	**Brought to theatre**	**Loading door:** 6′ wide, 8′ high separate from scenery door. Adjacent on loading platform.
	Unpacked	**Receiving space:** 100 sq. ft. minimum. Property crates stored in this space when empty.
	Fitted to sets of scenery **Stored on stage**	Floor space, racks, shelves.
	Operated during show **Repaired** **Struck and shipped out**	

		Lighting Equipment
Brought to theatre	Loading door (may use property loading door).	
Unpacked	Receiving space: minimum 100 sq. ft. additional to space for properties. Crates are stored here when empty. May be in alley or on loading platform.	
Installed	Lighting equipment may be placed in any position on the stage floor, in the space at the sides of the stage, above the stage, in slots or ports in the auditorium ceiling or on the fronts of balconies or boxes. See Chapter 12. *Portable switchboards* are set in areas up to 200 sq. ft. on the working side. Power supply through company switches up to 300 KVA.	
Operated Dismantled and shipped out		

With less bulk by 75% essentially the same as lighting equipment. **Sound Apparatus**

Costumes

Brought to theatre	Loading door: property door above.
Taken for Inspection	via Passage: 5 ft. clear width, no stairs, ramps where needed. or Lift: minimum 6 ft. by 8 ft. to Wardrobe room: minimum 120 sq. ft. Equipment: costume hangers 12 linear feet, ironing board and iron, electric ironer, outlets, sewing machine, and table.
Hung in dressing rooms	castered garment trucks a la 34th Street.
to actors' persons to stage and return	Passages: 5′ clear width for widest costumes, no protuberances on which costumes may catch.
Cleaning, pressing, repairs to trunks and shipped out.	Wardrobe room.

Animals

A common requirement in theatres planned for vaudeville was the animal room. The Hippodrome in New York contained provisions for housing a menagerie. An occasional performing animal or troupe must be accommodated today. Hence a completely equipped theatre must have an animal room, adjacent to the stage but separated from it by masonry walls, with separate outside door, ventilation, drainage, and water.

9: scenery

Most of the types of production listed in Chapter 1 require scenery. By the same token, most theatres, except perhaps drive-in motion picture theatres, are likely to try to employ scenery at some time. Using scenery where only concert or motion pictures were originally contemplated results in waste of labor, time and money, and in artistic compromises. Inferior productions often come about because people will not be deterred by such drawbacks. Since the theatre planner cannot cure this insistence on using scenery, it behooves him to learn its nature and uses and make its effective employment structurally possible.

History

The development of scenery has paralleled that of theatres. The most generously designed and ingeniously mechanized theatres provide the greatest scope in the use of scenery and maximum latitude in the production of plays. Good plays are extremely durable, and while many plays are susceptible of being set in a number of ways, it is unlikely that there will be more than one way, often the original one, as in the case of Shakespeare, in which the total emotional value of the play is most effectively projected.

As is the case in most arts, the passing generations have introduced new materials and new ways of using them, but almost nothing has been discarded. HIGH TOR by Maxwell Anderson, 1937 A.D., includes the suspension of two actors high above the stage in a steam shovel. THE CLOUDS, by Aristophanes, 423 B.C., contains the stage direction: "The machine swings in Socrates in a basket." Three-dimensional structural scenic units were used in ancient Greece, and the wing and border set was developed in the Renaissance. This century has given us projected backgrounds and so increased the flexibility of the stage, but not necessarily its scope.

Functions

Scenery contributes an essential element to the total effect of a theatrical production. It is used to establish locale, atmosphere, mood, to assist in the revelation of character and may contribute to the advancement of the plot.

Because playwrights set their plays in all conceivable and imaginable times and places, scenery must be capable of representing any time or place, real or imagined. Furthermore, since playwrights find it necessary to change the locale of their action from place to place, scenery must be capable of quick and easy changes.

In addition to its function of projecting the playwright's concept, scenery has the following purely technical functions:

1. It encloses and delineates the acting area.

2. It supplies openings of proper form and in sufficient number and location so that the actors may enter and leave the acting area as required.

3. It masks the stage walls, machinery, crews, and actors awaiting entrance cues.

Scenery is essentially fake, temporary, light in weight, and portable. The structural elements conventionally consist of light weight soft wood frames. Surfaces visible to the audience are light weight, durable fabrics, board materials, or wire and plastic substances, mounted on the frames, and painted to resemble whatever the scene designer requires.

Structural types of scenery are based upon the necessity of de-mounting and transporting it, and upon the available sizes of materials. A general rule is that all scenery must be capable of division, folding, or rolling into units. each with one dimension not greater than 5 feet 9 inches.

Structure

A drop, the simplest structural unit of scenery, is composed of widths of cloth sewn together and suspended from a wooden batten. Another batten is attached to the bottom edge to impart a stretch to the cloth. The drop and its variations, such as leg drops, scrim drops, translucent drops, cycloramas, borders, and teasers, provide large expanses of scenery, in great variety, by the easiest possible means. Since one dimension of the drop can be made very small by rolling it, the other dimension is limited only by the stage requirements,

Types of Scenery

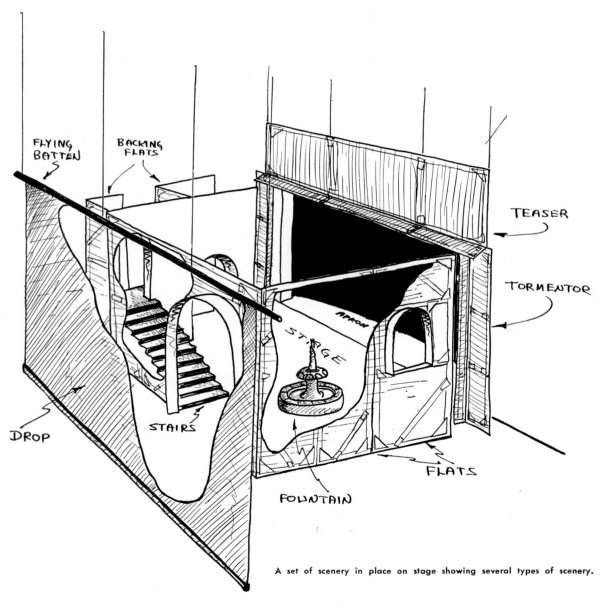

A set of scenery in place on stage showing several types of scenery.

the capacity of the storage space, and transportation facilities. The projection sheet for motion pictures or television is a drop, usually laced into a four-sided frame. The theatre planner must provide facilities for rigging, handling, and storing drops which are one-third wider than, and twice as high as, the proscenium.

Curtains or draperies are much used as stage decorations, occasionally as representational scenery, but more frequently as frank masking devices. Musical productions, which require little representational scenery and much stage decoration, make free and effective use of draperies, and achieve brilliant effects by clever operation and the use of novelty fabrics, dye, paint, and light. Draperies are rigged as curtains or drops, either hung from tracks above the stage to draw sidewise, hung from battens to be flown into the space above the stage, or rigged with lines, to be lifted vertically (contour) or diagonally (tab).

Flat Framed Scenery

Scenery of architectural derivation such as interiors and exteriors of houses is usually composed of frames, covered with cloth or board material hinged or lashed together, the joints concealed, and the surfaces painted. These framed pieces called flats or wings are generally rectangular, though they may be of any shape, seldom more than 16 feet high and 5 feet 9 inches wide. Any number of flats may be joined to form an expanse of wall. Details of architecture such as windows, doors, mantels, wall thicknesses, and cornices are attached to, or inserted into openings in, the flats. Small detail is painted. Ceilings are of cloth stretched on demountable frames. Ground rows for exteriors are flat framed pieces.

Scenery to represent nature is similarly built on frames. Surfaces simulating earth, bark, or stone are achieved by covering the frames with wire mesh and modelling thereon a plastic material, such as papier mâché. Standard limitations of size are observed as with flat scenery.

Three-dimensional scenery is an assemblage of demountable or collapsible frames, designed as structural members and calculated to carry specified loads.

Since it is rarely possible for scenery structures to be erected permanently on the stage where the performance is to be given, even bulky and relatively heavy weight bearing platforms must be made up of numerous frames, assembled in the scene construction shop with semi-permanent fastenings, taken apart, and reassembled on the stage before dress rehearsals begin.[1]

Space Requirements

The audience must see:

1. Significant contributive portions of the stage setting;
2. Scenery (backings, cycloramas, etc), extending to limits of vision.

The theatre planner must make it possible for the entire audience to see all or a large part of the stage setting (See Chapters 3 and 7—Proscenium), and must allow space offstage, at the sides and back, for scenery used solely for masking purposes.

Scenery occupies space, both when set in playing position and when stored, either on the stage or in the scene dock (Chapter 8).

[1] For a detailed presentation of kinds and types of scenery, materials, methods of construction, assembly, and handling, see Burris-Meyer, H. and Cole, E. C., SCENERY FOR THE THEATRE, Little, Brown & Co. (Boston, 1938).

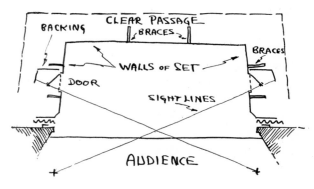

Plan of the simplest interior setting.

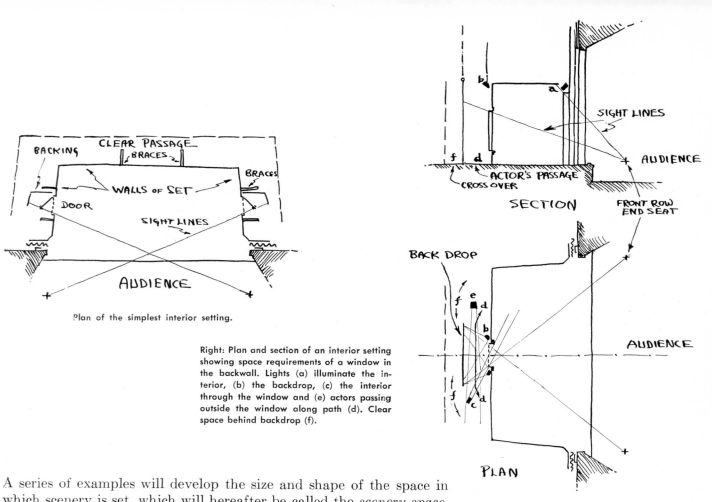

Right: Plan and section of an interior setting showing space requirements of a window in the backwall. Lights (a) illuminate the interior, (b) the backdrop, (c) the interior through the window and (e) actors passing outside the window along path (d). Clear space behind backdrop (f).

A series of examples will develop the size and shape of the space in which scenery is set, which will hereafter be called the *scenery space*.

The simplest kind of interior set, with the minimum number of doors and no windows, requires more space than is occupied by the portion of the set seen by the audience. Braces behind the walls support them and make them rigid. There must be entrance space outside each of the doors sufficient to allow actors to approach and prepare to enter the set. The entrance space, furthermore, must have a backing, that is, a unit of flat scenery to intercept extreme horizontal sightlines. Finally, because it is often necessary for actors, stagehands, and stage manager to get quickly from one side of the stage to the other, there must be a *crossover* passage behind the scenery. Thus this simple box set, the admitted minimum, with no openings of any kind in the rear wall, requires a zone of space at least 5 feet wide behind scenery where there are no openings, and at least 6 feet wide at the openings. Very few plays can be performed in sets as meager as this example.

As additional and more elaborate openings are made in the walls of a box set, to meet the requirements of action, locale, or pictorial design, additional demands are made for scenery space. A window in the back wall of the set is an example. The window reveals a world outside the set which must be plausibly represented if the locale represented within the set is to be believed. A simple backdrop, possibly painted with distant hill, skyline, and sky, may suffice. Space between the set and the drop is required:

1. to prevent light inside the set from casting shadows of the window on the painted landscape;

2. to allow sufficient spread of light on the drop from instruments outside the set;

Interiors

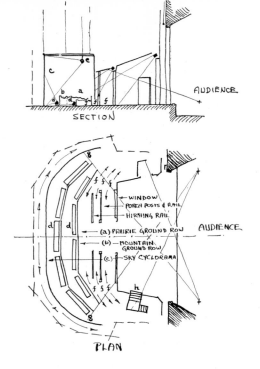

SECTION

PLAN

· WINDOW
· PORCH POSTS & RAIL
· HITCHING RAIL
(a) PRAIRIE GROUND ROW
(b) MOUNTAIN GROUND ROW
(c) SKY CYCLORAMA

AUDIENCE

Plan and section of interior setting having large openings in the backwall through which exterior landscape is seen by the audience. The text explains the space requirements.

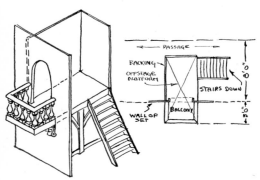

PASSAGE
BACKING
OFFSTAGE PLATFORM
STAIRS DOWN
WALL OF SET
BALCONY

Exterior Sets

A balcony cantilevered over the acting area requires considerable offstage space for landing and steps.

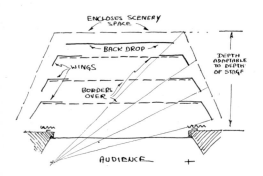

ENCLOSES SCENERY SPACE
BACK DROP
WINGS
BORDERS OVER
DEPTH ADAPTABLE TO DEPTH OF STAGE
AUDIENCE

The traditional wing-and-drop setting was economical of stage space but was lacking in illusion.

3. to allow lights outside the set to be directed through the window into the set;

4. to allow passage for actors whom the audience must see passing the window; and

5. to allow spread of light for illuminating such actors.

This space may have to be as much as ten feet. Furthermore, ample crossover must be provided if people are to pass behind the drop without causing it to move or ripple.

A complex, though quite common problem of masking openings in the back wall of a set is illustrated by the plan and section of the country store. The entire back wall is a series of openings through which the audience looks at rolling prairie (a), distant mountains (b), and sky (c). Diurnal light changes during the play require that the ground rows and cyclorama be elaborately lighted from instruments on the floor (d) and overhead (e). The action of the play demands passage for actors both on and beyond the porch of the store (f). Thus scenery space outside the set must aggregate more than the acting area inside the set. Dimensions given are normal, rather than maximum or minimum. The sightlines (g-g) indicate the great expanse of space outside the set which is visible to some members of the audience, and therefore the expanse of sky backing which must be provided.

Scenery and side space are conserved and adequate masking achieved by angling the scenery which represents mountains and prairie and curving the cyclorama. However, such saving cannot reduce the necessary spacing of parts below the dimensions shown.

The staircase in the side wall of this same set (h) illustrates another way in which scenery occupies space. This simple representation of a staircase requires an offstage platform and stairs down to the floor if actors are to use it. Similarly Juliet's balcony requires an offstage platform and stairs.

Combining the possible requirements of masking and auxiliary structure, a single interior set of scenery in playing position will often require a space twice as deep as the acting area and twice as wide.

Exteriors, with the exception of the conventional, implausible sets of another era, require more stage space than do interiors both in playing position and stored.

Realism demands that a scenery tree have as thick a trunk as one in a forest, that rocks and mountains on stage be rough and apparently solid, and that the sky be open and spacious rather than closed and floppy. In contrast to the old-fashioned exterior set with its arbitrarily smooth floor and rows of profiled wings and borders, the modern exterior scene consists chiefly of dummy or weight-bearing three-dimensional structures, ramps and levels to represent terrain, built-up or flat scenery to represent trees and shrubs, profiled ground rows to represent the horizon, and a great expanse of cloth, plaster, or plywood to represent sky. Sky borders and cloud borders are used sparingly above the stage, but foliage borders are used when the presence of tree trunks on the stage requires them. Convincing illusion in exterior settings is achieved chiefly by an emphasis on openness, a plein-air quality, which demands the elimination of all elements of scenery which tend to close in the set and places great importance on the ultimate background, the cyclorama.

Setting for Tennessee Williams' SUMMER AND SMOKE designed by Jo Mielziner. Imaginative stage design calling for unrestricted audience view of the background. Photo, Eiliin Darby.

Plan for the above setting. Masking wings and draperies are used to interrupt audience view arbitrarily. This is a theatrical convention which audiences and designers have to accept, if limitations of stage space force it.

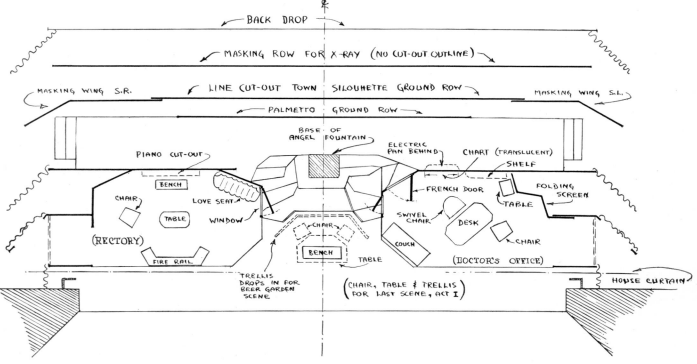

BACK DROP

MASKING ROW FOR X-RAY (NO CUT-OUT OUTLINE)

MASKING WING S.R.   LINE CUT-OUT TOWN SILOUHETTE GROUND ROW   MASKING WING S.L.

PALMETTO GROUND ROW

BASE OF ANGEL FOUNTAIN

PIANO CUT-OUT   ELECTRIC PAN BEHIND   CHART (TRANSLUCENT)
SHELF

BENCH   FRENCH DOOR   FOLDING SCREEN

CHAIR   LOVE SEAT   TABLE

TABLE   WINDOW   SWIVEL CHAIR   DESK   CHAIR

(RECTORY)   CHAIR   COUCH

BENCH   (DOCTOR'S OFFICE)

FIRE RAIL   TABLE

TRELLIS DROPS IN FOR BEER GARDEN SCENE   (CHAIR, TABLE & TRELLIS FOR LAST SCENE, ACT I)   HOUSE CURTAIN

Setting for Donald Ogden Stewart's HOW I WONDER designed by Donald Oenslager. The cyclorama serves as ultimate masking at top and sides, with a very high teaser emphasizing the sky and the stars as part of the plot. Open air effect completely achieved. Photo, Vandamm.

Setting for COMPANIONS OF THE LEFT HAND by Robert Meehan designed by Jean Eckart. Large set pieces mask at the sides. Commercial Photo Service. Courtesy Yale Department of Drama.

The Cyclorama

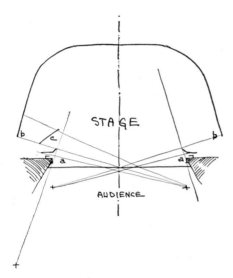

Plan showing the critical sightlines which demarcate the scenery seen by the audience. All members of the audience see scenery between the sightlines which do not cross the center line. Spectators sitting in the extreme front seats see across the center line to the tormentors (a) and to the downstage edge of the cyclorama (b) unless scenery (c) is set to force the extreme sightline further upstage.

The functions of a cyclorama are:

1. To supply the ultimate scenic background. With representational scenery, the cyclorama has some recognizable scenic aspects: commonly sky, less commonly landscape, forest, seascape. With abstract scenery the cyclorama may be a decorative curtain hung to enclose the scenery space, a black velour curtain hung flat or in folds to absorb all light and give a background effect of total darkness, or various other fabrics or combinations of fabrics, variously lighted to make the background an integral part of the stage design. The cyclorama may be used as a screen upon which light patterns are projected, from either front or rear, as a part of the scenic scheme. These light patterns may be abstract or representational, static or mobile, even motion pictures.

2. To supply the ultimate masking. For open scenes the cyclorama may mask the entire stage space as delineated by the extreme horizontal and vertical sightlines through the maximum proscenium opening.

Whether or not a cyclorama is part of the original equipment of a theatre, the stage must be planned so that one may be used. In 116 sets of scenery at the Yale University Theatre, a cyclorama was used 42 times.

Types of cycloramas are:

1. Cloth, sewn in horizontal strips, and dyed or painted.

(a) Laced, at top and bottom to shaped battens of pipe or wood and rigged to fly with guide wires at front edges.

(b) Laced to shaped rigid frame of pipe or steel, rigged to fly.

(c) Back section laced to rigid frame, side panels laced to separate frames, and all three frames rigged to fly independently or together.

(d) Rigged to travel horizontally on a curved overhead track and to roll into a vertical cylinder at one side. Bottom edge weighted with chain, to impart stretch. Cycloramas for special uses may be installed on the permanent equipment (battens, frames, or tracks) of any of these types.

2. Plywood or other semi-rigid building board. Fastened to shaped rigid steel frame, butt joints sealed with tape, the whole covered with fabric and the fabric painted.

(a) The whole cyclorama rigged to fly.

(b) Back section built permanently in place and side panels rigged to fly.

(c) The whole cyclorama rigged to travel backwards, rolling on overhead tracks.

(d) The whole cyclorama built permanently in place.

3. Plaster on metal lath, on a shaped steel frame, painted.

(a) Back section built permanently in place and side sections, of stretched cloth or plywood, rigged to fly or to roll backward.

(b) Rigged to travel backward, rolling on overhead tracks.

The cyclorama may be designed with widely spreading sides which intercept the extreme horizontal sightlines without extending downstage, thus providing free access to the scenery space without the necessity of clearing the cyclorama. This is a very space consuming arrangement. A rigid cyclorama, whether fixed or moveable, may have its top edge curved to follow the top sightline.

Plywood or plaster cycloramas may be part of the permanent

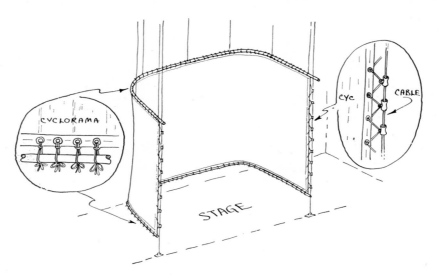

Types of cycloramas described in text. 1 (a)

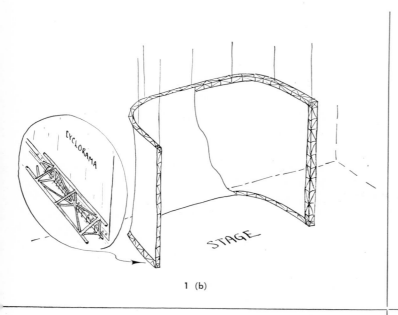

1 (b)

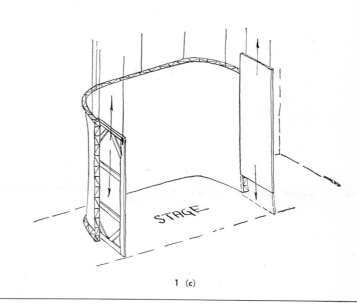

1 (c)

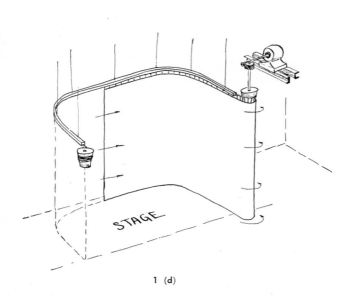

1 (d)

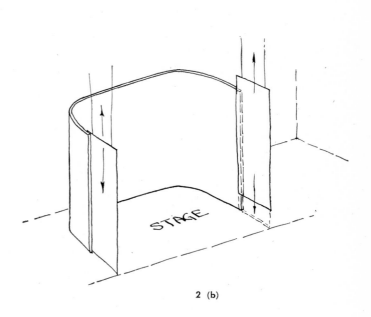

2 (b)

structure of the stage house. In these cases crossover passage at stage level must be provided behind the cyclorama.

Size and Shape

The theatre planner is concerned with the following aspects of the cyclorama as they determine the size, shape, arrangement, and equipment of the stage:

1. The size and position of the cyclorama is established by two requirements: It must not encroach upon the scenery space as developed above, and it must provide complete masking. Complete horizontal masking is essential. Complete vertical masking is desirable but is possible only in the case of a cyclorama which is not flown. In the case of a flown cyclorama the height to which the cyclorama must be flown to allow the passage of scenery under it added to the height of the cyclorama itself results in a disproportionately high and costly stage house. It is reasonable to plan to use a masking border which is visible to a small percentage of the audience, allows a considerable reduction in the height of the cyclorama and the stage house, and serves as concealment for the lights which illuminate the cyclorama from above.

2. The shape is established by four factors.
   (a) The cyclorama must surround the scenery space.
   (b) The cyclorama must, by its shape, and distance from the proscenium, permit uniform and adequate distribution and color mixing of light over its entire surface from lighting instruments located within the scenery space and flyspace, and possibly from instruments outside the cyclorama. This requirement dictates that there must be no sharp curves in the surface of the cyclorama in plan or section; all radii must be at least 12 feet; the surface of the cyclorama must be smooth. Wrinkles in a cloth cyclorama cause accidental streaks of light and shade, often in different colors. Unevenness in a plaster or plywood cyclorama causes patches of light and shade. Lighting the cyclorama from outside requires that there be no seams in the area to be lighted and that the cloth be treated to produce uniform translucency.
   (c) A hard cyclorama reflects sound. Its shape is determined as part of the acoustic planning of the theatre.

Movement

The cyclorama must perform its functions and at the same time not interfere with the normal operation of other stage equipment. Surrounding the scenery space as it does, it must be capable of rapid removal, entirely or in part, so that scenery, properties, and lighting equipment may be taken into and out of that space. If the plan for handling scenery involves movement to sides and back the entire cyclorama must either fly to a height which will allow movement of the highest scenery under it, or travel sidewise on a horizontal track and roll at one edge. The flying operation is the more rapid. If the plan for handling scenery involves only movement to the sides, the following methods of moving the cyclorama are possible:

1. The whole cyclorama to fly
2. The side panels to fly or roll back
3. The whole cyclorama to roll back
4. The whole cyclorama to travel on a horizontal track and roll up at one edge.

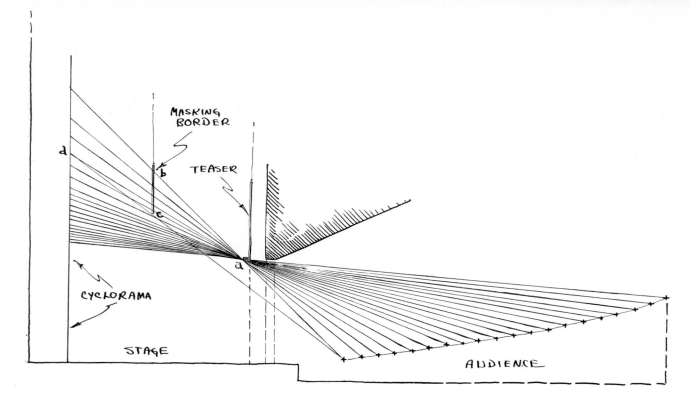

Method of determining the practical height of the cyclorama, of the fly space, and, consequently, of the gridiron and the roof.

1. Make a section of the theatre containing: the eye positions for each seating row in the orchestra; teaser drawn at highest working trim (level with top of proscenium opening); vertical line of cyclorama at back center; and sightlines from each eye position past the edge of the teaser to their intersection with the line of the cyclorama.

2. Record on the section: the height on the cyclorama of each sightline intersection; and the number of people in the orchestra audience who can see above the intersection.

3. At some point on the cyclorama the added height necessary to mask for a small percentage of the audience will appear disproportionately large. From this point draw a line to the edge of the teaser. On this line, at a point not less than 12 feet from the cyclorama, draw a vertical line c-b representing a masking border, high enough to mask from the front row. From the front row draw a sightline past the bottom edge of this border to locate the top of the cyclorama (d). We now have in the section a zigzag line a, b, c, d which is the top limit of the scenery space, and the bottom limit of the fly space.

To be completely useful, the fly space must be high enough (e) to accommodate the full height (n) of any piece of scenery set anywhere between the front of the stage and the cyclorama. The quantity n is a variable: downstage n equals little more than the teaser height; upstage n equals the height of the cyclorama. As the piece is set further upstage, its height increases, increasing the required fly space. Adding to the height e a minimum measurement for sprinkler pipes and gridiron steel (about 1'-6") we have established the height of the floor of the gridiron. The underside of the roof structure must be sufficiently higher than this to allow passage of workmen on the gridiron (minimum clearance under main roof girders, 6 feet). The necessary height of the fly space when no masking border is used is indicated by the lines e-j-g. It is unreasonable to construct a stage house so high.

Storage and Working Space

It is obvious that multi-set shows will need space to store sets and properties, while other sets are playing. The cyclorama usually establishes the largest single flyloft requirement. A loft which accommodates an adequate cyclorama can hold all other scenery which it is feasible to fly in or near its playing position.

While the fly loft can contain much scenery, considerations of speed, or simplicity of shift make it necessary to move settings intact, horizontally on wagons or discs between playing and storing positions. If such a shift is to be accomplished, space outside the scenery space, equal to one or more acting areas, must be available. Less space makes it necessary to dismantle scenery at least partly before moving it.

The theatre planner will easily realize that the fewer operations needed to bring in scenery, handle it on stage and take it out again (See Chapter 8), the more efficiently shows can be handled and the fewer people will be needed to handle them. This last item is often a critical and determining one in theatre operation (See Chapter 15). In the theatre in which the process of production is complete, the set can sometimes be built on a wagon, rolled intact with complete props into the acting area, and struck the same way. The ultimate inefficiency occurs when the sets must be pulled apart and elements moved individually. Stage area alone is no guarantee of efficiency in scenery handling. The area must be so planned that it can store large scenic units without thereby interfering with any other function of the stage. The principles here involved will be further developed in Chapter 10, Stage Machinery.

Projected Scenery

The creation of scenic backgrounds by projecting images in light upon large surfaces is of sufficient use to require consideration in the planning of the stage. Projection supplies scenic background but cannot supply solid scenery or properties required by the action of a play. Highly effective in some instances, projection cannot be substituted for built scenery.

Projection is of two kinds: 1. *shadow projection,* in which the light from a concentrated source (arc or concentrated filament) illuminating the projection surface is modified by a large slide or profile placed in the path of the beam; and 2. *lens projection,* which employs condensing lenses, slides, and objective lenses. The second kind of projection, by the concentration of light and the use of an optical system, produces images of greater intensity and higher definition than the first.

Projection may be in either of two directions: from the front, onto a near-white opaque surface, or from the rear, onto a translucent surface.

Front projection makes no special demand upon the stage space or equipment, but it is limited in scope. Surfaces suitable for front projection are easily made; drops and cycloramas are frequently used. Obviously the intensity of the image is affected by the efficiency of the reflecting surface, and mat surfaces of relatively high reflecting power, such as silver sheets and flat-white drops, are most useful. To cover the entire projection surface and neither light the actor nor cast his shadow on the surface, the projector must be either above the proscenium, or on the stage floor behind the acting area.

Rear projection makes exacting demands on both stage space and equipment. The distance of the projector from the projection surface

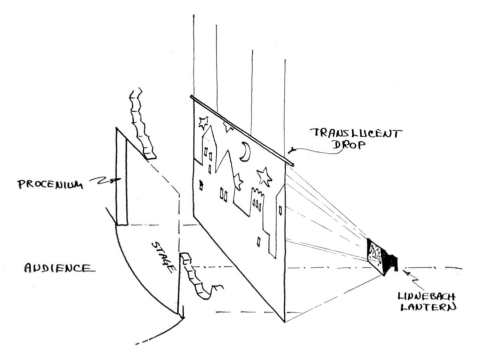

Scene projected upon a translucent drop from a Linnebach lantern (shadow projection). Outlines of projection are fuzzy because light source has extensity.

Setting for the 1944 Labor Day Pageant, Weirton Steel Co. Scenic backgrounds were projected onto three translucent screens. Designed by Peggy Clark, lighting by Stanley McCandless. Courtesy Weirton Steel Employees Bulletin.

must be at least equal to the largest dimension of the image desired. Thus to project images 30 feet high on a cyclorama from the rear requires a band of clear space outside the cyclorama at least 30 feet wide. Limited rear projection may be obtained by the provision of large openings through the stage walls into adjoining rooms. The openings between the stage and shop at the Yale University Theatre and in the projected Dartmouth College Theatre afford opportunities for rear projection of large images. Rear projection, to be most effective, must be on a specially constructed translucent screen which renders the light source invisible to the audience and equalizes the intensity of the image over its entire area. The screen must be seamless over the projection area. The best material for rear projection is an homogeneous acetate sheet having a graded opacity to correct intensity variation. Such sheets are at present prohibitively expensive and too inflammable for stage use, although they are much used in motion picture process shots and may be useful for open air productions. Development of a cheap, fireproof product with similar properties for stage use is anticipated.

Solid cycloramas are useful for front projection and are, obviously, of no use for rear projection. At least one solid cyclorama has been constructed with a flat translucent cloth panel in the center of the back for rear projection. The faults of this were: visible joints between the solid part and the translucent panel, and limitation of the projection area. Cloth cycloramas are suitable for both front and rear projection with the following reservations: a painted cyclorama has greater reflection and less transmission than a dyed one and is therefore better for front projection. On the same basis a dyed cyclorama is better for rear projection than a painted one.

Curves in the projection surface for either front or rear projection cause distortion in the image and variation in light intensity over the area of the image. Although correction can be made in the slide to eliminate distortion, it is difficult to correct for intensity variation. It is therefore desirable that the projection surface be flat or curved on a large radius (12 feet or more).

Requisites for front projection of scenery determine the minimum downstage position of the cyclorama and rear projection the minimum clear space outside the cyclorama. A one to one beam spread may be considered maximum.

Non-standard Types

While an effort is always made to keep scenery light, some sets cannot be so constructed. ROAR CHINA used a tank of water which covered the whole acting area. The water was only two feet deep but even so it imposed a load on understage structure which required special columns placed in the trap room. Such a requirement has a bearing on the kind of footing used in the trap room. TOBACCO ROAD with its many tons of genuine earth on the stage required similar special support. A tank of water for a diving act was flown in one of the Winter Garden shows.

It is, of course, impractical to design a theatre which will be adequate for the whims of some designers who usually feel it necessary to rebuild the theatre to accommodate settings worthy of their genius. Productions which involve extensive house alterations almost invariably fail. If a setting won't fit in the theatre, one should put it in a ball park.

The requirements from which stage size and shape are derived are many. The basic shape and maximum size are determined by the nature of scenery and provisions for handling it. Before shapes and sizes are frozen, however, they must be checked against requisites for lighting (Chapter 12), and the operation of the show (Chapter 8) and Economics (Chapter 15).

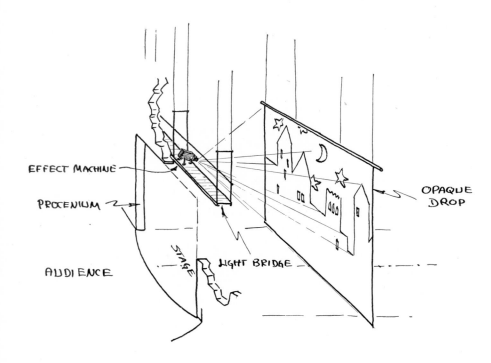

Lens projection of a scene from an optical effect machine on the light bridge onto an opaque drop.

10: stage machinery: on the stage floor

Basic Requirements

Plays require all possible variations in kind and amount of scenery. The production which requires varied and quickly changed sets represents the peak load on the stage space.

Existing theatres impose space restrictions upon scene designers. The designer's creative energies are often devoted to the problem of contriving scenery which will fit the stage rather than scenery which is suitable for the play. In some theatres it is even necessary to reduce the acting area in order to provide scenery space and working and storage space.

Scenery must be set up and struck quickly, often in a simultaneous movement consuming 10 seconds or less which the audience will accept as an instant. Five facts regarding the scene shift are important to the theatre planner: 1. The scenery space must be cleared of one set before the other can be brought into it. 2. There must be storage space to accommodate all the sets. 3. Paths of movement of scenery must be direct and clear of obstacles. 4. The fewer the pieces into which a set must be divided to strike it, and the fewer parts which must be fitted and joined to assemble it, the more rapid may be the scene shift and the better may be the scenery. 5. Scenery occupies space when stored.

A concept borrowed from Friedrich Kranich[1] is useful in appraising stages. Methods of handling scenery are divided into two categories:

The Old Stagecraft embodies those methods by which a set of scenery is assembled piecemeal within the scenery space and is struck by a reversal of the process. It is suitable to plays which allow ample intermission time for shifts. It is obligatory on stages where storage space for scenery is limited. If a skilled stage hand is assigned to each move of the shift, and performs only one operation, and that perfectly, there is still a sequence of operations which consumes time.

The Modern Stagecraft includes those methods by which whole sets or large parts of sets already assembled are brought into and taken out of the scenery space. This stagecraft recognizes the necessity of making scene changes in ten seconds, of changing scenery in a blackout without lowering the act curtain, or of changing scenery concurrently with the action of the play. The methods involve assembly of the set outside the scenery space in advance of its use; they predicate ample storage and working space outside the scenery space but within the stage walls. Present day American theatres are

[1] Kranich, Friedrich: BÜHNENTECHNIK DER GEGENWART. R. Oldenburg, Munich and Berlin, 1929.

not planned for this Modern Stagecraft, although, because of the continued production of multi-scene plays, some of its features have been laboriously and expensively adopted and used.

It is not possible to qualify scenery handling methods according to the type of production, because any type of production, except motion pictures, may call for any kind of scenery. A well-planned stage must have facilities for handling all kinds of scenery according to the five facts stated above. Proceeding from the proscenium and acting area to the scenery space, and next to the working and storage space, the planner must incorporate one or more of the methods of handling scenery set forth hereafter. He can then proceed sensibly to develop the size, shape, arrangement, and equipment of the entire stage space. There follows a table of the most common methods of shifting scenery, accompanied by illustrations. Types of stages which arise from the use of these methods are subsequently shown in plan.

In this chapter a system for rating the items of stage equipment will be used, to denote the authors' experience as to the utility of the various items, and as an aid to architects and clients in selecting equipment. Each item will be given a code index consisting of a letter and a number. The key to this code follows:

A equals essential. Necessary to adequately equip a stage for performance.

B, generally useful, but not essential. Recommended to be included if money permits.

C, occasionally useful, but by no means essential. To be included in all-purpose theatres if the budget is very liberal. Some of the items on this letter classification are downright luxuries.

1, must be installed during construction if at all. Later installation would require major structural alterations to the building.

2, may be installed after construction, but only at disproportionate expense and with great inconvenience to the occupant. Might even mean suspending use of the building during the work.

3, may be installed after construction with ease, and at not much more cost than if installed during construction. Items in this number category might be purchased and installed piecemeal if budgets require.

RUNNING

Description

Stage hands divide a set into pieces of size and weight to permit portability, and manually slide or carry the pieces to the storage space. Scenery is as far as possible reduced to two dimensions: thick-

Minimum allowance of stage space for setting and handling scenery by the Old Stagecraft. Space allowances below those indicated hamper the designer and the technician.

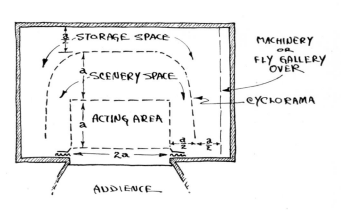

nesses are removed or folded, and platforms are collapsed. Movement is in the horizontal plane on the stage floor or, in connection with stage elevators, on the floor below the stage. The direction of movement is governed by the location of the storage space, which preferably should be at the sides.

Speed of Shifts

The minimum shift time from one full stage set to another cannot be less than two minutes even with an adequate number of expert stage hands.

Power

Manpower. Skill is necessary to the handling of large cumbersome, often topheavy, pieces.

Kinds of Scenery

All kinds of framed scenery which are supported by the stage floor. The size of individual pieces is limited.

Storage Space (A,1)

1. Stacking space for flat scenery with about 15 ft. of clear wall space on each side of the stage, and floor space for three dimensional scenery and properties aggregating minimum of 150 square feet on each side.

2. Clear height to accommodate highest flat scenery which will be used.

Equipment

Walls must be clear of openings and apparatus, or guard rails (A, 3) must be bracketted out from the walls to allow stacking over such apparatus. These are called *outriggers,* and are regularly placed over the sidewall elements of a counterweight system between 10' and 20' from the floor.

Pipe frames (B, 3) may be set either permanently or temporarily on the stage floor. If a stage contains a plaster cyclorama against which no scenery can be stacked temporary pipe frames are essential for the stacking of flat scenery.

Comment

This is the only method possible on the ill-planned and ill-equipped stages of many schools, town halls, social halls, and commercial theatres. It is wasteful of time and labor, prevents any attempt at a rapid sequence of scenes, and requires that the scenery be built in small pieces for *manhandling* and storage. Some scenery will be handled by this method no matter what other methods are also employed. Restriction to this method of handling imposes high labor and scene building costs on producers, indirectly inclines the producer to select plays which require no shifts of scene, and thereby indirectly influences playwrights to constrict the locales of their plays to one setting.

ROLLING: INDIVIDUAL CASTERED PIECES

Description

Parts of sets which are too heavy to run or too intricate to be divided for running are equipped with casters and propelled from the scenery space to the storage space. Movement is horizontal on the stage floor. Universal casters permit movement in any direction, and fixed casters establish straight line movement if it is desired.

This is the first and simplest addition of machinery (wheels) to the task of handling scenery. By increasing the size of the individual scenery units it reduces the number of joints which have to be fastened and unfastened, reduces the complexity of the shift routine and reduces the amount of physical effort. Current practice on inadequate stages is to limit the size of the castered piece by the size of the space into which it can be shifted.

Minimum shift time is faster than in running, but seldom less than 1½ minutes for changing from one fullstage set to another

Speed of Shifts

Manpower, sometimes aided by hand levers to overcome starting inertia. No lifting, consequently less physical effort and less danger of injury to scenery and stage hands than in running.

Power

All kinds which are supported by the stage floor. Generally complex or heavy assemblies, essentially three dimensional.

Kinds of Scenery

Variable. The larger the space, the larger the piece which can be stored. Any increase over the minimum storage space indicated for running is advantageous. Clear height to accommodate highest flat scenery which will be used. Located preferably at the sides of the stage, but space at the back is better than none.

Storage Space (A, 1)

None. Casters are considered as scenery and are supplied with it as required. Stage floor must be firm and level (A, 1).

Equipment

This is not a distinct method of handling scenery but rather an adjunct to running when storage space permits. Advantages are greater possible variety in settings, more three dimensional assemblies, freer use of platforms, some reduction in the time required to change scenes, and a slight reduction in the number of stage hands required to make a scene change. Because settings need not be divided into so many units, the appearance of scenery is generally better than in running.

Comment

ROLLING; DIVIDED WAGONS

Two wagons, each containing half a set, split in the center and rolled to the sides of the stage. Movement is horizontal in a straight line parallel to the proscenium.

Description

Stage space allowance for Divided Wagons.

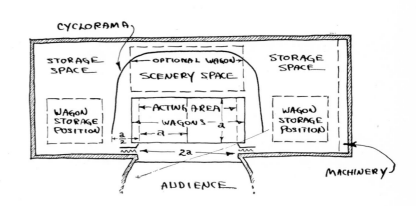

Speed of Shifts	The stage can be cleared in five seconds. The total shift time depends on the method of setting the next set.
Power	Manpower, applied by pull-ropes and pushing. May be applied through windlass. Electric power possible, using windlass and cables.
Storage Space (A,1)	Floor area equal to the area of the wagon at each side, plus space around this for storage of scenery and properties taken off and put on wagon, plus passageways. Clear height to accommodate the highest scenery used plus height of wagon.
Equipment	Two wagons (B, 3) each slightly larger than one-half the acting area. Stage floor tracks (B, 2) to guide the wagons, countersunk into stage floor if this method is contemplated when the theatre is planned, superimposed on the floor if not. Portable raised apron (B, 3) set in place and used when wagons are used, extending full width of the proscenium and from front edge of wagon to the footlights, height equal to height of wagons.
Comment	This method regularly requires the designing of settings to conceal a necessary break-line in the back wall. It is occasionally used in New York theatres where offstage space is barely sufficient to accommodate the wagons. Sometimes used in combination with a full-width wagon moving directly up- and downstage. This method permits changing scenes on the wagons, offstage, while action is in another set. This advantage is common to all methods employing wagons which move to storage positions, if sufficient scene storage space is allowed between the wagons and the stage walls. Costs and assembly time are lower than in the previous methods if the wagons and their tracks are part of the equipment of the theatre, greater if wagons and tracks must be brought into the theatre with a production.

ROLLING: UPSTAGE WAGON

Description	A complete setting is pre-assembled on a fullstage wagon which is propelled from the scenery space directly upstage to storage space. Movement is horizontal at stage level, and in a straight path.
Speed of Shifts	The wagon can be brought into or taken out of the scenery space in approximately five seconds. The total shift time depends upon what must be cleared before the wagon can be moved, and the method used to set the next scene. Range: twenty seconds to two minutes.
Power	Direct manpower; manpower with mechanical advantage through a windlass; electric power through windlass (B, 3).
Kinds of Scenery	All standing scenery. Hung scenery and background scenery must be cleared before wagon can be moved.
Storage Space (A,1)	Floor space equal to the wagon area upstage of the acting area and preferably upstage of the cyclorama, plus storage space for scenery off the wagon. Minimum clear height to accommodate highest

standing scenery (A, 1). Fly space over wagon storage is useful (B, 1).

One fullstage wagon (B, 3) slightly larger than the acting area, portable tracks (B, 3) to be laid only when wagon is to be used. Permanent tracks cannot be installed without interfering with the stage floor traps.

The depth of stage required for an upstage wagon will, if supplied, provide sufficient stage depth for all other purposes, including rear projection of light images upon translucent drops. Because so many settings contain elaborate background effects in scenery and light, which must be dismantled before an upstage wagon may be moved, this method is less useful than Traverse Wagons.

ROLLING: JACKKNIFE WAGONS

Description

Complete settings are pre-assembled on two fullstage wagons, each wagon pivoting around its downstage corner through 90 degrees to a storage position at the side of the stage. Movement is horizontal on the stage floor, and circular about centers near the proscenium.

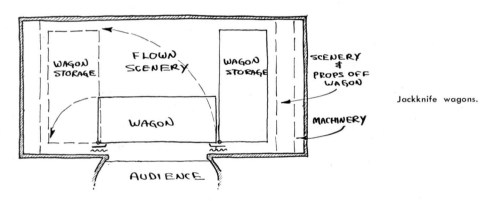

Jackknife wagons.

Speed of Shifts

Approacnes that of one-movement shift, but slightly slower because the arcs of the two wagons overlap. The first wagon must move through about 80 degrees before the second can move into position. Time: about 15 seconds. Fastest so far.

Power

Manpower applied directly by pushing and pulling; electric power applied through motor windlasses and cables (B, 3).

Storage Space (A, 1)

Wagons are stored in what is normally part of the scenery space, extending to the sides into storage space. Space equal to fullstage wagon extending offstage from the acting area plus stacking space and storage space off the wagons, plus passageways. Clear height equal to the highest standing scenery plus wagon (A, 1).

Equipment

Two fullstage wagons, slightly larger than the entire acting area (C, 3). Pivot mountings for each wagon near proscenium, portable forestage as for Divided Wagons. Wagons, pivots, and forestage must be removable because many shows will not require their use. Tracks to provide smooth surface for wheels of wagons must be portable (C, 3).

Comment   This method works best when a production requires two interior sets which alternate in a series of scenes. Side entrances are congested. Scenery may be shifted on one wagon while action takes place on the other. Flown pieces must be raised before the wagons can move. Because wagons swing through a large arc it is not feasible to have elaborate background effects. This method is better as a solution of a scenic problem in existing theatres than as a basis for the plan of a new theatre.

ROLLING: STRAIGHT PATH TRAVERSE WAGON

Description   Fullstage settings are assembled on fullstage wagons and propelled from scenery space to storage spaces at each side of the stage. Scenery may be shifted on one wagon while a scene is being played on the other. This process may be aided by the installation of flying equipment over the storage spaces, so that pieces of scenery may be flown off the wagons.

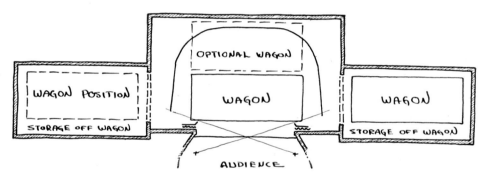

Traverse Wagons, straight path. Fly loft with high roof over center block only. Wagon rooms may be used as shop, rehearsal rooms, dance practice, or classrooms.

Speed of Shifts   The fastest possible change from one fullstage setting to another. Both wagons move simultaneously. If cyclorama is used it must be cleared before wagons can move. Time: 10 seconds.

Power   Manpower applied directly by pushing or pulling, about three men to each wagon; manpower applied indirectly through hand windlasses and cables; electric motor windlasses with remote control, automatic speed control and limit switches.

Kinds of Scenery   All standing scenery. Elaborate background set-ups behind the wagons are not disturbed by the movement of the wagons. Complete built-up exteriors may be mounted on the wagons.

Storage Space (A,1)   Floor area equal to the area of a fullstage wagon at each side of the stage, plus scenery storage around this for scenery and properties off the wagon, plus passageways. Clear height to accommodate highest scenery on wagon, plus 1'-6" for trusses above ceiling of set. Flying height over storage space useful but optional.

Two wagons (C, 3) each slightly larger than the entire acting area; tracks in the stage floor to guide the wagons; portable raised forestage optional (B, 3), electric windlasses and controls (B, 3) optional; auxiliary flying equipment over storage spaces (B, 1).

Equipment

Because of the advantages cited this method is strongly recommended. It requires generous allowance of space backstage, but the returns in efficient handling, variety of scenery, and speed of changes warrant it.

Comment

ROLLING: CURVED PATH TRAVERSE WAGONS

Fullstage settings are assembled on fullstage wagons which are propelled from the scenery space to storage space flanking the auditorium at the sides. Architecturally, certain walls of the storage space become party walls with the auditorium, rather than exterior walls. Permits shifting fullstage wagons without disturbing the cyclorama or background scenery. The cyclorama may be integrated with the backwall of the stage.

Description

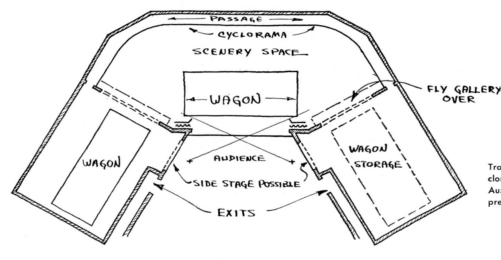

Traverse Wagons, curved path. Fixed cyclorama is out of the way of wagons. Auxiliary uses for the wagon rooms. Impressive open-air effects possible.

Fullstage change in about ten seconds.

Speed of Shifts

Same as for Straight Path Traverse Wagons.

Power

All standing scenery. Ceilings may be placed on sets and move with them.

Kinds of Scenery

Same as for Straight Path Traverse Wagons. In both these methods the storage space may be planned for auxiliary uses and partitioned from the stage by rolling doors or overhead doors.

Storage Space (A,1)

Tracks to guide wagons (A, 2), either countersunk permanently into the stage floor, or portable (A, 3) to be laid when wagons are used. Permanent tracks should not conflict with stage floor traps.
Two fullstage wagons (A, 2).
Auxiliary flying equipment over the storage spaces (B, 1).

Equipment

ROLLING: REVOLVING STAGE OR REVOLVING DISC

Description

A revolving *stage* (C, 1) is built-in, the stage floor structure being designed so that the floor of the revolver is level with the surrounding floor. In some elaborate examples, the structure of the revolver extends below stage sufficiently to contain elevators. A revolving *disc* (C, 3) is essentially portable and is placed on the permanent stage floor. The surrounding floor must be built up to the level of the disc when it is used.

Speed of Shifts

Change of scenes which are preset on the revolver can be truly instantaneous. Scenes can be changed while action goes on in other scenes.

Power

Manpower applied directly at edge of disc by pullropes or push-bars (A, 3); electric power applied either through drum and endless cable around revolver, or through pinion and rack gears, or motor drive contained in revolver (C, 1).

Kinds of Scenery

Sets of scenery are designed to fit onto sectors of the revolver, which is rotated to bring successive sets into position. Sets are changed during stage action on other sets. It is difficult to use exterior and interior settings in combination. All interiors tend to have triangular floor plans. Background effects are limited to what can be achieved above the scenery. Hung scenery must be flown before stage can revolve. Some scenery must be run and set to fit between the revolver and the proscenium.

Storage Space

Storage space off the revolver must equal and resemble that required for running. As any of the rolling methods may be combined with this method, the storage space must follow the requirements of any method selected.

Equipment

Revolving stage (C, 1): stage floor with built-in circular track in which the wheels of the revolver run. Revolving portion, being unsupported from below, must have heavy beams of deep trusses to support the long spans. A deep revolving stage may be built up from tracks far below stage and contain elevators.

Revolving disc (C, 3): portable tracks laid on the stage floor; central pivot; driving mechanism. The disc may be built in portable sections for transportation and storage

ROLLING: RECIPROCATING SEGMENT

Description

A wagon, large enough to hold at least two fullstage settings, in the shape either of a sector of a circle, or a segment of a ring stage is pivoted about an upstage center so that the scenery assembled on it is propelled from the scenery space into the rear corners of the stage. This method has been adapted to the shallow stages of American

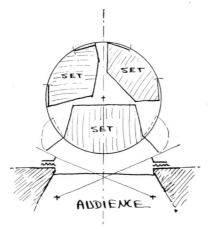

Revolving stage or disc.

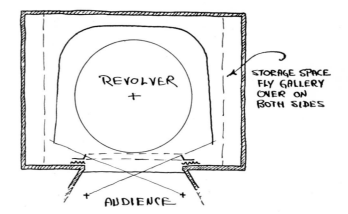

Sectional, portable revolving disc.
Photo, courtesy Joseph Vasconcellos,
Inc.

Driving mechanism of revolving disc.
Photo, courtesy Joseph Vasconcellos,
Inc.

commercial theatres in preference to revolving stages, because the large radius permits sets which are nearly rectangular. It is more a method to be used on existing stages than one to be recommended for new stages.

Speed of Shifts	Fullstage change in ten seconds, of limited kinds of settings (see below).
Power	Manual or electric through motors, drums, and cables.
Kinds of Scenery	All standing scenery. Because the wagon moves through space which background scenery and the cyclorama occupy, full stage exteriors are difficult. Hung scenery must be flown before wagon can be moved.
Storage Space	Space equal to acting area at each side for wagon. Floor space at least equal to that required by Running for storage off the wagon, on each side. Clear height to accommodate the highest standing scenery, on the wagon.
Equipment	Wagon, tracks, and motor mechanism.

ROLLING: RING STAGE

Description A ring, or doughnut of stage floor with its center on the centerline of the stage. Scenery is set on the ring and rotated into the scenery area. 1. Rotation may be about an upstage center, toward sides and rear of stage. Used occasionally in combination with a revolving disc or stage. 2. Rotation may be about a center located in the auditorium, around and under the seating bank. This is the extreme development of Curved Track Traverse Wagons, and exists in project only. Requires the development of the entire plan of the theatre around the ring stage, with all audience facilities fitted over or under the ring tunnel. Either type of ringstage is an ultimate development on the shifting of many settings by rolling. The cost of installation and the fact that comparatively few productions require them deter the use of ring stages.

ROLLING: MULTIPLE DISCS

Description Two or more circular discs are used to revolve scenery into and out of the scenery space: 1. Small discs rotated to change sidewalls and properties, 2. two large discs tangent at the center of the stage, each disc carrying sidewall, half the backwall, and half the properties, 3. one large disc and two small discs to change the entire set. The first type permits the use of hung scenery, the second and third limit the use of hung scenery. These methods are not versatile, and are not recommended as permanent installations.

Variations and combinations of the foregoing methods of handling scenery on the stage floor are numerous in project though rare in actual existence. To attempt a detailed listing, description, and criticism of them all would require more space than their importance warrants. An exhaustive listing with description and illustration may

Reciprocating segment.

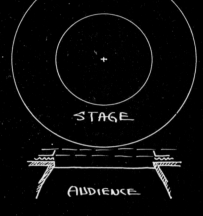

Ring stage with center upstage.

Ring stage with center in the house. An extreme concept.

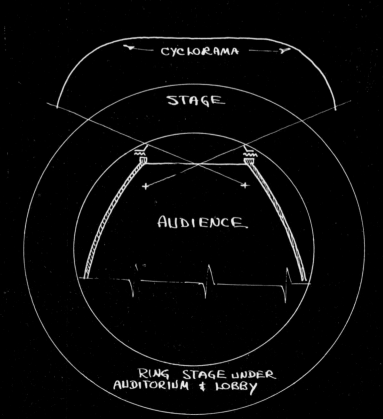

be found in Friedrich Kranich's BÜHNENTECHNIK DER GEGENWART, Volume I, pages 281-346.

Countersunk or Superimposed

A question of considerable importance is whether or not the portion of the stage floor on which the wagons travel should be countersunk to allow the surface of the wagon to be flush with the forestage and apron when set, and flush with the scenery storage floor when struck. If this is done, some device must be provided to raise the sunken portion of the stage to the general level for productions which do not use wagons. Since the sets for which wagons are impossible or unnecessary will outnumber those for which wagons are used, it is wrong to plan the stage solely for the use of wagons. Twenty-eight sets out of about 120 analyzed could have been handled best on full-stage wagons. In the Kirby Theatre at Amherst College where there is storage space offstage on one side for a fullstage wagon, in almost every production all or part of at least one set is mounted on casters or a wagon and rolled into that space.

Inertia and Momentum are involved in the operation of rolling stages. The greatest motive power is required to start the stages in motion; speed must be reduced as they approach the end of their motion; the stop must be precise but not abrupt. For electrical motive power there must be four adjustments of speed or power: 1. starting power, which after starting immediately reduces to 2. running power, which continues until near the end of the run and where 3. a slow-down takes effect until 4. the stop is reached. For some rolling stages, mechanical stops can be placed at the ends of the run. In manual operation, either by direct application (pushing and pulling) or indirectly through a windlass the operators may apply the correct amount of power.

Tracks and Guides

Tracks are necessary for all types of rolling stages whose direction of movement is established. Temporary tracks (B, 3) may be superimposed on the stage floor to provide truly level surfaces on floors which are uneven, and to provide directional guides.

When the use of rolling stages is contemplated in the planning of a theatre, it is sensible to include built-in tracks in the plan.

Tracks

Tracks may have two functions: to provide a level, smooth surface for the casters or wheels, and to control the direction of movement. Stages with rotary movement have their direction of movement governed by fixed pivots and require tracks only as surfaces under the wheels: jackknife stages, revolving discs, revolving stages, multiple discs. For stages the direction of which cannot be controlled by a pivot (divided wagons, traverse wagons, ring stage, reciprocating segment) direction must be controlled by the engagement of the casters or wheels and the track.

Tracks to provide surface only may be flat steel countersunk into the stage floor. Tracks to control direction may be: 1. two pieces of flat steel spaced about ½" to ¾" apart on a third piece, the whole countersunk into the stage floor, 2. steel angles 1½" x 1½" back to back set into the stage floor and spaced ½" to ¾" apart.

If the stage floor under the rolling stage is firm and level, only a few of the casters need engage the tracks, or all of the casters may be clear of the tracks, and rigid metal rods or straps attached to the rolling stage and inserted into the tracks as guides only.

Wagon stages, and revolving discs are not used frequently enough to warrant their being left permanently in place on the stage floor. Methods of storing them are:

1. Reduction to units small enough to permit easy transportation to storage rooms outside the stage.

2. Subdivision into sections small enough to permit vertical storage against a back wall or a side wall of the stage house. Suspension from the gridiron is forbidden by law in most states.

3. Up-ended and sunk through a slot, to be stored vertically, whole or in parts, in the space below stage.

4. A wagon stage may be stored by rolling it, whole or in sections, onto an elevator and sinking the elevator so that the floor of the wagon is level with the stage floor.

Except for differences in the details of the installation all rolling stages, whether with straight line movement or curved movement, may be propelled by similar methods:

1. Manpower, directly applied. Wagonstages may be pushed or pulled, generally with the aid of short pull-ropes; revolving discs, jackknife stages, and reciprocating segments by pull-ropes and push-bars, the latter inserted into sockets.

2. Manpower, indirectly applied through hand-operated windlasses and cables: either two winches and two cables, each to pull the stage in one direction, or one winch and endless cable reversed over pulleys to control movement in both directions.

3. Motor windlasses. Wherever hand windlasses can be used, electric motors may replace manpower and provide the added feature of remote control. Automatic stop switches may reduce the operator's job to the starting operation only.

4. Electric motive power may be contained in all rolling stages. A unit, consisting of motor, gears, and drive shaft may be mounted in the stage, to move it by one of the following drives: a) friction of a rubber-tired wheel on a track fixed to the floor; b) pinion on the drive-shaft and rack fixed to the stage floor; c) drum on the drive shaft and cable attached to the floor.

5. Revolving stages and ring stages may be propelled electrically by motors mounted outside the stages as follows: pinion of motor shaft engaging a curved rack on the edge of the stage. Motor bevel-geared to a shaft on which is a pulley, which in turn drives the stage by an endless belt or cable around the stage.

Figures show the size of stage wagons relative to acting area and proscenium. Certain direct benefits derive from integrating the design of wagon stages and other types of rolling stages with the trapping arrangement for the stage floor to permit entrances through the stage floor and the use of stage elevators when the rolling stage is in position. To meet this requirement, the framing structure of the rolling stage must coincide with framing of the stage floor when the rolling stage is in position.

For greatest stability wheels on rolling stages must be placed to run on the main beams of the stage floor, rather than on the floor between the beams. This design regulates the layout of the frame of the rolling stage to coincide with the frame of the stage floor, and facilitates the registering of openings in both.

Storage for Portable Wagons and Discs

Propulsion of Rolling Stages

Integration with Stage Floor Traps

Location of the Wheels on Wagon Stages

The Stage Floor

The stage floor must be considered as an important part of the stage equipment, to be designed expressly for its particular uses, which are: a suitable level upon which the actors may perform, adaptable to the requirements of several or all types of performance, and a level upon which scenery may be set, and shifted.

Excerpts from the Building Code, City of New York 1938:

"Section C26-722 Paragraph a. That portion of the stage floor extending from each side of the proscenium opening to the enclosure walls and from the stage side of the proscenium wall to the front edge of the apron shall be of construction having a fire resistive rating of at least four hours. Regardless of the height of the structure untreated wood flooring may be used on the stage floor. For a width of six feet more than the proscenium opening the stage may be constructed of wood.

"Section C26-344 Paragraph e. Live loads for public spaces and congested areas.—The minimum live load shall be taken as one hundred pounds per square foot, uniformly distributed, for——— theatre stages———."

The Stage Floor is the level upon which the show is performed. As such it must meet all the requirements imposed upon it by performances. These include 1. stability, 2. entrances for actors from below, and 3. alteration of the size and shape of the acting area by the provision of raised or sunken acting levels.

Stability: Floor Loads

The New York City Building Code, 1938, sets 100 pounds per square foot as the minimum allowable evenly distributed live load for stage floors but the National Building Code (1949 edition) recommended by the National Board of Fire Underwriters contains the recommendation of 150 pounds per square foot for the same load. Stages may be subject to a particularly violent form of live load in the form of vigorous ensemble dancing. The deflection of a stage floor, particularly if it is produced by a live load applied rhythmically may cause perceptible disturbance of the scenery which is set upon the floor. Therefore stage floors must be designed not only strong enough but stiff enough to withstand serious deflection under maximum loading. Deflection of more than 1/360 of the span must be considered serious.

Where two or more beams of different cross section have the same strength, the one with the greatest stiffness is to be preferred.

Scenery, properties, and lighting equipment are set up on the stage floor in and around the acting area by any of the various methods previously described. Salient features of this function are the following:

1. The stage floor must be firm, and truly level. The stage floor which sloped upward as it receded from the footlights has been obsolete for at least half a century.

2. Moveable beams and floor traps must be closely fitted and fastened.

Soft Wood Floor (A,1)

3. The stage must be floored with a tough wear-resisting wood which is at the same time receptive to nails and hand driven stage screws. Edge-grained yellow pine or similar wood (nominal 2 x 3 or 2 x 4, matched) is satisfactory. It is absurd to use maple, birch, oak, or other hardwood flooring on a stage.

4. Every precaution must be taken to counteract expansion and contraction of the flooring, especially in the trap area.

5. Thoroughly seasoned wood is essential for the floor beams, so that shrinkage or warping after construction will not throw the floor out of true level.

It has been the custom in America to floor the stage from the front of the trap area to the footlight trough with hardwood, such as maple. This appears to be almost as pointless as covering the whole stage with hardwood, since it is frequently necessary to drive carpet tacks, nails, screws, and even stage screws into this portion of the floor. Again yellow pine or a similar wood is recommended. An exception is the stage intended primarily for musical comedy, revue, or vaudeville, where a hardwood apron is a necessity for the tap dancers. Even in this case a portable *tap strip*, of matched hardwood cemented to a canvas back may be used instead.

In approximately twenty percent of the major productions in one theatre over a twenty year period, traps in the floor have been opened to provide entrances and exits of actors. Once a heavy stage property which could be set in no other way was elevated into position during a black-out. Once a mine shaft lift was operated through a trap in the stage floor. Twice instantaneous disappearance of actors was achieved by the use of sinking traps. Thus in about one production in every five, desired dramatic effects have been made possible by the presence of traps in the stage floor.

The smallest generally useful single trap must be rectangular, wide enough to allow two people to ascend side by side (3′-3″ minimum) and long enough to produce headroom under the floor framing using stairs or ladders. This is achieved in 7′ to 8′ of length.

The unit size of a trap may be established at 3′-6″ x 7′-0″ or 4′-0″ x 8′-0″. A few smaller traps based on even subdivision of these dimensions make possible small adjustments in position.

Flexibility of location requires that the floor framing under the trapped area be demountable.

Stage Floor Traps (B,1)

Stage traps must be wide enough to permit access to the stage from below by stairs of tolerable pitch.

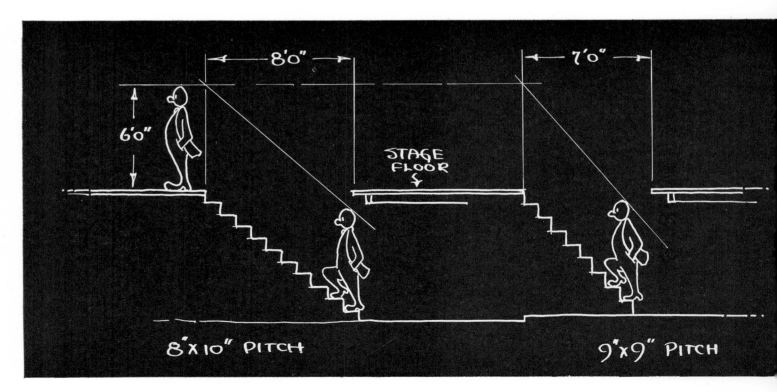

8′X10″ PITCH   9′x9″ PITCH

Four Systems of Stage Floor Traps

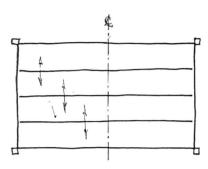

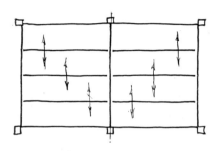

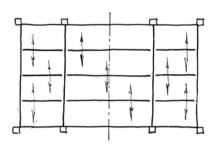

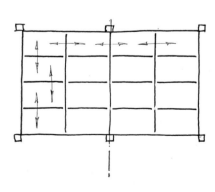

I Entire Trap Area Free of Permanent Beams
Transverse Beams moveable up and down stage

Advantages: Great flexibility in lateral position of traps.
        Beams at front and back of opening carry little load.

Disadvantages: Span makes necessary very deep transverse beams.
        Load makes necessary very heavy beams at sides of opening.
        Up and down stage location of traps limited to four positions. Flexibility beyond this requires considerable reconstruction.

II One fixed beam on center line of stage in middle of trap area.
Movable transverse beams.

Advantages: Shortened spans and reduced loads permit smaller beams than System I.
        Within limits set by the fixed beam, variety of location is obtained with less reconstruction than in System I.

Disadvantages: Fixed beam is in most important stage space where trapping is likely to be wanted.

III Two fixed beams ¼ in from each side of trap area.
Movable transverse beams.

Advantages: Flexibility of location and size within center area, with only moderate amount of reconstruction. Shortened spans and reduced loads require smaller beams than I or II.

Disadvantages: Fixed beams prevent trapping in two fairly important zones of the acting area.

To be preferred over System II.

IV No fixed beams in trap area. All beams moveable and removable.
Full-length moveable beams running up- and downstage. Short purlin beams across stage.

Advantages: Complete flexibility of location and size with only moderate amount of reconstruction. Possible to standardize on spare parts to allow considerable flexibility.

Disadvantages: Very limited flexibility without at least some reconstruction.

Columns in center of long spans at front and back of trap area may be used to reduce size of beams. To be omitted if possible.

It is sounder practice to plan and install a complete system of traps than to lay a solid floor. Traps built and fitted during construction can be carefully made and tested by skilled workmen. A system once established will be followed by the users of the theatre, provided it does not impose too much limitation. Traps cut at random in a solid floor to fit the demands of individual productions by the person who happens to be the stage carpenter at the time produce a mutilated stage floor soon in need of major repairs, for which the cost of a complete trap installation is easily spent.

Size and Location of the Trap Area

Study of 60 varied productions in one theatre has shown that traps have occurred in all parts of the normal acting area, and also beyond the sides and back of the acting area. The most extreme side traps have extended about half their length outside the acting

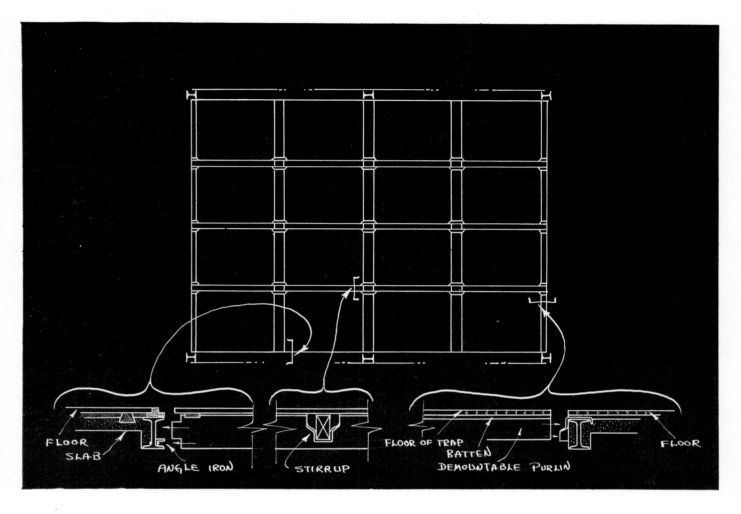

Removable framing for trapped area of stage floor.

Frequency of use of traps
from a study of 60 typical
legitimate productions.

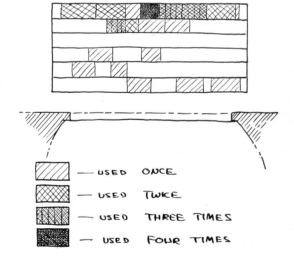

USED ONCE

USED TWICE

USED THREE TIMES

USED FOUR TIMES

area, and the upstage traps have been in a narrow zone across stage behind the acting area. From these facts, it may be deduced that the trap area should be slightly wider and deeper than the acting area.

Table of Proscenium Widths, Recommended Trap Areas, and Unit Trap Sizes

Proscenium Width	Trap Area Width	Depth*	Unit Trap Width	Depth[1]
26'	31'-6"	17'-6"	7'	3'-6"
28'	35'	21'-0"	"	"
30'	38'-6"	21'-0"	"	"
32'	42'	24'-6"	"	"
34'	42'	24'-6"	"	"
36'	45'-6"	24'-6"	"	"
38'	48'	28'	8'	4'
40'	48'	28'	8'	4'

[1] Horizontal distance perpendicular to proscenium.

Inasmuch as traps may be called for by playwrights, designers, or directors in any part of the acting area, the front edge of the trap area must coincide with the front edge of the normal acting area. When permanent side stages are provided it is advisable to provide at least one trap in each of these.

The design of the trapped area must permit the planned use of rolling stages.

Mentioned here and discussed fully in Chapter 12 are two other openings in the stage floor, the Footlight Pit (A,1) and the Cyclorama Base Light Pit (B,1).

Stage Floor Coverings

It is customary to cover the unfinished stage floor for most performances. Temporary coverings (B,3) of duck or carpet are chosen and laid at the option of the theatre user. Permanent floor coverings (B,1) which obviate the necessity for temporary coverings are the concern of the theatre planner. Materials for permanent coverings must be hardwearing but resilient. It must be possible to penetrate them with nails, screws, and stage-screws. They must reduce somewhat the sound of footfalls and other impacts and attenuate any sounds originating in the trap room below the stage. Battleship linoleum and certain other modern composition floor coverings satisfy these requirements.

It is inadvisable to lay a permanent floor covering on a stage floor in which traps may be cut at random. Such a covering is desirable only on a stage floor in which no traps may be cut, or on a floor which has been designed and constructed as a trapped floor. In the latter case, all of the traps are covered separately with the material and all edges are permanently finished with metal edging strips.

UNDERSTAGE MACHINERY

Raised and Sunken Acting Levels

The acting area is not always a single level of stage floor. Since the beginning of the century in Europe and since the early nineteen twenties in this country, there has been a steady increase of the use of *plastic form* in stage settings, with a resulting increase in the use of levels, steps, and ramps, in the acting area. The use of raised levels for emphasis is a stage director's axiom. Of 60 consecutive productions in one legitimate theatre, raised levels were used in 49.

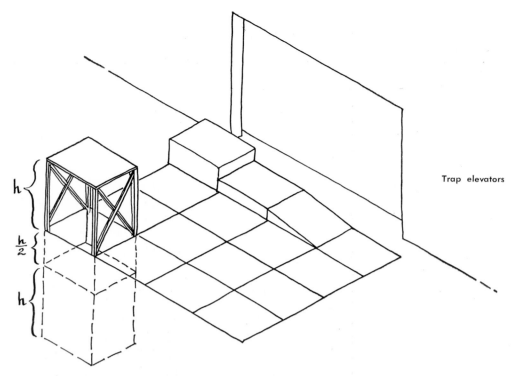

Raised levels within the acting area may be produced by two methods: by building platforms as scenery and setting them in the acting area; by elevating sections of the stage floor on understage machinery. The former method must be used on stages which have a solid floor and no elevating devices. It involves the maximum of effort in building and handling, the maximum of time and materials, and the maximum of storage space if platforms are to be kept for re-use. The second method reduces effort, time, and materials, and storage space. The desideratum is the greatest variety of size, shape, position, height, and slope.

There are similar reasons, though they occur less frequently for sinking portions or all of the stage floor below stage level: the creation of a scenic effect of a high place surrounded by open space, as a mountain top, a tower, or a plane; the creation of aquatic scenic effects by the use of a water tank; the creation of the grave in Hamlet or of trenches on a battlefield. Similarly, unless carefully designed equipment is provided for creating these effects, great effort, much material, time, and labor, and considerable jerry-building go into constructing them for particular productions.

Elevators

Vertical movement of the stage floor is produced by elevators, which may be considered under three main divisions: trap elevators, table elevators, and plateau elevators. Trap elevators and table elevators may be either fixed, that is, capable of operation in only one position, or portable, capable of being moved about horizontally below stage to be brought into action at various trap positions. Plateau elevators are entirely fixed in one position.

All elevators are operated by one or the other of two methods: hoists, which comprise cables running through pulleys fastened to the permanent understage structure; plungers, which by hydraulic force or screwjack action push the elevators up from below. The important difference to be noted between these two methods is that the hoist method requires the existence of understage structure extending upward to just below stage level, whereas the plunger method requires no such structure.

Trap Elevators

Trap Elevators provide means for moving a section of stage floor the size of a single trap or smaller. They make possible the raising and lowering of individual actors, single properties, and small pieces of scenery, and the creation of small raised levels above, or small sunken levels below, the stage floor. An entire trap area, equipped with trap elevators would provide the stage director with great variety in the location of appearances and disappearances and the scene designer with great variety in the location of raised and sunken levels. Grouped together, trap elevators may provide the elevating and sinking of larger areas which are multiples of the single trap.

Fixed Trap Elevators Operated by Hydraulic Plungers (C,1) under the whole trap area constitute a complete and flexible arrangement for elevating and sinking the stage floor. Remote control of the fluid pressure, with pressure variation and selective grouping, makes possible the movement at different rates of speed or together, in one or both directions, of separate or various groups of traps simultaneously. Irregular shaped raised levels can be produced by placing a section of beamed flooring of the necessary irregular shape upon one or more trap elevators and raising them to the desired height.

Fixed Trap Elevators with Screwjack Operation (C,1) supply the same variety and flexibility as the hydraulic plunger type, but without the possibility of speed variations, and without the expense of the elaborate hydraulic installation. Sinkage holes below the foundations of the stage must be made for either type.

Both the foregoing installations are extremely expensive. It is to be doubted whether any but the most elaborately equipped theatre should contain them. Other elevator installations, to be described below are less expensive and produce almost the same effects.

Fixed Trap Elevators with Hoist Operation (C,2) either electrically or hand powered, require the installation under the stage floor of a permanent structure of posts and beams from which the elevators are hung on cables. The presence of this structure precludes the possibility of lowering two or more traps combined in more than one dimension of the stage. If the beams run across stage, traps cannot be combined in depth;[1] if the beams run the depth of the stage, traps cannot be combined in width.

Fixed Trap Elevators with Manual Lift Operation (B,3) (sometimes called opera traps) afford a system for creating raised levels, and very limited sunken levels, which can be installed under an existing stage provided there is sufficient height below stage. Each trap rests on two vertical frames set in vertical tracks. The frames for each trap may be raised together to produce a level platform or singly to slope the platform across the stage. The frames are held at desired heights by steel pins or ratchets engaging the tracks.

When at maximum height the elevating frames must engage the vertical guides for about one third their height to insure stability of the raised level. Therefore the height of the understage space must be 1½ the height of maximum raised level. Generally useful platform heights rarely exceed 10 feet.

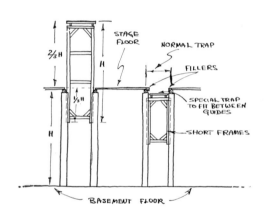

Fixed trap elevators, manual lift.

---

[1] In this chapter, and in general stage practice, the terms deep and depth refer to horizontal dimensions from proscenium to backwall; wide, width, broad, and breadth refer to horizontal dimensions across the stage, and high and height to vertical dimensions above or below the stage.

The probable value of an installation of trap elevators may be estimated from the following: In 13 out of 49 productions which used raised levels an average saving of 63% could have been effected with trap elevators. The net saving would have been 16% of all platforms used.

Portable Trap Elevators (B,3) are assemblages of vertical guides, elevator, and necessary containing structure, mounted on casters to be freely moved about in the space below the stage for use under any stage trap. Two or more may be used in combination to raise but not lower combinations of stage traps. For general legitimate production, a set of portable trap elevators sufficient to elevate approximately 20% of the trap area at one time is generally useful. Portable Trap Elevators may have either hoist operation or screw jack operation, with hand or electric power in either case. Portable Trap Elevators presuppose the existence of a trap area, with the traps resting on floor beams. If the beams are adjustable free selection of size, shape, and location of elevators is permitted.

Fixed Table Elevators are designed to raise or sink strips of stage floor, each strip one trap (about 3'-6" or 4'-0") in depth, and two or more traps (15'-0" and up) in width. They are mounted on plungers, or screwjacks, or set on steel trusses which are suspended on cables and run in vertical tracks at the ends. Because of the infrequent requirement for the elevation or sinking of a section of floor of one definite size in one definite location, their use is limited in theatrical and operatic production, although in stages of convention halls or concert halls, table elevators easily provide the desired stepped levels for speakers, choirs, or orchestras.

Portable Table Elevators (C,2) are of two types according to the method used to move them horizontally below stage. The wagon type is mounted on casters and rolls backward and forward on tracks set on the floor of the basement. The crane type is mounted on end rollers which travel on tracks suspended below the stage floor.

The portable table elevator is moved horizontally in only one dimension and brought into position under a selected row of floor traps. The traps are removed and the elevator raised into their space.

Table Elevators

Driving mechanism for fixed table elevators.
Photo, courtesy Joseph Vasconcellos, Inc.

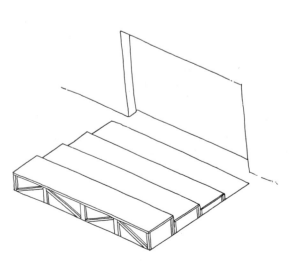

Fixed table elevators.

By setting the table elevator at a level lower than the stage and building platforms on it, a section of floor of any size, smaller than the table elevator, can be raised or lowered.

Sliding Floor Panels (C,3). For many uses of trap elevators and table elevators, it is necessary that the stage floor be intact above the elevator until the elevator is used. E.g., a scene is played on a solid floor and at a certain instant an actor rises through the floor. For such mechanical effects, a section of floor must slide sidewise under the stage to allow the elevator to rise. If fixed elevators are installed, permanent guides and operating mechanism for the floor panels are also installed; if a system of flexible elevators is adopted, the mechanism for sliding the floor panels may also be demountable, portable, and adjustable. Portable trap elevators may contain the mechanism for sliding out a section of stage floor.

Plateau Elevators

Plateau Elevators (C,1) are designed to move large portions of the stage floor. Rare in American theatres, they exist in isolated instances. The Philadelphia Convention Hall and the Radio City theatres are notable examples. They have three uses: to produce raised or sunken levels, to raise whole sets of scenery from below stage, and to produce spectacular production effects. Plateau elevators are permanently installed and have hydraulic plunger or screwjack propulsion. Of infrequent use in drama or opera, their greatest usefulness is in elaborate musical productions or presentation.

The ultimate in the installation of floor elevators conceived by Friedrich Kranich is a scheme which envisions the sinking and elevating of the entire stage floor inside the cyclorama, the subdivision of the central portion into plateau elevators, and the further subdivision of these into table elevators, with a moveable understage crane. The table elevators in turn are divided into trap elevators which may be operated singly or in groups. Kranich's system is designed for elaborate operatic production. Its greatest limitation is that the trusses running across stage between the table elevators restrict the depth (up and down stage dimension) of both table and trap elevators, and prevent location of elevators in the space occupied by the trusses.

Some theatres have been projected in which the only means of shifting scenery is by sinking and elevating wagons, which are rolled off and on the elevators below stage. By this system, it is promised, complete changes of scene can be effected in 30 seconds. This, however, is three times as long as a fullstage change takes in a well designed and equipped theatre.

Counterweights for Stage Elevators

Unless the operating mechanism can successfully sustain, overcome, and control the dead and live loads of the elevators, counterweight must be attached to at least balance the dead load. For hand powered elevators additional variable counterweight must be provided to balance at least a portion of the live load. Hydraulic, screwjack, and motor windlass types of operation may generally be designed with sufficient lifting power and holding power in the mechanism to render the use of counterweights unnecessary.

General precepts to be observed in planning of stage elevators are:
1. Modern theatrical production (drama, opera, musical comedy) demands versatility of stage equipment. The usefulness of equipment is more than directly proportional to its flexibility.

2. As the size of stage elevators increases and their mobility decreases, their versatility decreases, and the number of times and variety of ways in which they can be used also decreases.

3. Raised platforms in a variety of shapes and sizes are much used in stage settings and appreciable savings in cost can be effected if stage elevators can be used.

4. Sinking the stage is infrequently required but the possibility of doing one particular production may sometime depend on it.

Entrances through the stage floor, by stairs or ladders, and the elevating and sinking of sections of the floor postulate that the space below the stage be assigned to these functions. The following precepts must prevail:

Use of the Space Below Stage

1. There must be as few permanent posts and beams or trusses as possible, and none within the space under the acting area.

2. The height of the understage space must provide for the maximum desired sinkage of traps or elevators, and must be at least 1½ the desired maximum rise of elevators which are hoisted by cables, if such are used. The sinkage of elevators used for actors only need be just enough to clear the steepest balcony sightlines and to provide headroom under the stage floor. The sinkage of elevators for scenery must accommodate the highest scenery which will be set on the elevator.

3. Space at the sides for pulleys, drums, and counterweights, must be allowed in the case of hoist elevators, and for pressure tanks, pipes, and valves for hydraulic elevators.

4. The operating position for remote control elevators must be at the stage level where the operator can see the entire mobile area, preferably near the stage manager. Communication by telephone between the control station and the understage space is essential.

5. Access of actors from dressing rooms to understage stairs and elevators must be provided. This may be by a mezzanine gallery placed around the elevator pit, 8 or 10 feet below the stage floor. Automatic safety rails must protect this gallery except when the elevators are at the same level.

Two or more types of elevators may be combined in one installation. Plateau elevators on screwjacks may contain fixed table elevators, also on screwjacks. Plateau elevators may contain trap elevators on screwjacks or cable hoists, and plateau elevators may contain table elevators to work intact or subdivided to form trap elevators. Plateau elevators may contain revolving discs or wagons. All such elaborate combinations tend to multiply the amount of fixed apparatus, and the amount of structure, thus reducing the adaptability of the equipment, and limiting the ways in which it may be used.

Combinations

In planning an elevator installation the first consideration may well be given to providing a trap elevator in any part of the trap area. Other elevator devices when added must not sacrifice this function.

Stage elevators are expensive in comparison to other stage machinery on a basis of general usefulness. The theatre planner is well advised to consider carefully the possible uses of elevators before incorporating them in a theatre. Stage elevators have been but little used in American theatres generally, probably because of the cost. Some increased use, particularly of trap elevators, would improve the flexibility and efficiency of stages.

Evaluation of Stage Elevators

11: stage machinery: in the flies

Equipment Over the Stage

Equipment over the stage is used for the suspension and flying of scenery, lighting equipment, and other items which contribute to the performance. All large flat pieces of scenery can be easily cleared from the scenery space by flying. Without flyspace the clearing and storage of such scenery as drops, ceilings, wide flat backwalls, and cycloramas present a difficult technical problem.

Structural Elements

The gridiron, loading platform, head block beams, fly galleries, other working galleries, and pin rails are items of the overstage equipment which are normally included in the specifications and contract for the building. Because these items are installed before the more detailed items of stage equipment, and because the latter must be fastened to the structural parts, it is essential that the complete installation of overstage equipment be planned before the drawings and specifications for the masonry and steel are made. Too frequently, the steel work has been ordered without careful consideration of the detailed stage equipment with the result that expensive alterations or special stage equipment are made necessary.

Stage equipment companies offer free advisory service regarding the detailed lay-out of overstage equipment, which is of some value to architects. The weakness of this service, however, is that certain standardized lay-outs are recommended for all stages. Insufficient regard for variation in the conditions of use results in the installation of elaborate rigging systems in stages where use would require a limited installation.

It must be emphatically stated that conditions of use must guide the planner in the selection of methods of handling scenery, the specification of stage equipment, the determination of the size, shape, and arrangement of the overstage space. A high school stage will not require the same equipment as an opera house, a community theatre will not require the same equipment as a Broadway playhouse, nor the theatre in a women's college the same as a metropolitan presentation house.

Gridiron

The Gridiron is an open-work floor of steel located under the roof of the stage on which sheaves may be fastened either permanently or temporarily and through which ropes, either wire or hemp, may be dropped for the suspension of scenery, lighting equipment, actors, and anything else which the performance may require to be suspended. Examination of this definition will show the particular requirements which the gridiron must fulfill. Stage workers must be able to move about with safety and freedom; therefore

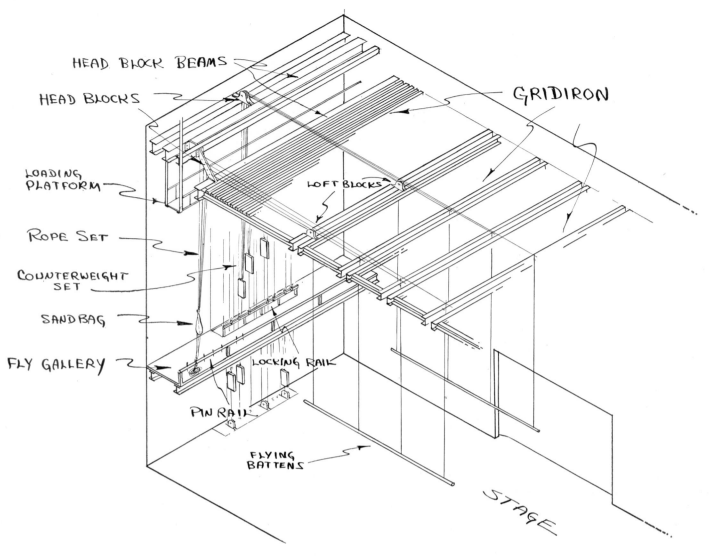

HEAD BLOCK BEAMS

HEAD BLOCKS

GRIDIRON

LOADING PLATFORM

LOFT BLOCKS

ROPE SET

COUNTERWEIGHT SET

SANDBAG

FLY GALLERY

LOCKING RAIL

PIN RAIL

FLYING BATTENS

STAGE

Stage block showing names and locations of flying equipment.

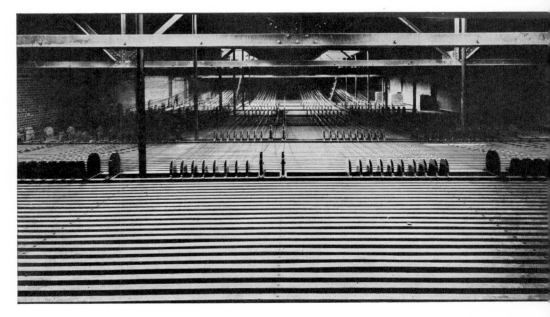

Gridiron, looking toward the head-blocks. Photo, Courtesy J. R. Clancy, Inc.

the gridiron must allow at least a minimum of headroom under the roof structure: six feet under the lowest roof girders.

Sheaves

Sheaves must be fastened to the gridiron, both permanently and temporarily. It is sound practice to consider even those sheaves which are part of the initial installation and to all intents permanent as temporarily fastened. Stage loft blocks are manufactured with fastenings which render them easily movable. The use of blocks of this type and the design of the gridiron to receive them save many hours of labor in the initial installation and in the preparation of shows.

Ropes are dropped through the gridiron. For the greatest possible use, it is essential that ropes may be dropped in the maximum number of positions. Standard steel gridirons, consist of 1½″ x 3″ channels laid web-up 3″ apart, on 6″ or 8″ channels (web vertical), and afford slightly less than 50% open space, allowing the location of spot lines (ropes through the gridiron) never more than 1½″ from a desired position, a satisfactory solution.

Cable Slots

As will be made clear when flying systems are considered most of the permanently installed ropes and blocks are arranged in rows perpendicular to the proscenium. The gridiron contains special steel to support the concentrated load created by this arrangement: pairs of channels set back to back, spaced by steel diaphragms, extend from the proscenium wall to the back wall and are suspended at intervals from the roof steel. The size of the channels is determined by the span and the safe load requirements of building codes. These cable slots are spaced according to the size of the flying system and this in turn is determined by the width of the scenery area.

Systems for Flying Scenery

The desired attribute of a system for flying scenery is that it facilitate the flying of any size, shape, or weight of scenery, lighting equipment, or other objects, set in any part of the scenery area in any position with relation to the proscenium and floor. Existing flying systems are designed on the premise that the most scenery will be flown parallel to the proscenium.

There are two established systems for flying scenery, called in stage vernacular the Rope System, and the Counterweight System. The Counterweight System, though by no means new, is the later of the two systems to come into use. A few recent installations combine the two to make available the good features of both.

Rope System

The *unit* of a rope system is a combination of three or more ropes (called lines) with their necessary loft blocks and head block, to form a *rope set*, or *line set*. The loft blocks are placed on the cable slots of the gridiron, 10 to 12 feet apart in a row parallel to the proscenium. The head block is placed on *head block beams* at the side of the stage outside the scenery space, generally, though not always, close to the sidewall. Each rope of a set extends from the stage floor, up through its own loft block, across the gridiron to and through the headblock, and down to a pinrail on the fly gallery. In some existing theatres, the pinrail is placed on the stage floor. This is mentioned only to be deprecated: the numerous activities which take place on the stage floor demand that the pinrail and its attendant gear be located above the stage. The ropes of a set are used together to hang and fly wide flat pieces. They are used separately or selectively to fly smaller pieces, and selectively in combination with ropes from other sets to fly pieces which extend up and down stage.

Briefly stated, the practice is to place the piece of scenery on the floor, attach the ropes, adjust them for equal tension and level *trim*, pull the piece into the flies, and tie-off the ropes on the pinrail. Sandbags may be attached to the ropes above the pinrail to partially balance a heavy piece of scenery.

Fly Gallery

A steel or reinforced concrete gallery is bracketed or cantilevered out from the wall on one or both sides of the stage for the operation of the flying systems. Its width ranges between four and ten feet; its height ranges between 20 and 30 feet above the stage floor. Factors affecting the height are: 1. Practical visibility into the flies for operation of hung scenery; 2. Clearance under gallery for the highest generally used standing scenery.

Pinrail

A steel pipe 3½" or more inside diameter is securely fastened to stanchions at the onstage edge of the fly gallery at a height of about 3'-0". Through holes in this pipe steel or hickory belaying pins are set vertically. Holes are oversized for easy fit. Rope sets are tied off on these pins. When many sets of lines are loaded and tied off, there is a great upward stress on the pinrail, requiring that the rail and its supports be designed to withstand an upward stress of at least 200 lbs. per linear foot in commercial, community, and college theatres, and 500 lbs. per linear foot in opera and presentation theatres. The floor load on fly galleries may be figured at the minimum for similar floors as given in the local codes.

Counterweight System

The Counterweight System for flying scenery employs steel in all its parts with the single exception of a manila purchase line for hand operation. It is therefore more expensive per unit than the rope system, loses some flexibility which the rope system possesses, but gains appreciable advantages of long life, dependability, and safety over the rope system.

A counterweight unit or set consists of pipe batten, three or more wire ropes, loft blocks for each rope, headlock, counterweight carriage, floor block or tension block, operating line, and rope lock. The pipe batten is hung horizontally on the wire ropes which are carried up to and over the loft blocks, across the gridiron, to and through the head block, and down to the top of the counterweight carriage where they are fastened by chains or turnbuckles which are adjustable for leveling (*trimming*) the batten. Because a batten will trim differently when loaded from its trim when empty, due to the sag of the ropes across the gridiron, the architect must specify that the theatre riggers trim all battens under a specimen distributed load about equal to an average load of scenery. The counterweight carriage runs up and down along the sidewall a distance equal to the vertical run of the batten. It is guided by wire guides attached to the headblock I-beams and the floor, or by T-section steel tracks which are fastened to angle steel crossbars on the wall. A purchase line runs from the top of the carriage up to and over the headblock, down through a rope lock, around a tension-block at the floor, and up to

Headblocks and headblock I-beams. The planks on the gridiron are not a part of the installation. The contractors just forgot them. Photo, courtesy J. R. Clancy, Inc.

T-track counterweight installation with locking rail at the fly gallery. A pinrail for a rope system may be installed at the outer (near) side of the gallery. Counterweights run below the gallery to the floor. Photo, courtesy J. R. Clancy, Inc.

Flymen operating the T-track counterweight system on the fly gallery of the Radio City Music Hall. Photo, McManus. Courtesy Plymouth Cordage Co.

Wire-guide counterweight installation with locking rail at the stage floor. Note: work-light strip, guardrails against which scenery may be stacked, and free-standing wire-guide units. These are badly located and should be so installed only if they are for temporary use.

tie to the bottom of the carriage. Counterweights are placed in the carriage at the loading platform.

Briefly stated, the operating procedure is to lower (*bring in*) the pipe batten to the floor thus raising (*taking out*) the carriage to the loading platform, affix the scenery to the pipe by snap chains or ropes, load counterweight into the carriage to balance the weight of the scenery, and fly the scenery by pulling down on the purchase line below the carriage. Many variations of this procedure are practiced by stagehands to handle diverse kinds of scenery.

Snap-chains are short lengths of passing link chain, with iron rings on one end to slide on the pipe battens, and snap-hooks on the other end for attaching scenery. They are furnished on each pipe batten in sufficient numbers to permit supporting scenery at intervals of about 10 feet.

Table of Recommended Maximum Working Loads per set of counterweight lines. (This does not include loads of light bridges, fire curtains, act curtains, or motion picture screens and horns.)

Legitimate theatre **College theatre** **Community theatre** **and summer theatre**	**700 pounds per set**
Opera, **Presentation** **Spectacle**	**1000 pounds per set**

Recommended optimum and minimum ratios of sheave diameter to rope diameter for wire rope.

Construction of rope	optimum ratio	minimum ratio
6 strands 7 wires each	72 to 1	42 to 1
6 " 19 " "	45 to 1	30 to 1
6 " 37 " "	27 to 1	18 to 1

Counterweight carriages are of three types, depending upon the kind of vertical guides used.

Wire Guides

The carriage runs up and down on two taut stranded cables stretched between head blocks and floor. This type is the least expensive, and is flexible in that sets may be moved up and down stage. No fixed steel or wall anchors are necessary. The wire guides, however, allow certain horizontal sway in the carriages, requiring that the counterweights be spaced at least 12″ apart to prevent fouling.

T-track Guides

The offstage side of the carriage is fastened to vertical steel tracks of T section by means of sliders of H section. Each carriage fits between two tracks and each track between two carriages, making the grouping of carriages desirable. Limits to this grouping are set by the allowable angle at which wire ropes may enter the head blocks. The T-tracks are fastened by steel U clips to horizontal battens (L-section) which are in turn bracketed out from the stage wall. When the wall has set-backs to reduce its thickness toward the top the brackets must become increasingly longer for each set-back.

Lattice Track Guides

Both sides of the counterweight carriage engage vertical T-tracks. The webs of the Tees fit into slots in the top and bottom members

Detail: Wire-guide counterweight sets. Photo, courtesy Joseph Vasconcellos.

Lattice track (left) and wire guide (right) counterweight sets. Photo, courtesy Joseph Vasconcellos.

Detail: T-track counterweight sets. Photo, courtesy Joseph Vasconcellos.

143

(draw irons) of the carriage. Cross spreaders of steel, fastened between the tracks at intervals, form the lattice. This type of track is particularly useful for isolated counterweights, such as those for the fire curtain or the act curtain. The track may be set perpendicular to a wall or flat against a wall.

Extra Counterweight Carriages

Useful additions to a counterweight installation are two or more extra carriages with head blocks, purchase line, rope lock and tension block, but without wire ropes or pipe battens, strategically placed among the complete counterweight sets. These have four uses: 1. to be fastened to adjacent carriages and supply extra weight capacity when very heavy pieces are to be hung, 2. to carry weight which is applied intermittently to balance scenery which is detached from the batten at the floor (*carpet hoist*), 3. to counterweight special sets of lines which are installed in spot positions for individual shows, 4. to receive lines attached to side walls of box sets which are flown intact when the backwall is hung on an adjacent batten.

Location of the Lock Rail

The generally accepted position for the lock rail in counterweight systems has been at the stage floor, so that stagehands might have ready access to the purchase lines while performing work on the floor. Under certain conditions it appears advisable to locate the lock rail on the fly gallery: 1. When rope system and counterweight system are used in combination, 2. When operation of the flying equipment is delegated separately to certain stagehands (flymen) who do none of the work on the floor, 3. when it is planned to move scenery, whether on or off wagons, in the space ordinarily occupied by the lock rail on the floor, and especially when it is planned to move wagons through that space into storage docks. The numerous demands on the stage floor space make it generally desirable that all flying operations and as much of the flying equipment as possible be kept above and clear of the stage floor.

Counterweight System for Stages with Wagon Docks Offstage at the Sides

When it is necessary to keep all sidewall parts of a counterweight system above the level of the fly gallery as when a wagon stage is to pass through an opening in the stage wall, a combination of pulleys having a mechanical advantage of two in favor of the scenery may be introduced above the counterweight carriage, whereby the vertical run of the counterweight is only half the vertical run of the scenery.

Loading Platform

Essential to a Counterweight System and occasionally useful for a Rope System, the loading platform is a steel gallery about 2'-6" wide hung between the gridiron and the head block I-beams below the level of the gridiron a distance which allows convenient loading of weights into carriages, i.e., level with the bottoms of the carriages when they are at the top of their run. The platform is open on the side toward the counterweights, and protected by a railing on the stage side. Access to the loading platform is by ladder, stair, or elevator from the stage floor or fly gallery; a ladder or stair leads from the loading platform to the gridiron.

Head Block Beams

Parallel I-beams are set 2'-6" or 3'-0" above the level of the gridiron, near the sidewall. The elevation above the gridiron lifts the wire ropes above the gridiron and prevents rubbing and wear. All ropes of the counterweight system change direction through about 90 degrees from approximately horizontal to vertical at this point.

Hence there is great stress in both vertical and horizontal directions. Wide flange beams are used, and a channel is fastened to the onstage beam to resist horizontal stress. The size of the beams depends upon the total load. This is specified in some building codes.

There is a great spread possible in the cost of flying systems. The theatre planner to be successful must design a flying system which is suited to uses of the particular theatre and neither insufficient to those uses nor too elaborate for them, and in any case within the building budget. It profits a theatre owner very little to be able to point with pride at the most elaborate flying system in America if the productions in his theatre never require the use of it.

A rope system requires less structural steel, generally cheaper parts, and less installation labor than a counterweight system. Counterweight systems can be economically laid out to cost not much more than a rope system or can be very elaborate, requiring much steel work, expensive parts, and much installation labor. Neither rope system nor counterweight system alone is adequate to all problems of hanging and flying scenery. Each system possesses advantages which the other lacks. Counterweight sets are best for flying curtains, lighting equipment, light bridges, heavy framed pieces of scenery, and sets flown intact. Rope sets are best for hanging light-weight framed pieces, drops, borders, leg drops, and unframed pieces generally, for the special spotting and selecting of lines, and for the hanging of scenery perpendicular and oblique to the proscenium. Counterweight sets are fixed in position; rope sets may be moved about the gridiron with ease. Rope sets require greater man power to operate than do counterweight sets. Rope system operation requires a higher degree of stagecraft than does counterweight operation.

The maximum use of a flying system is attained when the following vague condition is satisfied: any and all items of scenery, properties, lighting or sound equipment, and even actors, are flown and operated in the space over the stage to meet the demands of production. No specific criteria of adequacy can be derived from this. The most reliable source of criteria is the record of a number of productions. An examination of the flying problems in these productions shows that flown objects divide into two categories: those which occur with sufficient frequency and in sufficiently standard sizes that a suitable installation may be designed to handle them; and those which are so diverse in size and character and so infrequent in occurrence that each must be handled as a special problem by the stage technician, either by adapting standard equipment or by installing special equipment. The theatre planner can design equipment to fit the requirements of the former category, and he can supply some equipment whose flexibility will contribute to the solution of problems in the latter category.

Examination of some 200 sets of scenery for legitimate drama, musical shows, and opera discloses that elaborate musical productions make the greatest demands upon flying systems, both in sheer numbers of sets as well as in special effects.

Averaged, the different types of production require line sets per show as follows:

Elaborate musical production	30 or more sets
Ordinary musical and revue	10 to 20 sets

Comparison of Rope and Counterweight Systems

Opera	5 to 15 sets
Presentation	5 to 10 sets
Elaborate drama	15 sets
Ordinary drama	5 to 10 sets

Because of the variety of positions in which scenery is hung in different shows, a stage must be equipped with more sets than these figures indicate.

Although all kinds of scenery may occur in all types of productions, certain kinds of scenery occur with sufficiently greater frequency to warrant the design of flying equipment to handle more of those kinds. For dramatic production, which employs about 65% box sets involving backwalls and ceilings to be flown, the width of pieces to be flown is usually less than the full width of the proscenium. In musical production, opera, and presentation, all of which require side entrances, and spectacular scenery, involving drops, borders, and curtains, the width of much flown scenery exceeds the proscenium width by 10 to 20%.

Therefore on a stage intended for dramatic production wholly or to a large degree, the length of the pipe battens may be equal to or shorter than the proscenium width, whereas for the second group of productions, the battens may be 25% longer than the proscenium is wide. The proscenium here is taken to mean the *working* proscenium, that is, the actual opening which is generally used; if it is planned to *close in* the structural opening with tormentors or curtains, the *net* opening is the working opening.

If the stage is intended for all types of production about equally the shorter battens are recommended, because temporary extensions can be added to short battens but long battens cannot be made short without permanent alteration.

Motor-driven Counterweight Sets

Application of electric motive power to the operation of counterweight sets has various forms but relatively few existing installations. Expensive if applied to all sets, it is nonetheless effective and efficient if applied to the sets most frequently to be used, including the light bridge, the motion picture screen, and the cyclorama. Motors engaging the purchase lines of individual counterweight sets are located either below the stage or on the fly gallery.

Projected Systems

There is opportunity for the further application of portable prime movers to the problem of flying scenery. Two systems are projected but have not yet been reduced to practice, one employing variable speed electric motors on individual lines, remotely positioned, selected, and controlled, and one employing high-torque hydraulic motors, similarly controlled.

Heights

Heights backstage are determined from the probable maximum heights of scenery as follows: 1. the clear height of the stage house must accommodate the highest piece of hung scenery which will be used when it is flown to expose another piece of equal height. 2. Clear height under galleries and through openings into storage spaces must accommodate the highest piece of standing scenery which will be used, plus the height of stage wagons if they are used. The highest standing scenery rarely exceeds 16 ft. for legitimate drama and 30 ft. for grand opera and musical comedy.

The use of the upper space in wagon docks to store scenery flown off wagons expands considerably the capacity of the storage space. Such storage is only necessary for handling the most elaborate scenic ensembles and must be considered marginal in planning and budgeting stage equipment.

This equipment may be used when any of the following methods of handling scenery are used: divided wagons, traverse wagons with straight path, traverse wagons with curved path.

Types of flying equipment over storage space:

1. Steel pipes hung under the ceiling to which blocks may be tied where and when needed. A short pipe for headblocks and a short pin rail at the floor or on a gallery.

2. Exposed I-beams to which underhang blocks may be clamped. Short I-beam over a short pin rail.

3. Complete gridiron with rope sets or counterweight sets.

Optimum height of this space for flying is slightly more than twice the highest scenery which is set on the wagon.

Certain items of the permanent equipment of a stage are hung either on regular units of the flying system or on special units employing similar equipment and principles. These are: the fire curtain, the act curtain, light bridges, teasers, light battens, cycloramas, and part or all of the inner proscenium. Only those items which require equipment different from that of the regular flying systems already discussed need be considered here.

Fire curtains may be of three types, the type selected for use depending upon the requirements of the National Board of Fire Insurance Underwriters and local building codes: flexible asbestos, asbestos cloth on rigid frame, and sheet steel curtain on rigid frame.

A flexible asbestos cloth curtain is made of wire-woven asbestos cloth of approved weight, tensile strength and fire-resistive rating, stretched between top and bottom steel pipe battens, hung on wire ropes the number and spacing of which are specified by code, and permanently counterweighted with just less than enough weight to balance it.

Wire rope is regularly larger than that furnished in the counterweight system to give an added safety factor.

Loft blocks and Head blocks are larger than those in the counterweight system and are mounted either on the gridiron (spaced as required by the spacing of the wire rope without regard for the regular cable slots) or on special channel brackets set into the proscenium wall. The headblock is of the parallel type but with the groove for the operating line at the side of the wire rope grooves rather than in the center as in the counterweight system.

Counterweight carriage and track are of the lattice type and are located on the proscenium wall as close as convenient to the side of the opening. The track must be long enough to allow a run of the counterweight equal to the run of the bottom of the curtain (at least equal to the height of the proscenium opening).

Safety devices pertinent to the asbestos curtain are:

The Release Line, commonly called the cut line, which is the only device for securing the curtain in the high position. It is rigged in such a way that the curtain may be lowered by releasing or cutting it at either side of the stage or by the melting of fusible links placed

Flying Equipment Over Storage Space

Permanently Installed Equipment Which Is Hung

Fire Curtain

Steel-framed asbestos curtain, seen from the stage side, before back asbestos was applied. Purdue University Music Hall. Designed and erected by J. R. Clancy, Inc.

Asbestos curtain driving mechanism. Photo, courtesy J. R. Clancy, Inc.

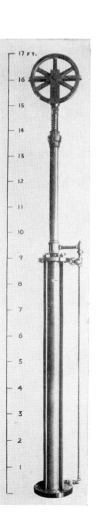

Hydraulic check for asbestos curtain. Photo, courtesy J. R. Clancy, Inc.

in three or more strategic positions along its length. Knives for cutting the release line are required standing equipment on each side of the proscenium.

Check chains which are attached to the gridiron and to the top batten of the curtain, of such length as to hold the top of the curtain above the proscenium opening.

Hydraulic curtain check which reduces the downward speed of the curtain during the last few feet of its descent. This device is optional for lightweight curtains, whose downward velocity does not become destructive.

Guide wires are attached to the gridiron and the stage floor inside the smoke pockets to assure the straight running of the curtain.

Framed fire curtains are regularly too heavy to be operated manually. Electrically driven machines are installed on the gridiron. Regular operation is by electric switch located at the stage manager's station. Limit switches actuated by the counterweight stop the curtain at the top and bottom of its run, and a clutch release mechanism allows the curtain to descend when the release line (see above) is severed.

One type is connected by chain drive to the head block; another drives a shaft and drums upon which the wire ropes suspending respectively the counterweights and the curtain wind and unwind.

Code Requirements

Excerpt from the Building Code of the City of New York (1938) Article 13, Sub-article 5, Paragraph C26-725.0:

"a. The proscenium opening shall be provided with a curtain of incombustible material constructed on a rigid frame approved by the superintendent, having a lap of two feet at the top and eighteen inches at each side, sliding at each side in steel or iron grooves, which shall have a minimum depth of twelve inches. The curtain shall be fastened to the proscenium wall and at its lowest position shall rest on masonry at least twelve inches thick extending from the foundation to the curtain, or upon a strip of linoleum, cork or rubber composition directly affixed to such masonry. The footlights shall be placed at least two feet away from the curtain line. The curtain shall be raised only at the commencement of each performance and lowered at the close and shall be operated by approved machinery.

"b. Satisfactory proof must be submitted and filed with the application that the curtain is so constructed and mounted as to prevent passage of fire, to permit the passage of only a minor amount of smoke, and to show no glow on the auditorium side, when exposed to a temperature rising to seventeen hundred degrees Fahrenheit in thirty minutes."

Excerpt from the Building Code recommended by the National Board of fire Underwriters 1949 Edition, Section 1201-6. Curtain:

"(a). Except as provided in paragraph (g) below, proscenium openings shall be protected with a proscenium curtain conforming to the following paragraphs (b) to (f), inclusive.

"(b). The proscenium opening shall be provided with a curtain of noncombustible material constructed on a rigid steel frame, having a lap of 2 feet at the top and 18 inches at each side, sliding at each side in a rigid steel groove, which shall have a minimum depth of 12 inches. The curtain grooves shall be securely fastened to the proscenium wall and the curtain at its lowest position shall rest on masonry at least 12 inches thick extending from the foundation to the curtain or upon a strip of linoleum, cork or rubber composition directly affixed to such masonry.

"(c). The proscenium curtain shall be so arranged and maintained that, in case of fire, it will be released automatically and instantly by an approved heat-actuated device, and will descend safely and close completely the proscenium opening. It shall also be equipped with effective devices to permit prompt and immediate closing of the proscenium opening by manual means.

"(d). No part of such curtain shall be supported or fastened to combustible material.

"(e). The curtain with its mounting shall be so designed as to close the opening, prevent the passage of flame, hot gases and smoke from a severe fire on the stage and to show no glow on the auditorium side for a period of 15 minutes.

"(f). Complete details of any proposed proscenium curtain and curtain installation, including mechanism and structural supports, shall be submitted, together with satisfactory proof that such installation meets the requirements as to strength, fire resistance and smoke-tightness when subjected to a fire test with exposing temperatures reaching not less than 1700 degrees F. at the end of 15 minutes. Approval shall be obtained before erection is started. After completion, operating tests of the curtain shall be made and approval of its functioning obtained before a public performance is staged.

"(g). Where the stage does not have a rigging loft or fly gallery, the proscenium curtain may be of roll type, lift-up type, or overlapping close-in type, of noncombustible materials so constructed and mounted as to prevent the passage of flame, hot gases and smoke, and show no glow on the auditorium side when exposed to a fire temperature rising to not less than 1350° F. at the end of 15 minutes."

Appendix J of the same volume describes and illustrates satisfactory construction of fireproof curtains and curtain guides.

The fire curtain is purely a protective device, is maintained in perfect operating condition as such and its use for any other purpose in connection with performance is generally forbidden. In some states the legal requirement is that the fire curtain be raised within a short specified time before the beginning of the performance, and lowered immediately at the close of the performance. In such cases the assembling audience must look at the fire curtain for a considerable time; there is good reason that the fire curtain be designed and decorated in harmony with the auditorium. Paint used must be noncombustible.

Act Curtain

In all cases except those cited above, the act curtain is the device which separates the stage from the auditorium, before the performance, during intermissions, and after the performance. It is the largest single feature within the auditorium and it is directly in the line of audience vision. It is used to begin and end all performances, acts, and scenes, making the necessary transition into and out of the stage action. In operation and appearance, therefore, it must be both sure, smooth, and pleasant.

Up-and-down, Fly Action

The curtain is tied to a pipe batten and is operated like a unit of the counterweight system. Differences from a counterweight unit occur in the following parts: wire rope, loft blocks, head block and purchase line are larger to provide a greater safety factor and easier operation; counterweight and carriage are of the lattice type, fastened to the proscenium wall with the operating position near the stage manager's station.

Draw or Traverse Action

(The term traverse seems to be the basis for the stage vernacular corruption *traveller*.)

The curtain is divided at the center and is suspended at short intervals from carriers which slide or roll on a horizontal track located above the top of the proscenium opening. An endless operating line is rigged so that the curtain is parted in the middle and drawn to the sides of the opening, gathering in spaces allowed for it behind the proscenium on each side. Allowances must also be made for overlap of the two halves of the curtain behind the proscenium at both sides and at the top. Curtain tracks and carriers are designed to assure smooth and quiet operation. Devices are available which permit starting the whole curtain in motion simultaneously.

Tableau Action

The curtain is divided at the center and is suspended from a pipe batten. Two operating lines are run from the offstage top corners down through guide rings which are secured to the back of the curtain

Curtain actions: fly, draw or traverse, tableau, contour.

Detail: a draw curtain track. J. R. Clancy, Inc.

along carefully plotted diagonal curves to pick-up points on the meeting edges. By pulling these lines the curtain is caused to part at the center and rise diagonally to form a drapery.

Tableau curtains are spectacular and decorative but impractical as working act curtains. It is seldom possible to expose the entire acting area.

Contour (or Brail) Action

Several operating lines are run vertically, at regular intervals, down the back of the curtain through guide rings to pick-up points along the bottom edge. By manual or motor operation of these lines, the curtain is caused to rise to selected heights. The shape, or contour, of the opening thus formed is variable. The limit to which one operating line may be raised above those next to it is determined by the amount of fullness made into the curtain.

Combination of Curtain Actions

It is possible to install an act curtain rigged so that a choice of actions is available to the users. It is desirable to install a combination rigging allowing the choice between fly and draw actions.

General Comment

Fly action requires flyspace above the proscenium equal to the height of the opening. The other four actions may be installed in stages which lack flyspace. The fly action is the most common in American theatres with the draw action a close second.

The act curtain is the most used single piece of apparatus in a theatre. It must be durable and dependable. It is an important decorative element in the house since the entire audience looks at it for a considerable time before the performance and during intermissions. The expenditure of money to procure attractive and durable fabrics, sturdy construction and dependable operation is warranted. Fabrics which are permanently flameproof or capable of being flameproofed without deterioration are essential.

Proscenium Framing Equipment

It is generally considered desirable to have some type of device directly upstage of the act curtain by which the height and width of the proscenium opening may be varied when the act curtain is closed. There are several suitable devices.

Cloth Teaser and Tormentors

These consist of a drapery (teaser) hung with fullness across the top of the opening, attached to a pipe batten and rigged to fly, and two tall, narrow draperies (tormentors) hung from short traverse tracks and rigged to draw at the sides of the proscenium. By raising or lowering the teaser and drawing the tormentors on- or offstage the height and width of the opening may be varied.

Cloth teaser and tormentors are decorative if made of the same fabric as the act curtain but they do not assure a definite limit to the opening because drafts may blow the curtains, and they may be displaced by various accidents. Furthermore, since the sightlines past their edges are very acute, it is necessary to place lighting instruments or other stage apparatus well above the bottom edge of the teaser and well offstage from the edges of the tormentors in order to conceal them.

Framed Teaser and Tormentors

These consist of a horizontal unit (teaser) across the top of the opening and two vertical units (tormentors) at the sides, each having a plane surface parallel to the proscenium wall and another narrow

Luxurious draping of a proscenium by use of a contour curtain. The shape of the draping is variable. Theatre. Photo, courtesy J. R. Clancy, Inc.

View toward the proscenium, Adams Theatre, Williams College, showing the light bridge and teaser, the tormentor, the lighting cables for the bridge, the fire curtain operating line, the stage manager's control panel, a lighting panel, and the underside of the fly gallery.

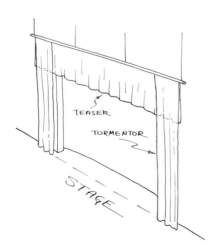

Cloth teaser and tormentors.

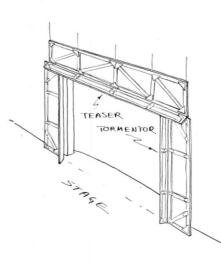

Framed teaser and tormentor. As shown, built of scenery materials. May be developed into steel towers, on casters, telescoping in height and width, and carrying light-mounting pipes and ladders.

plane surface at the lower edge in the case of the teaser and the onstage edges in the case of the tormentors, the second plane surface being set at an angle of from 90° to 135° to the first. The result is a rigid frame surrounding the proscenium opening with a reveal or thickness receding upstage. The construction is of lightweight wood or metal covered with either fabric or rigid sheet material. The teaser is suspended from a flying unit. The tormentors are either set on the stage floor or mounted on small castered platforms to allow movement on and offstage. The narrow reveal affords concealment for stage lighting instruments placed close to the acting area.

The framed teaser may be made an integral part of a flying light bridge (q.v.) and the tormentors may be developed into tormentor light towers, containing mounting positions for lighting instruments, platforms for operators, and access ladders.

The ultimate development of the proscenium framing device is a Telescoping Inner Proscenium, constructed entirely of metal, motor driven, and controlled from a remote position, incorporating the first flying light bridge and tormentor light towers.

Overhead Light Battens

The permanent stage equipment installation includes apparatus to provide mounting positions for lighting instruments and power supply for those instruments in space above the stage. Requirements of these positions are stated in Chapter 12. Certain battens of the counterweight system (q.v.) are selected as light battens, are equipped with counterweight carriages large enough to balance the heavy loads of lighting instruments, and are fitted with power outlets fed by multiconductor cable suspended from the gridiron.

Because there must be flexibility in the overhead light mounting positions the cables must be installed so that they may be attached to any of several battens. There must be a take-up device to remove excess hanging cable from the flyspace when light battens are raised high in the flies.

Light bridge at the Adams Theatre. The teaser is integral with the bridge. Note the swivel arms on the vertical stanchions of the bridge, the position of the borderlights, and the worklights for the stage.

Flying Light Bridge

The most important overhead light mounting position is directly behind the teaser. Here are located spotlights for lighting acting areas, striplights for blending and toning both the acting area and the settings, and special instruments for a number of particular uses. It is very desirable that operators be stationed in this position for manipulation of instruments during as well as between scenes of performances.

A flying light bridge constructed of metal, suspended from wire ropes, counterweighted and rigged to fly satisfies this requirement. The bridge may be lowered to the stage floor to facilitate the mounting of the many instruments which must be attached to it. Access to the bridge is afforded either by a rope ladder from the stage floor, or by side galleries connecting with the fly galleries.

Very large stages, as for opera and presentation, may require additional flying bridges for the mounting and operation of lighting instruments in the flyspace further upstage. These take the place of upstage light battens.

Motion Picture Screen and Loudspeaker

Necessary to the projection of motion pictures, the screen and loudspeakers must be cleared if the stage is to be used alternately for live shows. Most effective clearing is achieved by flying the screen with speaker in place on a motor driven counterweight set.

Almost all types of production listed in Chapter 1 require lighting as part of the performance. This chapter treats of light that is part of the performance in the theatre.

Stage lighting has four functions:

1. Visibility: To make it possible for the audience to see, and for the director to control attention by variations in intensity and color.

2. Naturalism: Lighting on the stage must imitate the natural or artificial lighting of the supposed place where the action of the play occurs so that a believable illusion is created. This function includes the whole gamut of sunlight to moonlight, city to country, interior and exterior, in any real or imaginable place.

3. Design: In theatre organization stage lighting is considered a part of scene design. The standard union contract provides that the designer is responsible for the lighting of the show. Designers' sketches, prepared as the first step in scene design, show the sets in color as they are to appear under playing lights. Light sometimes is scenery. It is as truly a material for the scene designers' use as are the more tangible materials—wood, canvas, and paint. It must therefore be flexible enough to be useful in conformity with any stylistic idiom of the plastic arts.

4. Mood: Many designers and directors depend upon light as an important facility for creating and sustaining the desired mood.

Visibility is listed first among the functions of light for the stage. The most important visual element of the performance is the actor. The actor's face is the focal point of audience attention. Lighting which fulfills completely the other three functions and does not provide the best of visibility on the actor's face is bad lighting.

An actor is seen by virtue of light reflected from his person toward the spectator. The spectator sees the portion of the actor's person which the light strikes. Thus the degree to which an actor is seen depends upon the direction of the light with relation to the spectator's line of vision. Light directed at the actor at right angles to the spectator's line of sight, whether from above, below, or horizontally from the side, illuminates very little of the actor which the spectator can see. From above, for example, the top of the head, the ridge of

---

[1] The best statement of the theory of stage lighting as an art and a science is made by Stanley McCandless. Summed up it is that the lighting designer and technician must design and control the properties of light (intensity, color, form, and movement) to achieve the theatrical functions of light (visibility, naturalism, design, and mood).

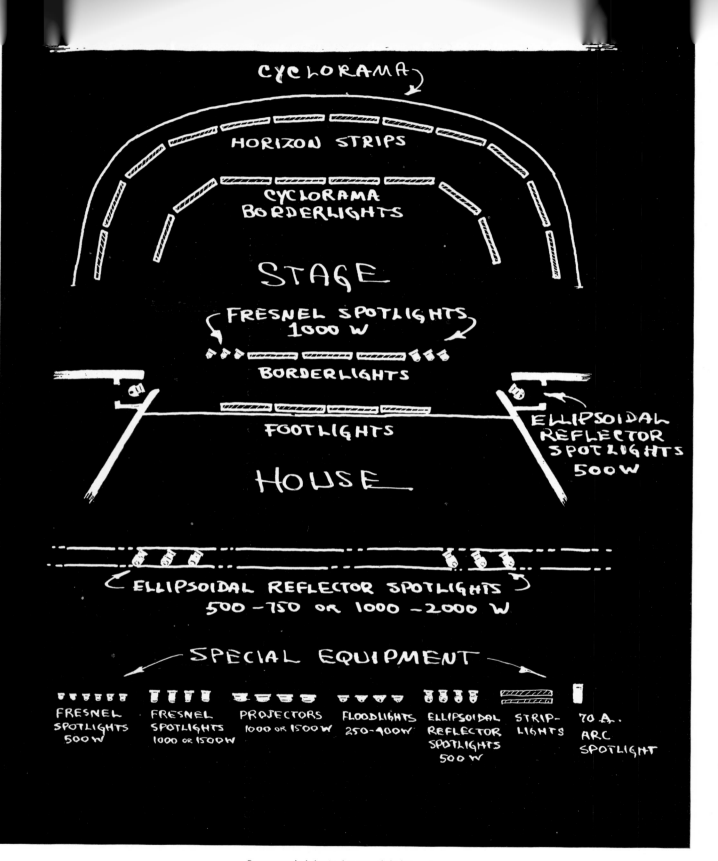

Recommended basic layout of lighting instruments for a stage having a 36' wide proscenium. Special instruments are intended for use in other positions above or at the sides of the stage and from the house. Courtesy Century Lighting, Inc.

INSTRUMENT SCHEDULE FOR MEDIUM STAGE

Item	No. of Units	Type of Unit	Position	Use	Lamps — No. Per Section, Wattage, Bulb, Filament, Service	Lens — Diameter and Focal Length	Reflector — Shape Material	Mounting	Connecting Provisions Per Unit or Per Section
				ESSENTIAL FOR AVERAGE INTERIOR SETS					
1	6	Ellipsoidal Reflector Spotlights	False Beam or Balcony Front	Front Acting Areas	500w. T-12 C-13D Spot[1] or 1000-2000w. T-30 C-13D Spot	Pl. Cx. 8"x10" or Step 8"x7½"	Ellipsoidal Alzak	Yoke and Pipe Clamp	Pig Tails and 15 Amp. Pin Connectors
2	6	Fresnel Spotlights	First Pipe	Rear Acting Areas	1000w. or 1500w. G-40 C-13 Spot[2] or 500w. T-20 C-13 Spot	Fresnel 8"x4¾" or Fresnel 6"x3½"	Spherical Alzak	Yoke and Pipe Clamp	Pig Tails and 15 Amp. Pin Connectors
3	4 or 5	6' Footlights / 5' Disappearing Footlights	Front Edge of Stage[3]	Toning of Faces and Set	12 — 150w PS-25 / 9 — General	See Footnote[4]	Compound Aluminum / Compound Alzak	In Trough / Recessed	3 Pig Tails and 15 Amp. Pin Connectors On Each End
4	3	6' Borderlights	First Pipe	Blending of Acting Areas	12-300w. R-40 Flood	See Footnote[5]		Trunnions and Fipe Clamps	3 Pig Tails and 15 Amp. Pin Connectors on Each End
				IN ADDITION: ESSENTIAL FOR EXTERIOR SETS					
5	8	6' Borderlights	At Top of Cyc.	Lighting Cyclorama	12-300w. R-40 Flood	See Footnote[6]		Trunnions and Fipe Clamps	3 Pig Tails and 15 Amp. Pin Connectors on Each End
6	12	6' Cyc. Footlights	At Foot of Cyc.	Lighting Cyclorama	12-150w. Par-38 Spot	5⅝" Dia.[7] 55° Spread		Castered Carriages	3 Pig Tails and 15 Amp. Pin Connectors on Each End
				FOR SPECIAL PURPOSES: HALF OF EACH ITEM ESSENTIAL					
7	12	Fresnel Spotlights	Stands or Pipes	Special Spots	500w. T-20 C-13 Spot	Fresnel 6"x3½"	Spherical Alzak	Yoke and Pipe Clamp	Pig Tails and 15 Amp. Pin Connectors
8	8	Fresnel Spotlights	Stands, Towers or Pipes	High Intensity Accents	1000 w. or 1500w. G-40 C-13 Spot	Fresnel 8"x4¾"	Spherical Alzak	Yoke and Pipe Clamp	Pig Tails and 15 Amp. Pin Connectors
9	8	Projectors	Towers or Pipes	Sunlight or Moonlight	1000w. or 1500w. G-40 C-5 Spot		Parabolic Chromium	Yoke and Pipe Clamp	Pig Tails and 15 Amp. Pin Connectors
10	8	Floodlights	Behind Flats or Set	Backings	250w. or 400w. G-30 C-5 Spot or Flood		Ellipsoidal Aluminum	Universal Clamp	Pig Tails and 15 Amp. Pin Connectors
11	8	Ellipsoidal Reflector Spotlight	Stands or Pipes	Side Lights	500w. T-12 C-13D Spot	2 Fl. Cx. 6"x9" / 1 Step 6"x3½"	Ellipsoidal Alzak	Yoke and Pipe Clamp	Pig Tails and 15 Amp. Pin Connectors
12	4	Striplights	Floor, Pipes, Stands or Set	Ground Rows or Backings	150w. R-40 or Par-38 Spot or Flood			Trunnions	3 Pig Tails and 15 Amp. Pin Connectors on Each End
13	2	Arc Lights	Stage or Booth	Follow Spotting	70 Amp. Arc.	Pl. Cx. 6"x9"		Rheostat Stand	25 Ft. Stage Cable and Full Connector

[1] For throws of 30 to 40 feet use 500w. For longer throws use 1000-2000w.

[2] For low teaser trims 500w. units may be used. For high trims and large areas use 1000-1500w.

[3] Six foot portable sections of footlights to be used in trough of stage. Disappearing footlights to be used for uninterrupted floor space if stage is used for purposes other than dramatic performances.

[4] Red, green, and blue (the primary colors) are recommended for the three-color circuits.

[5] Magenta, blue-green, amber (the secondary colors) are recommended for the three-color circuits.

[6] Dark blue, light blue, and amber are recommended for the three-color circuits.

[7] Red, green, and blue are recommended for the three-color circuits.

by courtesy of Century Lighting, Inc. and Stanley R. McCandless

the nose, the shoulders, and isolated outcrops are lighted; all else is not lighted and is therefore practically invisible. Similar results with respect to different parts of the figure obtain when the light is directed from below or from the sides. Such lighting is sometimes dramatically useful, to be sure, but not primarily as a means of seeing the actor. It accounts for the bizarre results when, as is too often done in schools, someone tries to light actors with footlights and borders.

Pursuing this logic, it would seem that the best direction of light would be on the line of the spectator's vision, since thus the whole expanse of the actor as seen by the spectator would be illuminated. This is not the case. Light from a full front direction, as from lights mounted on the face of a first balcony, actually illuminates the actor too completely for good visibility. The actor is a mobile form and his face is a plastic medium of expression. It has three dimensions and surface modeling, the changing character and quality of which cannot be distinguished by a spectator without some play of light and shade.

It has long been axiomatic of architectural drawing that light striking an object in the direction of the diagonal of a cube gives the clearest impression of the essential form of the object and its position in space. The application of this principle to the problem of lighting the actor anywhere he may be in the acting area has been proven sound in extensive practical application. Light striking the actor from the front, diagonally above, imparts the same appearance to the face as does natural illumination, lights around the figure to delineate form, and blends light and shade so that facial expression is emphasized and clarified. A balance of light from the opposite diagonal intensifies the modeling and provides illumination in the shadows. Light diagonally from above, furthermore, strikes the floor after passing the actor, projects the actor's shadow or shadows where they are least noticeable and least distracting, and keeps hot spots off the scenery.

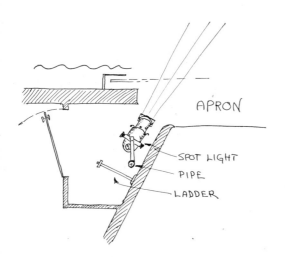

Plan Detail of Proscenium Lighting Slot.

Instrument Mounting Positions

The architect must provide facilities for mounting lighting instruments at 45° in plan and elevation from every position at which an actor is able to be seen, within the sightlines of most of the audience. This requirement calls for mounting lights in a ceiling slot at 45° to the downstage half of the acting area, another near the stage for use particularly when the proscenium opening is high, and one further back in the house for use when the apron or orchestra pit are playing positions. Ceiling slots should extend the whole width of the theatre. In a small theatre (capacity under 1000) one cut may suffice, particularly if there is not a broad apron. Visibility also requires spotlights mounted on a lighting bridge or light batten (first pipe) immediately upstage of the proscenium to light upstage acting areas and towers behind and at either side of the proscenium for lighting offstage sides and upstage areas.

Lighting the Scenery

Lighting the scenery fulfills first the function of naturalism. It also is a major element in design and mood. It blends the visibility light and establishes the dominant color. Light directed at the scenery is usually diffuse and general. Since scenic surfaces are very large in comparison to actors' faces, they must have a much lower illumination, or they will take attention away from the actor.

No matter how important it is to have the scenery appear to be lighted from the source naturalism indicates—the fireplace, the win-

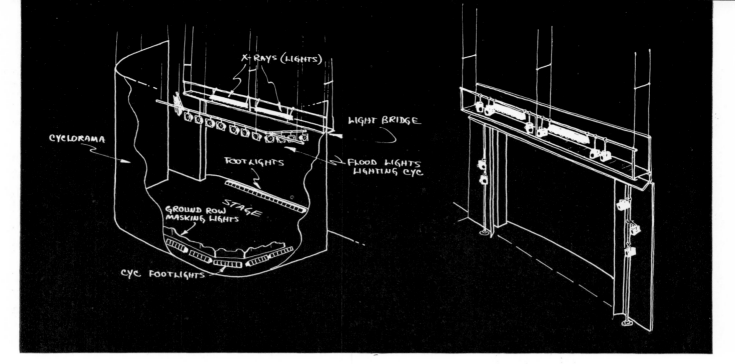

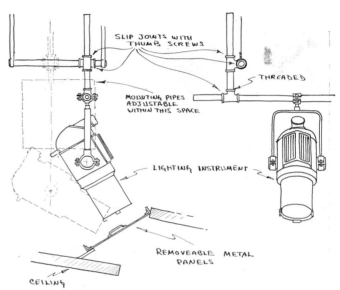

Above, left: Light mounting positions about the scenery space. In addition, lights on stands may be placed anywhere on the stage floor as needed. Cyc footlights (horizon strips) may be in a sunken trough. Above, right: Light mounting positions on a flying bridge and tormentor pipes.

Right: Light mounting above ceiling of auditorium.

Below: Light mounting at slot in auditorium ceiling. Catwalks are necessary for access to these instruments. Kirby Theatre, Amherst College. Below, right: Spotlights mounted on vertical pipe in space formed by the sidewall splay. A good position for lighting. Prompter's station at stage level. Kirby Theatre, Amherst College.

dow, the horizontal rays of the setting sun, the chandelier—the audience won't see much if those are the only sources. The most used devices for lighting the scenery are border lights, one row hung immediately upstage of the proscenium; one or more rows further upstage as necessary.

Footlights are second in importance for this purpose, and have the additional function of providing much illumination where it is most needed in some dance sequences. Footlights have the great limitation, if inexpertly used, of creating a wall of light between actors and audience and making everything on stage to appear two-dimensional. Footlight designs must be complete before the design of the apron can be finished.

Many special effects conventionally requiring footlights, among them the lighting of front curtains, can be achieved most efficiently by instruments either mounted on the balcony face, or set into a hollow balcony parapet.

Backgrounds

The principal background surface is the cyclorama, or sky dome. There are two architectural requisites for cyclorama lighting:

1. Provision for flying a bridge, frame or batten on which overhead cyclorama lights may be mounted;

2. Essential with a permanent cyclorama, usually desirable: a horizon lighting trough, to provide upward projection of light onto the cyclorama with minimum masking. The size and position of the cyclorama trough must be established by detailed planning of the cyclorama before the trapped area can be laid out or the stage floor structure designed.

In lighting scenery and background, the smaller the angle of light projection to the audience line of vision, the more even the distribution of light can be. When the cyclorama is lighted from a source close to it, it is difficult to keep it from being bright near the source and dark far from it. This situation accounts for the distances prescribed between ground rows in Chapter 9. Backings other than the cyclorama are lighted from overhead (border battens), towers or tormentors, or special instruments mounted on stands or on the scenery itself. They require only outlets, usually floor receptacles, where they may be conveniently connected to switchboard circuits.

Special Effects

Compartment striplights used as horizon lights in a pit at the base of a skydrop. Pit covers are raised and lowered automatically. Kliegl Brothers.

Motivating lights, the sunlight streaming through the window, the flickering light from the burning barn, are produced by instruments mounted in any mounting position which will accomplish the task.

Lights used for emphasis, to give one area more prominence than another, and for purposes of definition may often be mounted on balcony facia, from which position the curtains and drops for scenes played in one may also be illuminated.

Other locations for specials include:

1. Extension of the optimum ceiling slot down the sides of the auditorium.

2. Ceiling and side proscenium slots for gauze and tormentor lighting, transformations, disappearances, fog and clouds.

3. Spotlight booths at the rear of the balcony at either side of the projection booth.

4. Pockets in the stage floor located at either side and behind the acting area.

The long finger of light from the follow spot, is a dramatic element in itself. It is used in spectacle, presentation, opera and musical shows. Follow spots require room. If used at all, it is often well to use many. The Radio City Music Hall uses eighteen. Follow spot operating positions require a substantial portion of the back of the balcony.

Instruments

Though stage lighting instruments change in size and power, the essential principles on which they are based, and the places where they are used, remain standard. There are four basic types: 1. spotlights: used for front lighting; acting area, special emphasis; 2. strip lights: borders, footlight, cyclorama strip; 3. floodlights: motivating lights, backings; 4. projectors: effects, scenery, shadows.

Specials include any type of instrument required for a particular function, designed and built for the job: fireplace glow, electrified oil lamps.

In designing ceiling side and tormentor slots, and recesses in balcony facia, the architect must first obtain the specifications of all the types of instruments that may be used in all locations. Their size and balance dictate provisions for mounting. He will not need to provide much tolerance since, as stage lighting instruments are improved, their size tends to decrease. He must provide:

Spotlight, plano-convex lens. Century Lighting, Inc.

1. Clear space for all necessary movement of the lighting instruments through a predetermined directional range.

2. Surface jogs, setbacks, beams or coffers to permit beams of light to pass from instruments to stage without spilling unwanted light on wall or ceiling surfaces. The breaks supplied by ceiling slots may facilitate adjusting the ceiling and wall sections to the optimum angles for sound distribution.

3. Access to all concealed lighting positions from backstage by direct and unobstructed routes apart from the routes of audience traffic.

4. Adequate working space for operators in each lighting position.

5. Mounting apparatus adjustable to allow the use of various types and sizes of instruments. Modern practice keeps all stage lighting instruments in a theatre interchangeable as to location. This practice is essential in community theatres, most of which can afford only limited amounts of lighting equipment.

6. Electrical outlets equal to the maximum number of instruments which may be placed in any position. Connectors on all instruments standardized to fit all outlets.

Power

The bigger the audience, the farther away is its farthest member, the more light is required to illuminate the show satisfactorily. Also, the biggest shows—pageants, etc.—draw the biggest audiences. Power requirements vary directly with the size of the audience, except as follows:

1. The motion picture theatre, not equipped for stage shows, seldom needs more than 200 to 300 KVA backstage (not including house lights or projectors).

For presentation, opera, pageant or legitimate productions, the rule holds at about 300 KVA per thousand of audience, for all stage and house lights.

This specification is admittedly very rough, but most designers will be able to do satisfactory lighting with the indicated amount

Spotlight, step lens (Fresnel). Century Lighting, Inc.

Projector parobolic reflector. Century Lighting, Inc.

Spotlight Ellipsoidal reflector. Century Lighting, Inc.

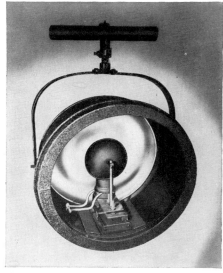

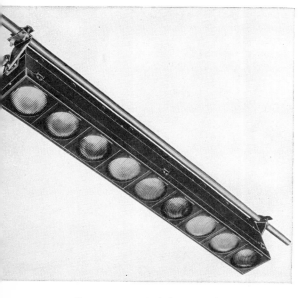

Compartment strip light, roundels. Overhead mounting. Century Lighting, Inc.

Disappearing footlights. Century Lighting, Inc.

Compartment strip light. Floor mounting. Century Lighting, Inc.

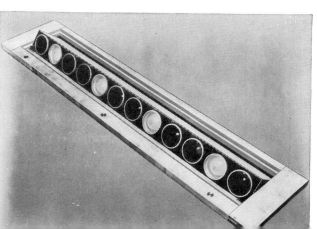

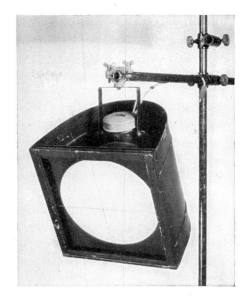

Floodlight. Kliegl Brothers.

Linnebach. Kliegl Brothers.

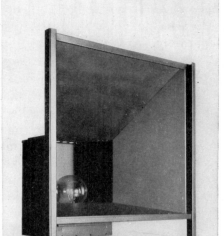

Follow spot. Kliegl Brothers.

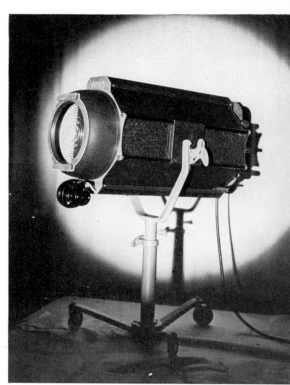

Izenour Dual 5,000 watt rear scene projectors. Optical systems identical for each channel and designed to produce an 18' x 20' image from a 4" x 5" kodachrome transparency. Each channel is separately cooled and focused, and the carriage is designed to compensate the horizontal axes so that two overlapping images can be formed with exact matching of screen area for electrical lap dissolves. Photo, Bullock.

163

of power available. As in the case of space for lighting instruments, power requirements tend to decrease as equipment improves in efficiency.

Control

To balance and change intensities and colors, each light must be susceptible of intensity control. Not all the lights are used on any one scene nor all the outlets on any one show. It is therefore not necessary to have every circuit in the theatre permanently hooked to a dimmer, except where a standard setup is used as in the motion picture theatre or the concert hall, and the house lights in any theatre.

House Lights

House lights are conventionally all dimmed together. Where colors are used as in Radio City Music Hall, it is standard practice to control all circuits of a color together. Balcony lights, under balcony lights, chandelier may be controlled separately: progressive dimming from the back of the house toward the curtain coincident with bringing up of lights on the curtain sometimes serves to settle the audience and focus attention on the stage. There is no point in controlling circuits at the sides of the theatre separately.

Circuits

As in the case of power, the number of circuits used in stage lighting can only be suggested on the basis of the needs of past shows. The Yale University Theatre has 136 circuits permanently installed, of which 65 (or 43)[1] can be controlled through dimmers at any one time. The Radio City Music Hall has about 350 circuits, all with dimmers. The legitimate combination production carries its own dimmers, and while this system is highly inefficient, the production is at least sure of having what it needs. Except where the theatre is to be a boarding house, in the sense that the current commercial legitimate theatre is, permanent circuits in conduit should be established to all front house lighting positions, cyclorama trough, footlights and pockets, downstage towers and such battens, bridges and frames as are permanently installed for overhead lighting. The minimum motion picture house schedule will call for circuits for ceiling spots to light the apron for speeches and Bingo, and four colors in foots, tormentors and borders to light the curtain, gauze, and screen, for opening and closing effects and trailer color.

Control Board Location

Stage and house lighting control are operated from a control board. In its most elaborate (European) form, this is a multi-bank board requiring as many as six operators, by which direction, focus, and color of many lights may be controlled. In repertory such a system is highly economical of time in setting up and lighting the show. It also makes possible the most consistently high standard of technical performance. European control boards are conveniently placed under the apron with a cut for the operator to see the stage. The Metropolitan Opera House has a switchboard located under the apron.

The obvious desirability of making it possible for the operator to see what he is doing has resulted in bringing the control boards out into the house in several American theatres built since 1930. The position on the audience side of the orchestra pit, center, seems to be optimum. There is ready access to the stage, and easy communica-

[1] Resistance dimmer board: 65
Electronic control console: 43
Both may be used simultaneously but it is not usual.

tion during set up. The operator can see all the stage and the orchestra and so can run most of his show on dead cues. The location below the apron cuts out the view of the apron and the orchestra leader.

A number of plans for college and community theatres have called for (some have even been built) control boards at the back of the balcony. The operator in such installations sees the effects he creates from a position inferior to the poorest seat, which is not good enough to exercise control sufficiently precise to be satisfactory if viewed from the best seats in the house. Obviously the motion picture theatre should use remotely controlled dimmers operated from the projection booth. This eliminates cueing.

Resistance dimmers are the conventional means of controlling light intensity. They vary from water barrels (The Alhambra in London still had some before the war) to plates engineered to compensate for the non-linear output of the incandescent filament. Where only DC is available, resistance dimmers must be used, hence they are employed in portable equipment because DC is still encountered in numerous theatres, notably most of the legitimate houses in New York. The resistance dimmer wastes the power it does not pass to the lamp. It will not dim to out lights of lower wattage than the dimmer. It is cumbersome, heavy, and in operation, hot.

The auto-transformer is an excellent dimmer where AC is available. For school and community theatres it is particularly appropriate. Since it controls voltage, current not used at the lamp is not drawn from the mains. The resulting economy in power is important. The auto-transformer will dim evenly to out any load up to its rated capacity. This makes it very flexible in that it can be switched from circuit to circuit irrespective of the circuit load. Auto-transformers run cool, do not arc, and occupy no more space than resistance dimmers. Their only drawback for trouping is the fact that they must be limited to AC houses.

In the early 30's the thyratron-reactor system was in considerable vogue. This system depended on a regulation of the DC current on the center leg of a transformer by an amplifier whose gain was remotely controlled.

The virtue of this system is that it makes possible a very compact control board capable of elaborate pre-setting facilities since its currents and moving parts are so small. Amplifiers and reactors can be located where there is room, need not be near the switchboard where space is at a premium. Several boards of this type were built, the most elaborate being one installed in Radio City Music Hall. The Metropolitan Opera House also has one. This system is obviously not suitable for trouping. It has many virtues for theatres where large loads must be handled.

As in the case of the control of all electrical equipment, the most flexible and precise principle is that of electronic control. This principle has been developed in three systems. The American Transformer (Brettell) system, the Sharples system, and the Izenour system. Of the three, only the Izenour system is in use at this writing. These systems are, of course, confined to locations where AC is available. They have the virtue of small convenient consoles, easy pre-setting, and simple operation. Amplifiers can be located in a room where space is not at a premium. Circuits can handle loads up to rated capacity to out. To date, electronic control systems have been built

Control Systems

Auto-transformer stage lighting control. Kirby Theatre, Amherst College. A metal hood conceals board and operator from audience. Cross-connecting panel for selective plugging of stage load circuits on dimmer circuits is in the trap room under the stage.

Portable resistance dimmer boards as used in most commercial legitimate productions. Installed on stage floor. Cables run to all stage lighting instruments. Courtesy Century Lighting, Inc.

Thyratron-reactor, 10 preset, stage lighting control console in Radio City Music Hall, located at the front of the orchestra well.

Electronic, 10 preset, light control console (right) and preset panel (left) in the Yale University Theatre. Designed by George C. Izenour. Installed in a control booth at the rear of the auditorium. Photo, Bullock.

Tube bank for Izenour Electronic console control system. 44 Electronic switching and dimming units: 38-1500 watt units; 6-6,000 watt units; a total control capacity of 90,000 watts. Yale University Theatre. Photo, Bullock.

with capacities up to 6,000 watts per circuit. Circuit capacities up to 10,000 watts are anticipated.

Pre-set Operation of Control Boards

Legitimate and musical shows, pageants, operas, etc., may employ rapid change from scene to scene as a device directed toward achieving a cumulative impression on the audience. Such changes are often accompanied by a change of lights without moving of any props or scenery. Changes of this sort are particularly striking when projections are used. Lighting changes must be accomplished by simple easy fading from the setup of one scene to that of the next. If each circuit has to be handled manually and the number of circuits per scene is normal, i.e., 25 or more, it is almost impossible to accomplish an even fade from scene to scene in a matter of from five to twenty seconds. It is therefore desirable to have provision for setting up two or more scenes in sequence, using in many instances some of the same instruments in both scenes, but not necessarily at the same intensities, and fading from the first scene to the second scene by a single operation. As many as 10 pre-sets are desirable, although two or three usually serve.

It is apparent from the foregoing that the optimum position for the switchboard is in front of the orchestra center, a place at which space is at a premium. It is therefore desirable to have the smallest practical board. Electronic control is indicated by this requirement.

Follow Spots

Follow spots are spotlights generally having arcs for light sources. They are specialized instruments having little use except in spectacle, but they are well-nigh indispensable there. Follow spots are conventionally manually operated (even an automatic-feed arc needs an operator).

View of the rear wall of Radio City Music Hall showing (left to right) observation port, spotting port, sound monitoring port, viewing ports for projection booth. Photo, courtesy Radio City Music Hall.

They are seldom directed at a fixed point on the stage, but follow performers about the stage. They are precisely controllable in color and shape and extensity of beam. Arc spot hoods must be ventilated and bases must be free from vibration, which requires a location which is not varied from show to show. Follow spots are usually operated from a booth or platform at the rear of the top balcony. Some theatres have provision for operating them in rooms built into balcony facia and in the ceiling slots. In Madison Square Garden they are operated from a spotting gallery extending around the arena above the audience gallery. Arc spots need DC current.

Motion Picture Projection Booth

To build any theatre without a motion picture projection booth is to limit its usefulness. Even legitimate shows require projection of motion pictures from time to time: SPREAD EAGLE, PERSONAL APPEARANCE, I'D RATHER BE RIGHT. Moreover, it is economically unsound to build a booth which is not adequate for continuous run motion pictures.

No part of the theatre has been the subject of so much careful study and planning as the motion picture projection booth. Building codes treat of it extensively. Excellent recommended specifications may be obtained from the Society of Motion Picture Engineers. It is shocking to note the number of booths containing code violations and built with no apparent reference to the recommended specifications, which are to be found particularly in school and community theatres where space is not always at a premium, and safety is certainly important. It is difficult to understand laxity in booth design when the legal requirements may be easily obtained.

It is theoretically possible to run a motion picture show with two projectors. Despite the reliability of modern projection equipment, a third machine is an insurance against mechanical breakdown. In many large theatres the third machine is used for the news and shorts, leaving machines one and two for the feature picture. The use of effects involving grandeur screen requires at least one grandeur projector, which although not used often, is an inexpensive means for achieving a lot of spectacle and therefore is an essential element in the presentation bag of tricks. On the basis of these requisites, even if it is planned to equip the theatre with only two projectors, the booth should be adequate for four. It is much easier to change production policy than it is to change a building.

Another requisite which must be stressed is the importance of having space enough for machines. It is also important to have space for its own sake. The operators spend a long time in the booth, the work is highly responsible and often trying. The psychological factors accompanying unwarranted cramped quarters are not to be lightly dismissed. Moreover, it is easier to make a big booth a safe booth. Reels of film not in the vault can be physically so widely separated that combustion of one will not set off another. Moreover, with a big booth, it is less likely that one operator will get in another's way if it becomes necessary to leave the booth in an emergency. For inspection of film and making up the show, the operators should have a separate room which is in itself a film vault ventilated to the open air, located behind the projection booth. This need not be large. The splicing table can be located against the wall into which is built the closed rack containing individual reels. This room should contain one or more motor-driven re-wind machines. Adjacent to the projection booth itself there should be an office for the chief projectionist. In motion picture houses there is a certain amount of paper work for the projectionist. It is also desirable to have a place to use an outside telephone during the show as distinct from the intercommunication system used in operating the show which has its station in the booth itself. The functions of office and light maintenance shop are sometimes combined so that the same room contains the desk and rack for carbons, parts, oil, and small accessories. Finally, the projectionists need a lavatory.

Projection machines, however quiet, emit a certain amount of high-frequency noise which probably contributes to the fatigue of those exposed to it day after day. A sound absorbent ceiling and sound absorbent material on the walls are therefore requisite. Also, it is necessary to cool the booth even in the winter time. Despite the safety requirement that all lamp houses be ventilated direct to outside, the lamp house picks up and re-radiates enough heat to make the booth an exceedingly uncomfortable place. With the tightening of the building codes, tuberculosis has ceased to be the projectionists' occupational disease. However, it is asserted, and not without confirming evidence, by some operators that certain booths will "turn you into an old man in three years."

One of the best ways to insure a good performance is to do all that is possible for the safety and comfort of the operators. It is not pleasant to earn one's living under conditions which are trying because of the theatre planner's negligence or ignorance. Fortunately there are numerous booths which can be cited as models, notably Radio City Music Hall, and the Brooklyn Paramount Theatre.

Requirements for follow spots and projection booths, if generously met, will provide operating facilities across most of the back of the balcony. When this section of the theatre is being laid out, the facilities for sound control (Chapter 13) will also be located in this area, and thus make necessary the use of the whole back of the house as operating area.

To serve his client properly, the architect will make architectural provision for the most elaborate and advanced means of stage and house lighting, even if the lights and apparatus are not available at the moment. By this means, the theatre can be progressively improved without architectural alteration. Moreover, the building cost where such provision is made is seldom appreciably more than that of a theatre in which architectural features render improvement impossible.

Motion picture projection booth, Radio City Music Hall. Photo, courtesy Radio City Music Hall.

Spotting booth at the rear of the balcony, Radio City Music Hall. 150 ampere, automatic feeding, arc follow spots are equipped for the control of color and the shape of the beam. Photo, courtesy Kliegl Bros.

13: sound and inter communication

Chapter 4 outlined the means by which audibility of the show could be assured within the limits of what can be achieved architecturally. Even with the best acoustic planning, however, there is a limit (about 3000 seats) to the size of a theatre in which unamplified speech can be satisfactorily projected to all listeners. Larger houses may seem satisfactory for opera or orchestral music, but speech is not very effective.

Even in the small theatre where the actor can easily be heard by the whole audience, the play often demands projection of sound in ways which cannot be satisfactorily achieved by mechanical means. Ariel, invisible, flies about above the audience, playing his tabor and pipe. The ectoplasmic figure of Hamlet's father must speak in a voice acceptable as that of a ghost. The laughter of Lazarus must fill the house. The voice of Mephisto must interpose itself between Marguerita and the entrances from which she successively tries to escape from the church. Church scenes to be artistically credible must sound highly reverberant.

For purposes of the show, the audience must be able to hear any sound, at any intensity, from any apparent source or sources or moving source, or no source, and the sound must have any predetermined frequency spectrum and any desired reverberant quality or echo. All this must be possible for not only a single sound but a group of unrelated sounds simultaneously employed.

A large proportion of legitimate productions use electronic sound control equipment for one or more of the purposes above outlined. Many theatres would be unusable without electronic facilities for sound intensity control. However, the development of completely flexible apparatus for control of sound has been slow. The first equipment answering this description was developed at Stevens Institute of Technology and was first publicly employed by the Metropolitan Opera November 24th, 1940. As showmen and technicians learn the technique of controlling sound electronically many values traditionally assigned to light, scenery, and business are undertaken by auditory means. The most notable example of this is THE LIVING NEWSPAPER. Time, locale, atmosphere, and mood may be created by auditory means, and arbitrarily designed sounds may be used as direct emotional stimuli. Up to the time of this writing, no theatre has been planned with complete provision for electronic sound control equipment. In legitimate production, and motion pictures using multi-channel sound systems, equipment is usually trouped with the show and suffers from varying limitations imposed by house structure and acoustics, in the same manner as stage lighting is rendered inefficient because of architectural restriction of equipment and instrument placement. As has been pointed out previously, architectural restriction on any phase of production limits the use of the theatre and raises production cost. Therefore, provision for electronic sound control installation must be incorporated in the original design.

BASIC OBJECTIVES

1. Reinforcement

Sound reinforcement consists of achieving intelligibility for speech and acceptable intensity for music or other sounds, the actual source of which is in sight of the audience. This involves recreating at the auditor's position the intensity level and frequency spectrum which is characteristic of the source, less a small amount of intensity at certain frequencies which would be absorbed in free air at the desired aesthetic distance. In the case of music, the desired reverberant characteristic must be added. In practice, these objectives can be accomplished only by control of frequency spectrum and reverberation, as well as intensity.

The intelligibility of speech depends upon the projection to the hearer of the high frequencies which give consonants their character. Reinforcement often may be limited to reinstating in the sound the high frequencies absorbed by the house to the extent to which they are absorbed. Reinforcing the whole speech spectrum often results only in noise with little or no increase in intelligibility.

2. Motion Picture Sound

Motion picture sound reproducing equipment is powerful, and to a limited extent capable of being adjusted in frequency response to compensate for acoustic limitations of the house. The knowledge of those facts has too often made the builder of the motion picture theatre neglect acoustic planning and use too much sound absorbent surface material. The result is that sound distribution is uneven, and the current reigning film siren pants like a 200-ton locomotive if heard in the first row, while she is just comfortably audible in the last. When a theatre is designed for good sound distribution from the stage without benefit of reinforcement, the motion picture sound will not have to be unconvincing in some locations to be heard in others.

3. Legitimate Productions and Opera

In live shows, the sound is limited in point of origin, direction of movement and essential characteristics only by the imagination of the playwright. Problems vary from simple reinforcement to creation and projection of synthetic voices in auditory perspective. Where the human voice is used in speech or song, it must be reproduced with such fidelity that the audience will not suspect that electronic control equipment is being employed. If this condition cannot be met, it is better to abandon electronic sound control. After all, there are many productions and theatres that do not require it.

Speaker Mounting Positions

Sound comes to the audience from the stage, orchestra pit, from above and from either side of the proscenium, from the auditorium walls, the auditorium ceiling, from the back of the house and from the floor. The architect must, therefore, provide speaker mounting positions which will enable sound to come directly or by reflection from all these locations.

Man's directional preception of sound is notably weak in the ver-

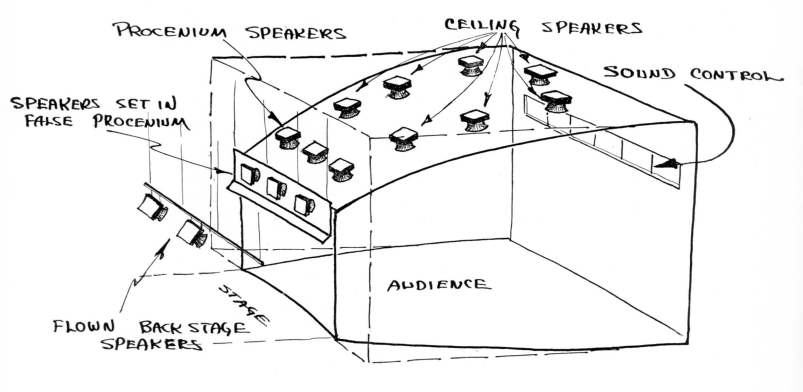

PROCENIUM SPEAKERS

CEILING SPEAKERS

SOUND CONTROL

SPEAKERS SET IN FALSE PROCENIUM

STAGE

AUDIENCE

FLOWN BACK STAGE SPEAKERS

Above: Speaker mounting positions necessary for auditory perspective about the house. Permanent proscenium speakers or false proscenium speakers for stereophonic reinforcement. Speakers hung upstage for projection through proscenium arch.

Below: Sound motion picture speaker unit rigged to travel left on traveller and fly offstage where fly space is not at a premium. Purdue University Music Hall. Courtesy J. R. Clancy, Inc.

tical plane, owing to the fact that his ears are at the same level. This fact enormously simplifies the problem of PA. The loud speaker can be located above the source, and project its signal to the audience just as the unamplified first reflection of the voice is projected. The audience, watching the source, and probably hearing a little sound directly from it, need not suspect that most of the sound comes from above the source. This is well exemplified in the Radio City Music Hall where almost every sound except from the motion picture is projected to the audience from speakers above the proscenium.

Man's directional sense is so good in the horizontal plane that he will instantly identify the reproduced sound when, as is too often the case, speakers are placed at either side of the source or proscenium. Unless he is on the center line of the house, he is lucky if he can understand speech, and music will sound fuzzy due to the sound from the two sources not being in phase when it reaches him. This misuse of the sound system for many years made grade B performances out of the New York Philharmonic Summer Concerts at the Lewisohn Stadium, and even now condemns many open air concerts, pageants, operas, etc., to artistic mediocrity. Except where highly directional speakers are necessary to project sound under badly designed balconies, and cannot reach their segment of the audience from above the source, no speaker should be used for reinforcement except above the source or proscenium, and unless the sound is stereophonic, speakers must be located on the center line of the house.

The motion picture screen is within the sight lines, so sound projected through it can reach every part of the house directly.

Stereophonic Projection

When music from an orchestra or an opera, or speech from a play is picked up from a number of places on a line perpendicular to the center line of the house, and each section is separately reproduced from a speaker above the pickup position, the resultant stereophonic reinforcement can give the performance a definition and dynamic range beyond what is possible with the unamplified performance. First demonstrated by Leopold Stokowski and the Bell Telephone Laboratories, this system supersedes others wherever the requisite musical taste, knowledge and funds are available.

Movement of sound is achieved by varying the signal intensity progressively between adjacent speakers. The installation of speaker mounting positions must be so planned as to make possible the apparent movement of sound source in any direction—about, above, around or below the house or stage, without interruption or apparently jumping from point to point. This means that the points of origin or reflection of sound cannot be more than approximately 30 degrees apart. The closer they are to the audience, the closer they must be together: the smaller the point of origin, the closer it must be to the adjacent points. For example, when the sound source is a speaker with a diameter of a silver dollar and it is used not more than 20' from the first row, it must be not more than 12' from the next unit if the sound source is to appear to pass smoothly along the path between the two units. If the point of apparent sound origin is a wall area of 100 square feet, the edge of that area may be 15' from the next similar wall area provided, of course, that the audience is not close. Sound appearing to originate from the ceiling of the theatre may appear to come from any point between two units placed as much as 50' apart, provided the sound comes by reflection.

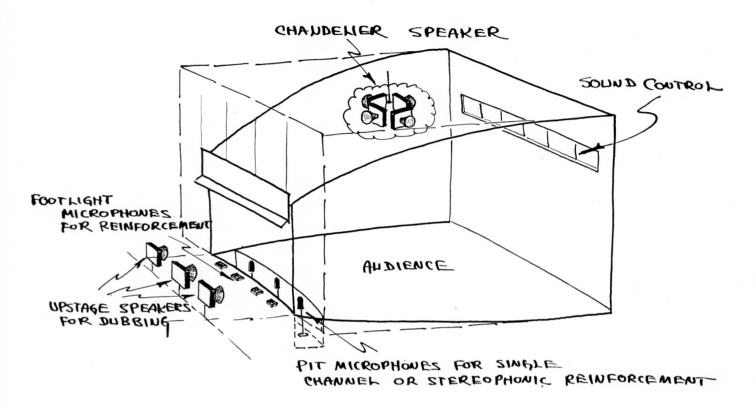

CHANDELIER SPEAKER

SOUND CONTROL

FOOTLIGHT MICROPHONES FOR REINFORCEMENT

AUDIENCE

UPSTAGE SPEAKERS FOR DUBBING

PIT MICROPHONES FOR SINGLE CHANNEL OR STEREOPHONIC REINFORCEMENT

Speaker mounting positions in chandelier for auditory perspective in the house. Upstage speakers at head height for voice dubbing (now you too can sing like Adelina Patti). Principal microphone positions.

For maximum usefulness, there must be as much flexibility in mounting position and in direction in which the speaker is pointed as there is for a lighting unit. Moreover, all speaker mounting positions must be concealed. It is often unwise to point speakers directly at the audience, if the nature of the source of sound is not to be disclosed.

Speaker mounting positions may be determined by calculating distances between sound sources and from reflection angles as indicated. These must be numerous and of sufficient size to permit flexibility in pointing the speaker. The architect's ingenuity in determining mounting positions is called into play to provide means of concealment. Speakers in the chandelier can cover almost all the ceiling and wall areas. Speakers mounted behind grilles, for ventilation and house lighting, can be very useful though the areas they cover are often restricted. Ceiling slots or false beams used for front mounting of stage lights or similar to them, can often be effectively employed. Concealment for speakers mounted on the back wall of the house and pointed toward the ceiling must usually be provided by special architectural devices. The most useful area for speaker location is, as previously noted, above and about the proscenium. If much of this area is grilled to conceal organ pipes, etc., speaker mounting position becomes very flexible and will be varied according to the demands of the individual production.

As in the case of architectural provision for the mounting of stage lights, mounting positions for speakers must be equipped with permanent speaker outlets.

Stevens Sound Control System Mark I. Speaker flown upstage of teaser to project through proscenium arch. Metropolitan Opera production of ORFEO. Photo, Otto Niederer.

Sound control booth, Radio City Music Hall. By LIFE photographer Herbert Gehr, Copyright TIME, Inc.

Dubbing
When speech or other sound is made to appear to come from an actor or a location on stage which is not the actual source of the sound, speakers must be located upstage of the apparent sound source. This condition requires the largest number of speaker outlets on-stage, i.e., one at each side of the acting area and one for each 15' or fraction thereof of proscenium opening for each signal channel at each useful elevation above the stage floor. In practice, the maximum demand seldom exceeds one series of outlets below stage, three outlets onstage, and three outlets in the flies.

Pickup
Provision for picking up the sound to be controlled is no less important than speaker placement. For sound reinforcement, microphones must be placed wherever the performer is to appear. This requirement calls for a larger number of microphones than any other condition. The original installation in Radio City Music Hall provided for 55 microphones for stage and orchestra pit.

Distance between microphones and their position with respect to the performer must be planned with reference to the characteristics of the microphone. The smallest stage will need at least three in the footlights and an equal number in the orchestra pit, and provision for three more to be hung overhead.

Offstage Pickups
Offstage microphone connections will be necessary for all sounds which originate on the stage but not in the acting area. The most arduous operatic demands have not to date required more than three on either side.

For recorded sound, when the source of the sound is a record, disc, film, engraved or magnetized tape, efficient operation demands that the pickup apparatus be handled by the sound technician who also operates the distribution equipment. Pickup apparatus must, therefore, be located in the sound control booth.

For motion pictures all control is most efficiently handled in the projection booth. Pickup from film sound track, but not in connection with projection, can well be made from the projection machines, in which case an operator in addition to the sound technician will be necessary. However, pickups from records of any sort operated at locations remote from the sound control console are inefficient because they require elaborate intercommunication systems and involve duplication of personnel and waste of rehearsal time.

The sound control console must be located so that the operator can see and hear the show. The best installations are in a booth with open front at the back of the balcony. The booth must be acoustically live so that the operator can hear as well as the audience. Obviously, there should be direct access to the motion picture projection booth from the sound control booth. The control system consists of two parts: the input mixing panel and the output mixing panel with appropriate provision for input and speaker switching on either side. All electronic equipment is located at this point except where very long microphone lines are necessary, in which case the necessary voltage amplifiers must be located close to the microphone position (on a shelf in the proscenium splay or on the stage wall), and the control circuit carried to the console. This procedure involves only a change of location of certain items but no change in circuit or operation.

Sound Control Booth and Equipment

Standard radio wiring practice is satisfactory for theatrical sound installations. The following precepts embrace strictly theatrical procedure:

Wiring

1. It is good practice to assure isolation of microphone lines from speaker lines by carrying microphone lines down one side of the house and speaker lines down the other. As noted in Chapter 6, microphone lines must be kept as far as possible from electric motors, power lines, power transformers, motor generators.

2. Microphone cable to connect microphone to outlet should not be made up in lengths of more than 25 feet since repeated coiling of long lengths will result in breaking of shield. For flexibility all input lines should be made identical and be equipped with identical connectors.

3. Speaker outlets should be equipped with female twist lock connectors.

4. There must be a single ground for all electronic equipment.

Electronic sound control equipment varies so greatly in quality and performance that it seems important to note a few basic essential characteristics here. Inferior equipment will wreck any show. The best is in the last analysis the cheapest. Characteristics here cited are condensed from specifications of the Stevens Sound Control System MK I, as used in the Metropolitan Opera. Equipment which has such characteristics is good enough for any theatre. Any further restriction of response characteristic or power will serve not only to limit the unit concerned but restrict the use of the whole system and limit the manner and degree in which it may be increased in size and

Equipment Characteristics

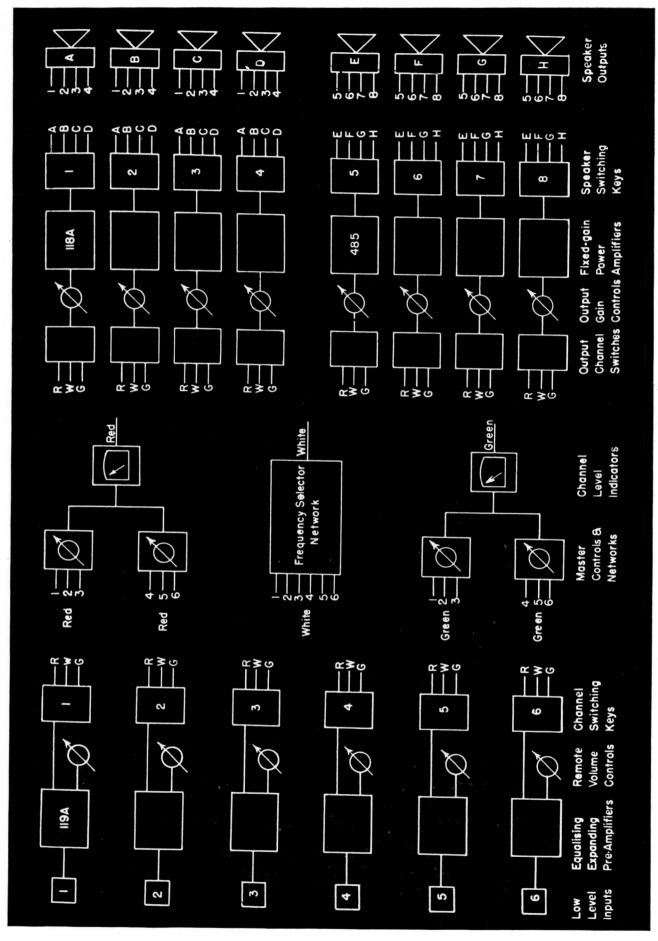

Block schematic, Stevens Sound Control System, Mark I, designed by Vincent Mallory, providing facilities for complete control of the auditory component of the show.

flexibility. The Block Schematic Diagram contains enough units to handle adequately any play or opera by any production means so far envisioned in any theatre up to a 1,000,000 cu. ft. capacity.

1. Microphones

1.1 Microphones to have a flat frequency characteristic from 30 cycles to at least 10,000 cycles, and a useful response to 16,000 cycles, preferably of adjustable directional characteristics.

1.2 Adjustable for unidirectional pickup.

1.3 Frequency response must be substantially unchanged when used for distant pickup and for close talking.

2. Reproducers

2.1 Magnetic tape reproducers to have a flat frequency response 30-10,000 cycles.

2.2 Turntable to be driven by a synchronous motor.

2.3 To take 16-inch diameter discs.

2.4 Reproducer to operate on both laterally and vertically cut discs by switch adjustment.

3. Voltage Amplifiers

3.1 Voltage amplifiers to be completely self-contained and to include its own power supply, operating from 120 volt 60-cycle commercial line.

3.2 Gain at 1,000 cycles to be approximately 80 db.

3.3 Gain of this amplifier to be adjusted by a remote type volume control of such design that it may be operated without frequency discrimination or noise pickup at 1,000 feet from the amplifier.

3.4 Undistorted output to be at least 0.3 watt with a maximum output noise level of -40 db, below 6 milliwatts.

3.5 Useful frequency range shall be from 30 to 16,000 cycles.

3.6 To be equipped with frequency equalizer between tubes.

3.7 Frequency equalizer to raise or lower the low frequency end of the audio spectrum to the extent of 15 db in each direction at 30 cycles, to raise or lower to the extent of 15 db in each direction 6,000, 8,000, 12,000 and 16,000 cycles.

Thunder Screen operated by August Lynch, Stevens Theatre.

Stevens Sound Control System console. Input left, output right, voltage amplifiers and equalizers below. Power amplifier group not shown. Photo, J. D. Jones.

4. Input Control

4.1 Input controls to be mounted on a $\frac{1}{8}''$ steel panel, slate gray, ripple finish, 19" x 12¼".

4.2 To contain the circuit which transfers the output of any or all of the voltage amplifiers to any of three channels.

4.3 Channels to be so color-coded.

4.4 Panel to contain four volume controls connected to the outputs of four voltage amplifiers, these controls to be "T" or ladder attenuators with vertical rather than rotary movement, 600 ohms to 600 ohms.

5. Frequency Discrimination Filter

5.1 To consist of a series of nine band rejection filters as follows: 30 to 65; 65 to 125; 125 to 250; 250 to 500; 500 to 1,000; 1,000 to 2,000; 2,000 to 4,000; 4,000 to 8,000; 8,000 to 16,000; all in cycles per second.

5.2 Minimum attenuation in any one band to be approximately:
    At center of band, 40 db.
    40% above and 30% below center, 35 db.
    54% above and 35% below center, 7 db.

6. Power Amplifiers

6.1 Each power amplifier to be self-contained, with its own voltage supply, to operate from the 120 volt commercial alternating current mains.

6.2 Amplifier, when used in a bridging connection across a 600 ohm line, to have a gain of approximately 50 db.

6.3 Output power to be 50 watts with less than 5% total harmonic distortion, or 25 watts with less than 1% harmonic distortion.

6.4 Unweighted output noise level to be 25 db or better, below 6 milliwatts.

7. Speaker Switching Panel

7.1 To contain a circuit using six sets of switches having ten push-buttons each.

7.2 To provide means of switching ten loud speakers to any of six power amplifiers.

8. Loud Speakers, Cable and Connectors

8.1 Speakers to consist of two parts—a low frequency speaker and a high frequency speaker.

8.2 Level of the high frequency speaker to be adjustable in four steps of 2 db each.

8.3 Speakers to have permanent magnet field.

8.4 Useful frequency range 35 to 18,000 cycles.

8.5 Overall dimension to be no larger than 33" x 33" x 31".

All equipment is to be assembled and connected in conformity with practices covering such installations established by I.A.T.S.E.

It will be noted that the specifications provide that each unit shall have a flat response characteristic or be compensated to a flat characteristic in itself, with the single exception that the adjustable compensation specified in the voltage amplifier may be used to flatten the ends of the microphone response. The necessity for interchange-ability and for increasing the number of units in the system, does not allow variations from flat characteristic in one unit to compensate for opposite variations in another unit.

While in small systems it may be argued that single amplifier units, instead of separate voltage and power amplifiers will do, a single unit arrangement defeats flexibility and therefore has no place except in a motion picture sound system or ballroom public address system.

For the purpose of coordinating the activities of a theatre, it is necessary that there be instantaneous communication between many parts of the plant. Cues must be transmitted to various parts of the stage, the trap room, the projection booth, etc., dressing room calls must be made, department heads exchange information and the audience called back into the house at the end of the intermission. All of these requirements vary in their special demands, and the satisfying of all of them by a single simple system is no small task. Nevertheless such a system must be installed unless the preparation of a show is to be difficult and wasteful, and its operation inefficient and unreliable.

The requirements will be here set forth by a progressive listing of the requirements of the various types of stations. First, the control for performance and rehearsal must be at the stage manager's station, for that is the point from which most cues originate and to which most information must be conveyed. The stage manager must be able to communicate by voice or cue with 1. the opposite side of the stage; 2. the fly gallery; 3. the trap room; 4. the switchboard; 5. the orchestra; 6. the spotting booth; 7. the motion picture projection booth; 8. the sound control station. He must be able to communicate by voice with 9. the dressing rooms; 10. the green room; 11. the box office; 12. the shops; 13. the offices; 14. outside telephone switchboard.

He must have voice (PA), chime, or buzzer communication with foyer, lobby, and lounge, to recall the audience at the end of intermissions. He must be able to communicate with a number of stations simultaneously. Communication between stations listed must be possible without turning the stage manager into a telephone switchboard operator.

When the theatre is large and active enough to make an intercommunicating dial phone system economically justifiable, such a system is satisfactory for communication between stage manager's station and all stations not directly connected with the operation of the show. If such a system is not justified, however, it must be possible to shift the control of all telephones in the system from stage manager's station to that of the house PBX, so that the system can still function at times when the stage is not occupied.

Intercommunication

Composite Cueing and Intercommunication System. When stage manager's control panel is shut down, telephones are operative through house PBX. Station details right.

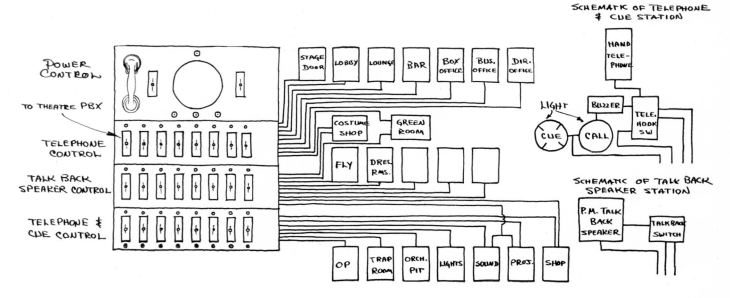

Dialing or calling numbers, however, takes too long to be satisfactory as a means of instantaneous communication. Therefore all stations involved in the operation of the show, and that excludes only the offices and sometimes the shop, must be called by a single movement connection, simultaneously if necessary. Where stations are isolated from the stage, the talk-back loudspeaking telephone can be used to further speed up communication by making it unnecessary for the wrong person to pick up the phone, call for the person to whom the message is directed, and pass over the hand set.

Stage Telephones

The talk-back loudspeaking telephone may be used on stage and at stations where it can be heard from the stage, during assembly, lighting, and rehearsal. On such occasions, a microphone may be used on an extension in the house for giving directions, and all stations ganged together, so that all directions go to all stations. This rehearsal and assembly technique has an added advantage in expediting the work in hand in that no station can talk back to the person giving directions, and much time often spent in discussion is thereby saved.

The fewer the cues which emanate from the stage manager, the more smoothly the show will run, since each cue passing from person to person suffers from the doubling of the human element hazard. It is therefore wise to run on dead cues as much as possible, and such operation is facilitated if all departments and persons who have to respond to cues hear the whole show, no matter where they are situated. The loudspeaking telephone system may be hooked up to stage microphones during performance as a means to this end. Whenever the stage manager wishes to, he can cut in with whatever other communication may be necessary. Whenever loudspeaking telephones are not so located as to be inaudible from the house, they can be equipped with automatic volume controls which vary the output level inversely as the signal. Whispers will come through such a system, while a loud signal will reduce itself to the same level as the whisper which cannot be heard in the house. The telephone with the loudspeaking features listed and provision for plugging in head and chest sets where quiet operation is required, is the most useful theatre intercommunication system and is an important part of a permanent installation.

Cueing Systems

Cueing must be simple, silent, positive, and must work in both directions. It must provide for difference between warn and dead cues so that the receiver will not mistake one for the other, and fail to initiate his operation, or get it early. Of the multitude of systems so far devised, only two seem worth considering. The first, particularly useful in elaborate productions, involves a box at the stage manager's station equipped with three or more numbered keys, and a pilot light for each station. All cues in the script are numbered. The stage manager sets up the number of the cue next in order and presses a master key which causes the cue number to light up all stations simultaneously. The lighting of the cue number constitutes the warn, and the stations which it affects acknowledge the warn by pressing a button which lights the pilot light opposite their station numbers at the stage manager's station. The dead cue is shot by opening the master switch, at which all stations black out.

A more conventional cue system consists merely of lights at various stations controlled by push buttons, switches, or keys at the stage manager's station, and in the best installations a return cue is provided. Cue keys are best pilot lighted and color coded. A system such as this is satisfactory for all but very elaborate productions, and for them it is perhaps better practice to run the show on dead cues which each person who normally receives cues takes them directly from seeing the show or hearing it or both. Monitoring the show by a PA system to all stations effectively eliminates the necessity for most cueing.

Opposite prompt side of the stage: Telephone, call light, cue light, (or cue number box) cue acknowledgment key. If the stage is large, loudspeaker for assembly and rehearsal.

Fly gallery: Same as opposite prompt (OP).

Trap Room: Same as OP plus a click signal on the cue light and telephone call. Loudspeaker included irrespective of the stage size. The click signal, a device similar to a buzzer, save that the magnet holds the clapper as long as it is energized, so only a click rather than a buzz is heard, calls attention to the cue or telephone call light, and is useful at all stations where the operator has duties which move him about so the lights are not constantly in his line of vision. The audience seldom notices a click but can hear a buzzer in the next block.

Switchboard: Same as OP.

Orchestra (conductor's stand): Same as OP.

Spotting Booth (and every position where house spots are operated): Same as trap room.

Motion picture projection booth: Same as trap room, plus outside telephone.

Sound control station: Same as trap room.

Dressing rooms: Talk back loudspeaking telephone, preferably one built into the wall between every pair of dressing rooms. Talk back button in each room.

Green room: Talk back loudspeaking telephone. Outside pay telephone in booth, more than one if casts are large.

Box office; other offices: Telephone with buzzer call.

Shops: If the shops are used as part of the stage, communication to them is the same as to the trap room. If they are not, the same system is used that is used for the dressing rooms.

Outside telephones form the theatre's intercommunication system not associated with the running of the show. The average legitimate house in New York uses so few extensions that it doesn't need a switchboard. The Music Hall, despite the fact that the process of production is far from complete within the theatre, has a large PBX. The decision as to how many extensions to put in, and where to put them depends upon whether they can earn their keep. It is safe to assume that they will, in all departments housed in separate rooms where the departments work all day throughout a considerable part of the season.

Talk back telephones must be pilot lighted at the stage manager's station. Lights must be associated with keys and the keys must return to the open position when they are released. It must be possible for the stage manager to cut out his microphone and loudspeaker and substitute therefor a telephone handset during performance. There must be provision for ganging all stations and feeding the system from a microphone in the house, during rehearsal, or on stage during the show. Amplifiers must be simple, rugged, and accessible. Class B will do.

All switches and keys must be silent. Mercury switches will handle voltages too high for telephone keys.

There must be provision for substituting head and chest sets and loudspeaking telephones for all telephone handsets used at operating positions, and button extensions for cue keys at all stations where cues may originate.

The stage manager's cue and telephone keys may well consist of one double throw key per station, which will stay closed in the telephone position and return from cue position.

Obviously, the intercommunication system must be designed for the specific theatre, and its characteristics will depend largely upon the uses to which the theatre is to be put. No satisfactory system has ever been designed by a person outside the theatre. Some elaborate and costly installations have proved so cumbersome and so unreliable that they gather dust while the stage manager shoots his cues by means of a muffled buzzer hooked to a couple of dry cells or by waving a handkerchief.

The most effective cueing is, of course, that supplied by the band at the circus. On signal from the ringmaster, it establishes the timing of the performance, and people and animals take their warn, entrance, and act cues from the music. The opera also operates on music cues, as can many other shows in which music is played more or less continuously.

14: production services

Up to this point the functions of the theatre involved in performance have been treated. This chapter is concerned with the preparation of the production that must precede performance and the architectural requisites arising therefrom.

There are six major steps in the theatrical process prior to performance:

1. Script is written
2. An organization is formed
3. The production is designed and planned
4. The production is prepared and manufactured
5. The production is assembled
6. The production is rehearsed

Steps 5 and 6 have been treated in Chapter 8. The first four steps must receive consideration, because they are integral functions of the total theatre plant, whether they take place under the same roof as the performance or in a separate building or buildings remote from the theatre. Where the process of production is carried through by one organization there are many advantages in the former situation.

Organization

There are two basic types of the theatre organization: 1. the organization within which the process of production is complete and often within the single building; 2. the organization in which all technical elements of the production are prepared by independent contractors. The first form is standard for most theatres in Europe, and for community, university and college, high school, stock (including summer stock), and repertory (including opera) theatres in this country. Most theatres in these categories are organized to plan and execute the entire work of theatrical production, including, in the case of professional and graduate theatre schools and music conservatories, writing and composing the plays and operas which are produced.

The second type of organization in which the functions of theatrical production are divided among many entrepreneurs is the American system of professional play production centered in New York, called the combination system. In it scenery, lights, costumes, are prepared by individual contractors and assembled with the other elements of production only when completed.

Some organizations, notably presentation, employ elements of both systems. Many factors influence the type of organization which will function in any theatre at any time. In the interests of efficiency, represented, if in no other field, by the saving of transportation costs, the theatre should be designed to be as self-sufficient as the tax rate warrants.

The theatrical organization has two principal functions: production and business. Production includes all of the activity of preparing and presenting the theatrical production: casting, rehearsing actors, music, dances, designing the production, and manufacture and assembly of the scenic elements. Business includes providing plant and procuring the facilities for the producing personnel, promoting an audience, receiving income and making expenditures, observing laws, and keeping accounts and records.

Theatrical organizations are extremely diverse; often functions and subfunctions are vested in the same person. Any categorical division stated here is schematic for purposes of exposition and must be subjected to modification in consideration of the factors in a particular situation.

The policies of any theatrical organization are in the hands of a managerial body which requires offices. From a single managing director, or general manager, this managerial body may expand to comprise producer, production manager, stage manager, dance director, art director, technical director, and numerous assistants, and in schools, acting and speech coaches.

An example of a completely expanded organization is Radio City Music Hall and of a completely contracted one is the combination producer who may maintain a small office and a secretary between productions, but engages a complete producing organization by contract, only when he has a play to produce, and only for the production of that one play.

The demand for working facilities for a theatrical organization ranges then from a single office to numerous specialized offices and studios for the staff of a resident, continuing, repertory or stock company.

The Play Is Written   The preparation of scripts, musical scores, libretti and choreography is seldom done in the theatre. During the preparation of a production, however, rewriting of script, rescoring of music and redesigning of dances are often necessary. The complete theatre plant must contain, then, studios for playwright, composer, and choreographer with appropriate equipment.

Opera and presentation houses will contain music libraries.

The professional theatre school will have seminar rooms for play writing courses.

Rehearsal room, Radio City Music Hall. Mirror wall, wall bar, acting area marked on floor. By LIFE photographer Herbert Gehr, Copyright, TIME, Inc.

Talent

Casting	**Waiting Room** Comfortable furniture. **Casting Director's Office** Standard office equipment.	
Tryouts or Auditions	**Audition Room** Minimum 15' x 20'. Platform at one end, several chairs. Acoustics good for voice. Piano, if for musical auditions. Audition room necessary only if theatre or rehearsal room is not available for tryouts and auditions.	
Rehearsals	**Rehearsal Room** Minimum size: acting area of same size and shape as that of the theatre for which show is being prepared, *plus* narrow strip of offstage space for actors, *plus* generous space for director, stage manager, and author on one long side. Washable floor without carpet, glareless general illumination minimum about 15 f.c. Acoustics good for voice.	

An NBC radio studio stage well suited to rehearsals, indicating the possible dual use of rooms. NBC photo.

Rehearsal Room
(continued)

Rehearsal Room, The Actors Studio, New York. Raised acting area, and provision for front lighting.

Equipment: 24 sturdy hardwood "kitchen" chairs. Three small sturdy tables, an assortment of strong standard household furniture (no upholstered pieces and no special pieces). Levels, ramps and platforms as they are to be in performance.

Use of the stage by other production departments often necessitates rehearsals elsewhere. Hence the rehearsal room is necessary to continued activity under good conditions. A Lounge may serve as a rehearsal room but it must meet the space and light requirements to do so adequately.

Rehearsal room may double as broadcast studio, in which case it should conform to studio requirements first.

Professional theatre school or repertory theatre often has several productions in process simultaneously, hence needs several rehearsal rooms.

For rehearsal in the theatre: easy passage between auditorium and stage. A ramp from the aisle to the stage, better than stairs which are dangerous in a darkened theatre.

Rehearsal lights. A set-up of lights independent of stage lighting control board

Optimum reverberation time for broadcast (with artists in place) shown as a function of studio size. Values within 30% of those shown can be compensated for by micro phone placement. (From an article by J. P. Maxfield in The Western Electric Oscillator, Copyright 1947, Western Electric Co., Inc.)

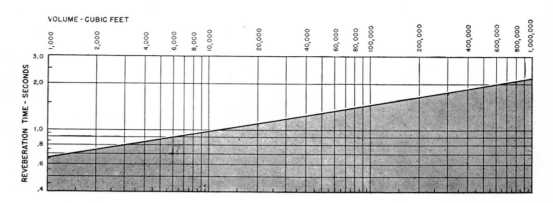

VOLUME - CUBIC FEET

to illuminate the acting area but not to shine into the eyes of the director, min. 15 f.c.

Rehearsal of singers requires:

1. Piano, light.
Rehearsal piano onstage. Performance piano in pit should *not* be used.
2. If not in the theatre, then a rehearsal room, preferably designed for broadcast pickup. Because of acoustic differences, a certain number of singing rehearsals must be held in the theatre.

Rehearsal of dancers requires:

Rehearsal room as above. Piano.

Rehearsal of musicians requires:

Orchestra pit, or rehearsal studio large enough to permit arrangement of instruments as in pit. Preferably designed for radio pickup. Lighting similar to rehearsal room above.

Some music rehearsals must be held in the theatre for acoustic reasons.

During the rehearsal period, the physical production (scenery, properties, costumes, lights, and sound) is being prepared on drawing boards, and in shops, and usually makes no demands upon the stage or its equipment. Rehearsals of any kind of production are best conducted in the theatre in which the performance is to be given. Other uses of the theatre often make this impossible, in which case rehearsals must be held in other space.

Dance Drill and Practice

Dance Practice Room

Rehearsal room as above, *plus* one mir-

	ror wall, wall bars on other walls, hardwood floor, piano.
	Comment: Dance requires rehearsal and practice space separate from the stage and in addition to the cast rehearsal room.
	Showers and dressing rooms convenient to the dance practice room.
Music Practice (Schools, conservatories, and some repertory companies.)	**Practice Rooms for musicians and singers** Minimum 100 sq. ft. each. Piano in each. Music stands. Acoustically isolated from the house.
	Orchestra Practice Room (See Rehearsal Room)
	Instrument Storage and Locker Room Minimum 200 sq. ft. Shape optional. Located near practice rooms but with good access to orchestra pit and outside, for loading and unloading instruments.
Rest Periods	**Recreation Room, or Lounge** The theatre Green Room (Chapter 8), if near rehearsal and practice rooms.

Costumes

A theatrical costume department must be equipped to fabricate any imaginable costume. The process is more involved than tailoring or dressmaking because theatrical production knows no limitation of style, material or color. Actor's shapes must sometimes be changed to conform to requirements of design or to make up for natural deficiencies.

Actors measured for costumes and wigs	**Fitting Room** (See below)
Materials purchased and stored	**Supply Room** Materials consist largely of cloth in bolts, sewing materials, small supplies, pattern paper in rolls. Deep shelves for bulk materials. Shallow shelves for sewing materials. Some moth proof storage space for woolens and felts.
Patterns drafted from measurements	**Costume Shop** Pattern drafting table. Minimum 3' x 6' with working space all around it. Hard surface. Clean area.
Muslin garment made up from pattern and fitted	**Costume Shop and Fitting Room** (See below)
Cloth is dyed	**Dye Shop** Storage for dye stuffs. Closed cabinet with shelves. Space for demijohns of acid. Small chemist's table with balance and weights. Dye vats, water supply, gas or electric heat, drying racks (preferably in sepa-

rate room). Air circulation supplying warm dry air to speed the drying of cloth, and separate from the system for the rest of building to isolate the odors associated with the dye process.

Cloth is painted	**Large Table** Surface must be proof against paint, water and acid. Clear working space around table.
Cloth is pressed	**Costume Shop** Hand ironing boards, electric ironers, steam presser.
Cloth is cut	**Cutting Tables** Minimum 3′ x 6′ with clear space all around. Preferably arranged so that two tables may be put together for big jobs (trains, capes, etc.).

Flow charts pertaining to costume fabrication and use.

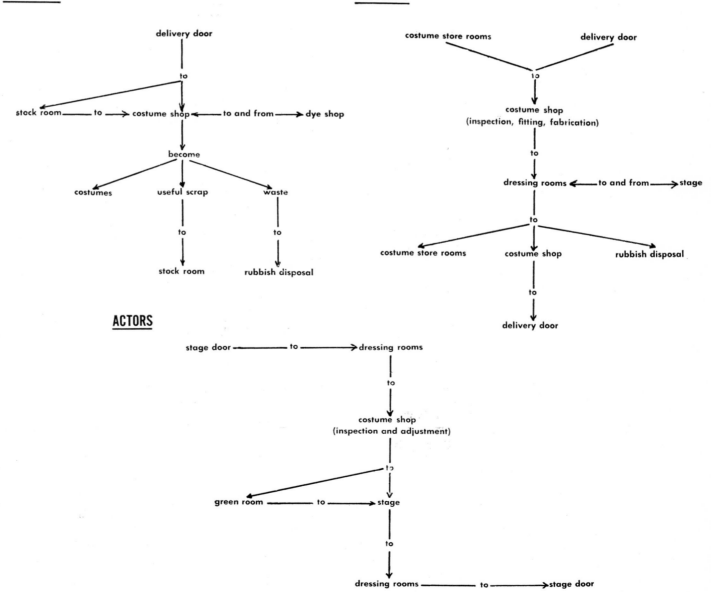

MATERIALS

COSTUMES

ACTORS

Cloth is sewn into actual garments	**Power Sewing Machines** Allow 5' x 8' floor space for each, including operator
	Hand Sewing Tables Allow 4' x 6' floor space for each, including operator
Garments are fitted	**Fitting Room** Minimum 100 sq. ft. Podium, 3' x 3' x 1' high Full length mirror Small cabinet for fitting supplies.
Garments are finished and trimmed	**Hand Sewing Tables** (See above)
Costume accessories are made and procured	**Accessories Shop** Minimum 10' x 15'. Small wood- and metal-working benches with tools. Accessories constitute hats and shoes, plus all decorative and useful implements which may pertain to costumes, from spectacles to broadswords. The craftsman in costume accessories is generally able to make use of wood- and metal-working tools and machines in the scenery or property shops. If such shops are not available, he must be equipped to work in wood, leather, sheet metal, wire, cardboard, and plaster of paris. In planning a theatre it is advisable to supply the shop space with cabinets. It would be either uneconomical or impossible, perhaps both, to attempt to furnish all the equipment which might be necessary for some unspecified future job.
Costumes are shipped	Shipping room, if the costume department is separate from the theatre. Minimum 10' x 20'. Assembly counters, space for hampers and trunks. Access to street via wide corridors or elevators.
Costume shop administration	Office. Minimum 100 sq. ft.
Scenery Scenery is designed	**Design Studio** Drafting tables, model building bench and equipment, reference files and bookshelves, cabinets for filing sketches and drawings. Cabinets for storage of drawing materials. *For professional schools and conservatories*, collection of source material, design library, models. Museum.

Costume Shop in the Radio City
Music Hall. By LIFE photographer
Herbert Gehr, Copyright TIME, Inc.

| Scenery is planned | **Technician's Office**
Desk, chair, and filing cabinet, drafting table, cabinet for drawings and materials.

Production Drafting Room
Drafting tables, model making bench and equipment, files for technical data, cabinets for material samples, wall board for moulding samples, wall covered with tack boards. |
| Scenery is manufactured | **Scene Shop**
Supply room for storage of bulky ma- |

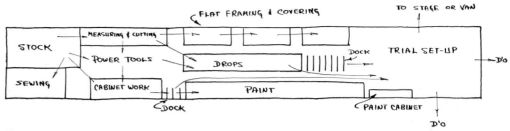

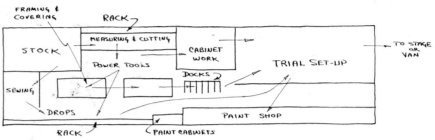

Schematic diagrams of scene shop layouts. Areas are proportional but not to scale. Sizes depend upon the size of the scenery to be built. Adaptable to other floor plans.

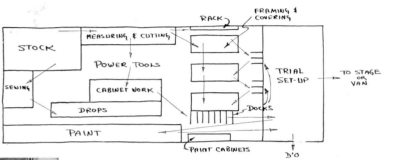

Scene shop, Kirby Theatre, Amherst College. A traverse stage wagon carrying a complete setting and properties may be rolled into the shop from the stage. Paint shop is out of the picture to the left.

A framing bench for scenery. Note the preset right angle corner and the hardware trays. Precut lumber is stored below.

terials, especially lumber, building board, and rolls of cloth and chicken wire. Cabinets for small supplies. Tool racks.

Measure and mark, cut, work-up
Power woodworking tools: cut-off saw, rip-saw, mortiser, jointer, drill-press, cut-awl, and router.

Join into frame, flameproof, cover
Woodworking benches, assembly benches, covering benches. Each 6' x 16' minimum with 3' of working space all around. Storage racks for finished and partially completed scenery.

Drops, ceilings and trial assembly
Trial assembly area big enough to receive sets of scenery assembled as if on stage. Rigging equipment over.

(Scene shops, except for a few in New York City, are too small for their uses. For shops planned with the minimum space for efficient work under the conditions stated, see the illustrations.)

Metal Working Shop
Lathe, break, drill press, saw, sheet metal shears, welding torch, hand tools.

Facilities for performance of the simpler processes of fabrication in sheet metals and steel (worked cold) are desirable. There is little demand for hot shaping of iron and steel; the small amount which is required may be most economically done at a smithy.

Scenery is painted

Paint Shop
There are two principal methods of painting scenery, on a paint frame or on a paint floor, neither of which is an adequate substitute for the other, because the effects produced differ.

Paint Frame
Minimum 1½ acting area width, full proscenium height, hung on counterweighted rigging against a blank wall so as to sink past the working floor to bring the top within easy working reach of a person standing on the floor. Sinkage equals height minus 6'. Access to bottom of sinkage well for clean-out and to retrieve dropped tools. Bottom of sinkage well troughed and pitched to high capacity drain. Automatic ejector or sump pump in well if bottom is below sewer main. Easily accessible cleanout trap in drainage line. No sharp turns in drainage line. Working floor at paint frame pitched

Two paint frames, back to back, one with scenery attached, are lowered through a slot made by lifting the traps in the floor. Painters stand on the floor and the scenery is raised as they paint it.

to drain, to allow washing. Slight curb at edge for safety.

Paint Floor

Minimum area somewhat greater than paint frame. In some instances the stage floor or scene shop floor may be used as a paint floor, but more often other uses of the stage and shop make this impossible.

Painting in the scene shop or on stage produces objectionable dampness, dirt and dust in these spaces.

Painting tools and supplies

Bins for dry colors. Fireproof locker for flammable paints and ingredients. Ventilated cabinets with flat shelves made of bronze wire mesh for storing brushes. Space for barrels of glue, whiting, and flameproofing.

Ventilating and heating of paint shop

The ideal situation comprises high-capacity circulation of warm dry air, separate from the system for the rest of the building, to produce rapid drying of painted scenery.

Sink with hot and cold water. Three-burner gas or electric stove. Double boiler tank to take three 12 qt. pails, with automatic heat and water controls.

Lighting of paint shop

Evenly distributed, about 25 f.c. minimum, white or daylight fluorescent or cold cathode lighting. Auxiliary circuit to supply evenly distributed incandescent light from stage-type flood lights, allowing test of the painting under stage colors. Projection space. Ideally there should be space in front of the paint frame to allow projection of an image from a slide for enlargement onto scenery. A pyramid of clear space with its altitude horizontal and its apex $\frac{1}{2}$ the width of the frame in front of the frame. Projection may be from a movable tower or step ladder at apex.

Access to the paint shop

Scenery is brought to the paint shop in large units. Frequently one dimension equals the width of the frame, and sometimes framed scenery equals the width and height of the frame. Therefore access to the frame should be in a straight line, preferably parallel to the frame. It should not be necessary to swing or turn scenery through spaces where other work is in progress.

Surface finishes in paint shop. Many ingredients of scene paint induce corrosion of metals. Much water is used both in scene painting and in cleaning the paint shop. Therefore surfaces must be either of wood which is replaceable if it rots, or of concrete, tile, or non-corroding metals or enamels.

Scenery is stored

A continuing theatre organization may effect considerable saving of time, labor, and materials by the storage and re-use of scenery. The apparent saving in labor and materials may be cancelled by the costs of land and building. This is true in New York City where rental of storage space is too high to make the storage of scenery economical. The apparent saving may also be cancelled by transportation costs if the storage space is not near the scene shop and stage. The saving in time is real in any case. In places where land costs are lower than in New York City there is the likelihood that a triple saving will be achieved by efficient storage and re-use of scenery.

A policy of storing only standard pieces of scenery which are most likely to be used again, guarantees against filling the storage space with useless items.

For efficient storage, scenery must be categorized according to its space-filling characteristics. There are four main categories: rolled scenery, flat scenery, architectural trim, and three-dimensional pieces. Each of these categories requires specially shaped storage space. The total space must be subdivided according to the expected quantities of scenery in each category to be stored. The entire space, furthermore, must be easily accessible from the stage and the scene shop.

Effective storage of flat scenery where there is little headroom. Access to such storage docks must be direct and clear.

	Scenery is stored (continued)	Storage of scenery under the stage in fireproof vaults is permitted in the current New York building code. Though its use may be restricted this space will be needed at times and should not be omitted.
	Scenery is shipped out	Loading doors, covered loading space, platform level with floor of motor trucks: Changes of grade necessary to effect this made outside the building. Straight paths of movement from shop to trucks. (See Chapter 8) If scenery goes directly from paint shop to stage in the same building, paint shop and stage on same level: clear, wide, straight paths of movement, as short as possible.
	Scenery is washed	High pressure hose connectable to hot water supply in paint shop. Force-control valve in nozzle. Scrub brushes, long and short handled. Drains at bottom of well and in working floor as described above.
Stage Lighting	Lighting is designed	Guided by the stage designer's concept of the visual aspect desired, the lighting required by the playwright's script, and the director's projected stage action as it expresses demands upon the lighting, lighting is designed by the stage designer himself or by an assistant called the lighting designer. If by the stage designer, it is done in his office or studio. If by a lighting designer, a studio-office is necessary. Equipment: standard office furniture, file cabinets, shelves for reference books, drafting table, racks or cabinets for the storing of blueprints.
	Lighting is planned	Lighting office or studio The plan for the lighting graphically implements the design. It consists of a *lighting layout* in the form of mechanical drawings showing the location of all lighting instruments on plans, sections and elevations of the set or sets, *instrument schedule* stating all particulars about each instrument and identifying each instrument by an index number for reference to the layout, and *cue sheet*, giving in sequence of performance all operations of lighting instruments with adequate cues taken from the script or the stage action.

Three sources: owned by the organization, purchased, rented.

It is most economical for a continuing theatrical organization to own the bulk of its lighting apparatus. This implies a large initial investment but ease of procurement, coupled with the savings effected by re-use, warrants it. Progressive purchase over a period of years allows a growing organization to acquire in time all necessary apparatus.

Instrument storage:

Adequate storage for a full complement of lighting instruments, accessible to the stage and to the lighting shop, and planned for efficient use of three-dimensional space, is a necessary part of the theatre plan, whether the apparatus is all procured initially or over a period of time.

Lamp and accessory storage:

Many small devices are necessary for the mounting and operation of stage lighting instruments. Stage cables are necessary to connect instruments to stage outlets. Used directly in connection with assembly of lighting instruments on stage, these objects should be stored close to the stage.

Fabrication, maintenance, repair, and experimentation:

The modification of instruments to perform special functions, the construction of new instruments and parts of instruments, repair, and maintenance require a small workshop equipped with machines and tools for the fabrication of sheet metal, steel (worked cold), and wire. There must be equipment for bending, cutting and threading iron pipe and conduit.

Rapid change of show in Presentation, Repertory and Stock productions demands that a standard layout of lighting instruments be kept mounted in performance positions. A plan for lighting, similar to that set forth by Stanley McCandless in A METHOD OF LIGHTING THE STAGE is made the basis of lighting all productions and special instruments, held to the irreducible minimum, are installed to meet nonstandard requirements of particular productions.

Properties are designed

The design of properties is a duty of the stage designer and is done in his studio. (See above)

Properties

Properties are procured

Properties are either bought, rented, or made. As with lighting instruments, the ownership of properties by a continuing theatre organization is warranted by the ease of procurement and the financial savings effected thereby. The more productions an organization presents the greater are the savings of time and money.

Property shop

Inasmuch as the category of properties embraces all conceivable objects, it is patently impossible to purchase and own all those which may be required. Hence there must be provision for the fabrication of properties in wood, metal, plastic substances, fabrics and other materials. Examples of made properties are a maguey plant native to Mexico but needed for a play produced in New England, a replica of an iron safe, made light enough for a quick scene shift, and leg shackles to make no noise because they are worn by the ghostly chain gang in the EMPEROR JONES.

Property storeroom

Adjustable shelves for small objects. Ample open space for large objects. Access to stage and property shop direct and wide. Largest object a grand piano. Planned for maximum three-dimensional use of space.

Sound: Electronics	Sound Control is planned	Technical Director's office
	Equipment assembled	Shop If equipment is not permanently installed in the theatre.
	Equipment tested and maintained	Shop (above). Equipment: Vacuum Tube Volt-ohm Milliammeter Tube Tester, Audio Oscillator, C-R-Oscilloscope, 5″ preferable, usual electronics shop hand tools. With the increased use of electronic control for stage lighting and machinery, electronic maintenance becomes increasingly important and may require more shop space than the electrical shop.
	Recording	Permanent studio for conservatories of music. Other theatres: portable equipment kept in sound shop, used in studios, etc. for making up show records, voice training, performance records.

Recording Studio, Juilliard School of Music. Microphone booms, intercommunications speaker, outlets, and playback speaker. Window into control room.

Control room and recording apparatus of the same studio. Photos, courtesy Juilliard School of Music.

SCHOOL

The theatre school or conservatory may start its training with the basic elements of the arts of the theatre. The plant will, in such cases, need standard school facilities for such a curriculum: class rooms, demonstration amphitheatre, seminar rooms, drafting rooms, and numerous rehearsal rooms.

ADMINISTRATION AND BUSINESS

Management

In presentation, opera, and the motion picture palace, the operation is large enough to require a large executive staff and an appropriate suite of offices. Even the smallest motion picture house has a manager's office which serves as the treasurer's office, necessary wherever ticket cages or counters are used.

Equipment: Standard office equipment for receipt and expenditure of money and keeping records: desks, chairs, files, accounting machines, safe.

Promotion of Audience

The public relations person of a theatrical organization is called a theatrical press agent, but his duties encompass the exploitation of all means of public relations for the promotion of audiences.

Equipment: Standard office equipment, plus large table for laying out publicity material. Large shelves for the temporary storage of same. Standard files for pictures and typescript.

Ticket Sale

The member of a theatrical organization who is charged with the sale of tickets and held accountable for the money received therefrom is called the treasurer. The treasurer's office is in essence an accounting office and is so staffed and equipped. In a small theatre the treasurer's office is connected with the box office or is combined with it. When connected, it sometimes also serves as the manager's office. (See Box Office, Chapter 5)

Secretarial Functions

General stenography and typing, and filing, are often augmented by the typing and duplicating of scripts under pressure of time limitations.

Equipment: for regular use, typewriter desks, chairs, files, and supply cabinets according to the needs of the organization. Reserve typing facilities for pressure periods.

This chapter treats those elements and factors of theatre planning which pertain to the theatre as a whole, to more than one part of the theatre or aspect of the theatrical function, and to the interrelationship of the various parts of the whole theatre insofar as the relationship is not implicit in the parts themselves.

Just as each part of the theatre must serve discrete functions, so the complete theatre plant must:

1. Accommodate an audience
2. Accommodate a performance
3. Bring audience and performance together in the most effective relationship.

These functions are interdependent and combine to make possible the total uniform effect which is the requirement of the audience and the purpose of the showman.

Failure to recognize the interdependence of theatrical functions has resulted in theatres in which each separate part fulfilled its own particular function but the theatre as a whole did not. For example, there was a tendency to build, usually on college campuses, theatres which had stages more or less adequate for legitimate or even musical production, but house capacities of intimate or news reel motion picture theatres.

The Interdependence of Functions

The tiny audience cannot contribute the kind or amount of response which is its part in a live performance. Despite an adequate production the show suffers and the audience doesn't get its money's worth.

Optimum audience-performance relationship, made possible by the correct size, shape, and arrangement of the house and the acting area, as dictated by the type of production being presented, may be vitiated by an unpleasant experience of difficult access to the theatre, too closely spaced seats, or poor ventilation. Undue concession to local social *mores* in the arrangement of the house may vitiate the basic audience-performance relationship. Concentration on the accommodation of the audience to the neglect of the performance may produce theatres in which the performance cannot possibly have an advantageous orientation toward the audience. Conversely, though of rarer instance, concentration on accommodation of the performance to the neglect of the audience predisposes the audience unsympathetically toward the efforts of the performers.

Functional requisites are identical irrespective of the origin of the theatre building project. The *origin* of a plan for a theatre is some-

Universality

times confused with function. The theatre planner must not be tempted to compromise basic function with the objectives of making money, affording a focal point for social activity, establishing or maintaining social prestige. The theatre which fulfills its basic functions adequately will titillate the sensibilities of the dilettante and make money for the impresario. It will not accomplish these ends to the satisfaction of anyone if any essential part of the theatre is sacrificed and the *total uniform effect* thereby compromised, to make possible a diamond horseshoe, an imposing façade or a tricky stage.

Theatre in Educational Institutions

The educational objective has two aspects: to teach theatre, and to teach other material *by* theatre. To teach theatre requires the existence of an exemplary theatre plant just as to teach surgery requires an exemplary operating room.

Teaching *by* theatre is the use of theatre, its plant and its techniques, as a direct or indirect medium for imparting other subjects. Directly, drama may be presented in a liberal arts program as the epitome or representation of past cultures, corollary to studies in languages, literatures, history, anthropology and sociology. Directly also, dramatization of situations may be a teaching method for numerous departments of instruction. Indirectly, participation in theatrical productions fosters creative imagination and expression, development of desirable character traits, and the discipline of co-operation. Even where theatre facilities must be incorporated in a building primarily for other than theatrical uses, theatre function must be borne in mind and the basic theatrical requisites supplied, or it cannot as a theatre contribute to the attainment of non-theatrical educational objectives.

Theatre Function and Architectural Style

The battle between function and historic style in architecture appears to have been won by function in those localities where architectural design has been allowed to develop most freely. In the design and construction of buildings suited to the needs of the mid-twentieth century all of the modern materials have been allowed to take their places not only in the hidden parts of the buildings but also in the visible frames, walls, ceilings and floors. Architects and engineers have accepted new structural theories and materials, have devised new building methods to use them efficiently and effectively and have learned to achieve beauty by their assembly and arrangement.

Not infrequently, however, conservative requirements of clients have compelled architects, while using modern materials and structural methods, to hide them under period surfaces and ornament, and occasionally to distort the function of a building in order to force it into an archaic shell.

A common objection among those in authority in the planning of theatres is to the height of the stage house. Failure to realize the function of that part of the theatre or a mistaken belief that that function is dispensable may motivate the order that the height of the stage house be held below an arbitrary limit. Using the stage house as an example although other parts of a theatre are often subject to such unenlightened decisions, it must be emphasized that *theatrical functions must be the primary determinants of the size, shape, and arrangement of the parts of the theatre building and that in no other kind of building is suitability of form to function more precisely demanded.*

Auditorium of the Crow Island Elementary School. Theatrical requirements of seeing (sloped floor) and performance (fore-stage) are recognized to make this simple auditorium much more like a theatre than are most elementary school assembly rooms. Eliel Saarinen, Eero Saarinen, Perkins, Wheeler, and Will, architects. Photo, Hedrich-Blessing Studio.

Plan of the Shorewood, Wisconsin, High School Auditorium. This building supplies the needs of both the school and the community as a place of public assembly, concerts, and performances. Herbst and Kuenzli, architects. Courtesy, Shorewood Public Schools.

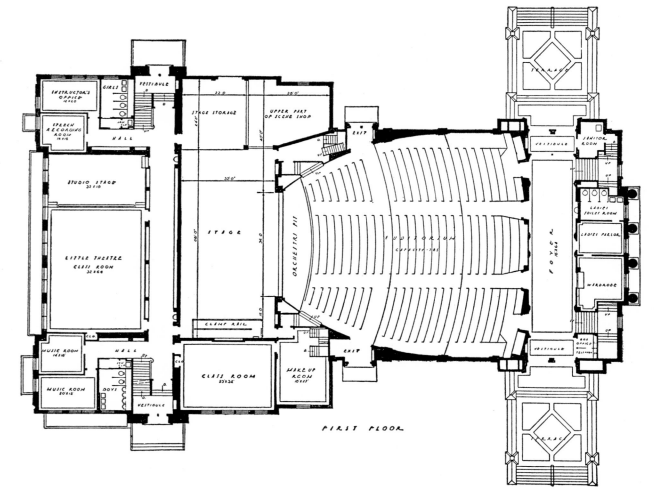

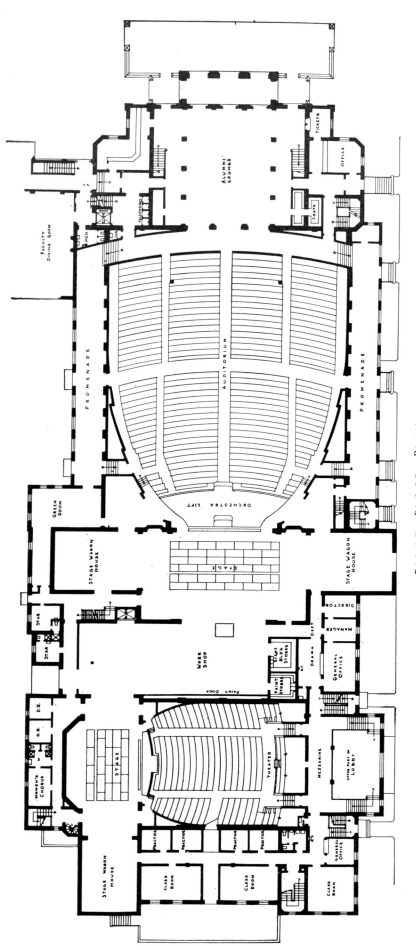

FIRST FLOOR PLAN

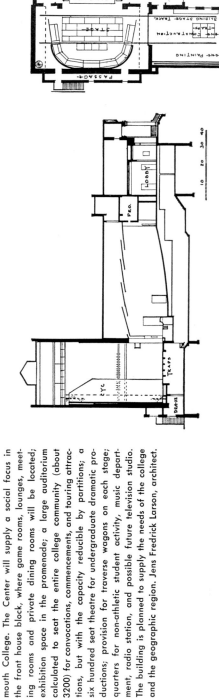

The Adams Memorial Theatre, Williams College. Cram and Ferguson, Architects.

Main floor plan for the proposed Hopkins Center at Dartmouth College. The Center will supply a social focus in the front house block, where game rooms, lounges, meeting rooms and private dining rooms will be located; exhibition space in the promenade; a large auditorium calculated to seat the entire college community (about 3200) for convocations, commencements, and touring attractions, but with the capacity reducible by partitions; a six hundred seat theatre for undergraduate dramatic productions; provision for traverse wagons on each stage; quarters for non-athletic student activity, music department, radio station, and possible future television studio. The building is planned to supply the needs of the college and the geographic region. Jens Fredrick Larson, architect.

The question of style, period or modern, and of exterior ornament, is a matter for the taste of the client and the artistic conscience of the architect. The question of distorting the function of the theatre to make it comply with requirements of appearance invades the province of the audience and the showman who care not a whit, except privately, whether the building be encrusted with Gothic limestone or Georgian white pine so long as its internal spacial disposition and equipment are conducive to the true functions of theatre as stated throughout this book.

Site

The theatre site must be big enough to hold the theatre and to provide access and outside audience handling facilities. This statement stands opposed to the idea that the building may be made to fit the land by adjustment and rearrangement of its interior spaces without regard for their optimum functional arrangement. Urban real estate is conveniently divided into predominantly rectangular parcels. The result is that urban theatres have been arranged to fit onto predominantly rectangular plans. High costs of urban land have prompted the building of theatres on sites so much too small that the functioning of the theatres, as analyzed in this book, has been impaired and the financial and artistic success and continuance of the theatres have been jeopardized. Prior to 1938, when no other occupancy was allowed in a building containing a theatre, high real estate taxes provided some justification for the niggardly use of land. Since 1938, however, the New York building ordinance has been liberalized to permit other income-producing occupancies in a theatre building.

The project of combining two or more theatres on one plot of ground so that a large building might be raised over their combined lobbies and auditoriums has been advanced with some prospects of adoption.

Theatres in schools and colleges have been frequently subjected to restraints imposed by preconceived master plans, in which either a site has been allocated to a theatre before determining adequately the theatre's space requirements, or considerations of campus design have imposed restrictions upon the physical size and shape of and access to the theatre building.

This book can only urge that consideration be given to the requisite functional shape and size of and access to the theatre building before a site is selected. The problem is as simple in its essence, though not in its execution, as buying a hat: no matter how handsome the hat is, it must fit or one does not buy it. No one cuts off an ear or slashes the hatband to make a hat fit. Yet a hat lasts one season, a theatre at least a generation.

Fortunately architectural design theory has veered sharply away from the concept that all buildings must be rectangular in plan and have imposing, balanced façades, toward the concept of allowing the exterior and plan of the building to develop logically from the optimum arrangement of its interior spaces, and its siting to evolve from traffic requirements. This concept favors the production of workable theatres.

Development of the Plan

The production type for which the theatre is intended determines the *audience-performance relationship* which the theatre must assure. In concrete terms this means:

1. The shape and size of the minimum architectural proscenium

The Kleinhans Music Hall, Buffalo, New York. Eliel and Eero Saarinen, designers; F. J. and W. A. Kidd, architects. Photo, Hare Photographs, Inc. Courtesy Kleinhans Music Hall Management, Inc.

Recognizing the place of acoustics in the design of a music hall, the architects accepted the specifications written by the acoustic consultants as the basis for this building. Concert artists and music critics acclaim its excellence. The provision for handling a large audience is good.

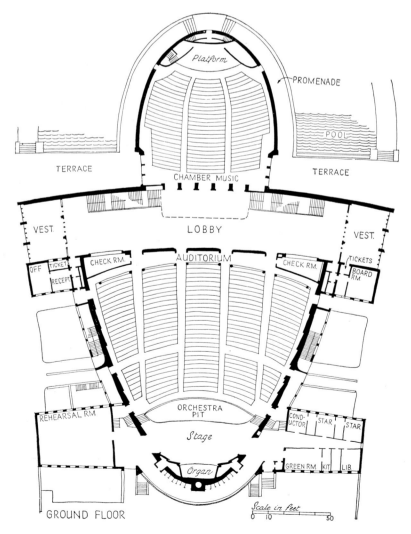

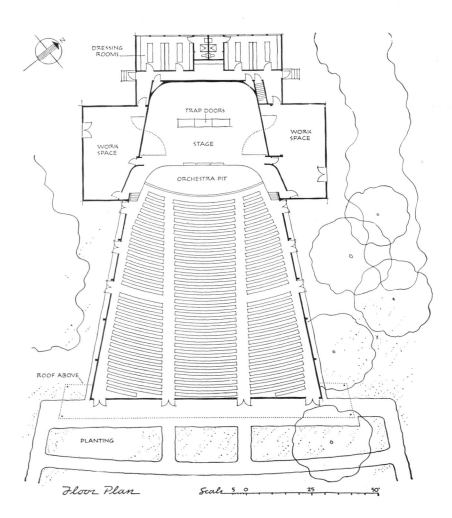

DRESSING ROOMS

TRAP DOORS

WORK SPACE

STAGE

WORK SPACE

ORCHESTRA PIT

ROOF ABOVE

PLANTING

Floor Plan

Scale 5 0   25   50'

Plan of the theatre at Tanglewood, Lenox, Mass. Saarinen, Swanson and Saarinen, architects, Charles C. Potwin, acoustical consultant.

The proscenium of the theatre at Tanglewood is flexible, allowing use of side stages, entrances from the sides, or sound reflecting panels for use during concerts. Photo Gottscho-Schleisner.

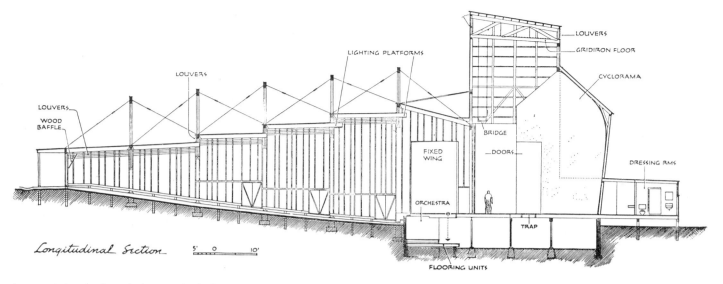

Longitudinal Section   5'   0   10'

Section of the Tanglewood Theatre. The built-in cyclorama is tilted backward to prevent unwanted reflected sound from reaching the audience.

Exterior of the Tanglewood theatre. Intended for summer use only, the theatre is of light construction, having ventilation slots and louvers which permit convective circulation. Ceiling panels are hung from external bow trusses. Photo, Gottscho-Schleisner.

opening and the provisions, if any, for its enlargement. Architectural minimum is usually production maximum.

2. Optimum audience.

3. Size and shape of apron, acting area, and orchestra pit.

These shapes and dimensions constitute the starting point from which design proceeds simultaneously to both audience and stage sides of the proscenium.

The two main divisions, as has been implied in the topical arrangement of this book are 1. the house and its related spaces, and 2. the stage and its related spaces. The first constitutes the accommodation of the audience in terms of reception, traffic, seeing, hearing, comfort and safety; the second constitutes accommodation of the performance in terms of preparation, reception, assembly, rehearsal, performance, removal and possibly storage. Either division taken by itself may be planned by a straightforward process of adapting the form to requirements which can be derived and stated. But *neither division can be planned by itself* until the fundamental relationship which exists between them has been established.

Variations

If there are several intended production types, the audience-performance relationship must necessarily embrace them all. The relationship selected must be the most flexible, allowing the provision of other relationships as necessary. If the program includes non-theatrical uses, care must be taken that theatrical functions are not slighted in the plan, inasmuch as theatrical uses exert the more exacting requirements.

Variable House Capacity

Many schemes have been advanced for varying the size of the house so that it may be used for productions varying from intimate chamber music concerts to grand opera. Schemes involving curtains, sliding panels, etc. are more often mechanically intriguing than satisfactory to the audience. Of those which have been installed many are never used. A few, such as the Malmö (Sweden) Municipal Theatre seem to work satisfactorily and merit study. A far cheaper system, not subject to the same hazards to acoustics and sight lines, is so to design the house that the audience in the orchestra is never aware of the balconies which are closed when a small audience is to be accommodated.

The capacity of the Malmö Theatre is variable by means of hanging panels which are stored in bays at either side and are drawn through ceiling tracks to reduce either the width or the depth or both. The transverse panels hung from a serpentine track produce a sound-diffusing form. Photo, C. G. Rosenberg.

An orchestra of a legitimate theatre providing optimum seeing and hearing conditions and exceptional comfort, is limited to less than 700 seats. A balcony brings capacity up to a number which is economically sound. All compromises with optimum audience conditions may be made in the balcony. Control of house lighting may effectively reduce the apparent size or capacity of an auditorium.

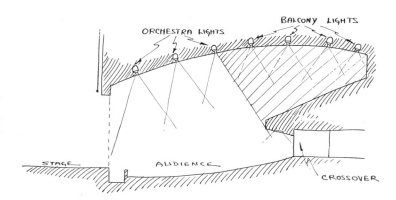

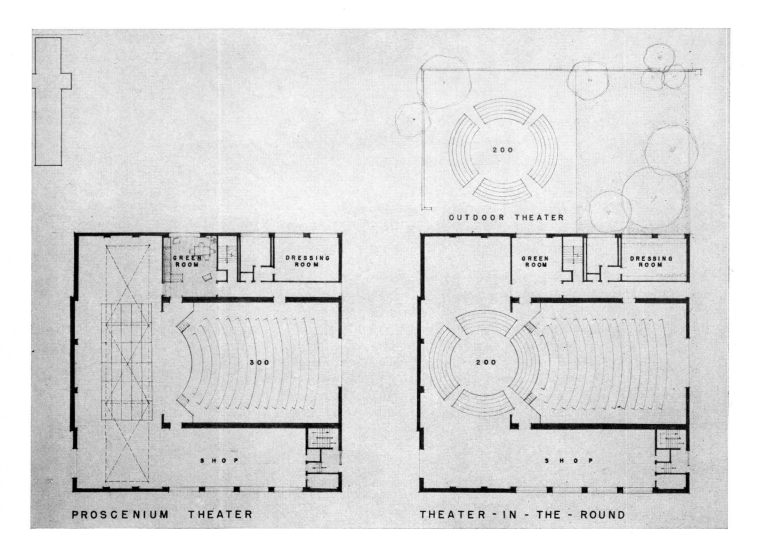

OUTDOOR THEATER

200

PROSCENIUM THEATER

THEATER - IN - THE - ROUND

300

200

GREEN ROOM

DRESSING ROOM

SHOP

Projected theatre for the University of Arkansas. Play production may have either conventional form, using the proscenium, or the experimental form of central staging. Stone, Haralson, and Mott, architects.

The designation Experimental Theatre is sometimes adopted by organizations which lack the patience or skill to learn or employ established production forms, or the facilities for adequate production, and undertake to hide their shortcomings under a respected banner. They merit no consideration here.

There are, however, a few specific theatre situations which admit the construction of experimental theatres. A theatre school which already has one or more theatres of conventional form and which uses them to the full extent of their potentialities can use, even needs, experimental facilities. It is only by experiment that new forms and techniques may be tested and the theatre school is the logical place for the tests to be made.

An experimental theatre must be a flexible theatre in which many production schemes may be put to test. It is *not* a theatre capable of only a single production type. To provide an untried form of theatre for an organization which has no other theatre worthy of the name is to ask that organization to turn its back on the whole body of accumulated theatre practice, both artistic and technical, and to undertake production in a milieu for which there is little precedent and less knowledge. The theatre planner must make sure that the people for whom he provides an experimental form of theatre are able and willing to experiment.

Neophyte, impecunious groups wishing to undertake a theatrical venture may benefit from attempting production in the mode of central staging. They may produce a play in any large room which has sufficient structural strength and sufficient exits to assure safety to the audience. They are relieved of the task of supplying scenery since scenery cannot be used. Platforms must be limited in height and lighting need be restricted to the creation of satisfactory illumination of the acting area. Thus a large part of the cost of play production and considerable of the effort is eliminated.

Schemes for the elimination of scenery and scenery-handling devices apparently arise from the valid realization that scenery requires both effort and expense, that scenery handling devices and the space they require constitute a large portion of the total theatre plant, rationalized into the supposition that since the play and the actors are, admittedly, the major conveyors of the illusion to the audience, scenery is unnecessary.

There has been ample opportunity in the course of the theatre's twenty-five hundred years for scenery to be eliminated. If it has not been, it is probably important to the theatre.

Plan of the Federal Theatre Project Theatre at The Golden Gate International Exposition. Timothy L. Pfleuger, architect.

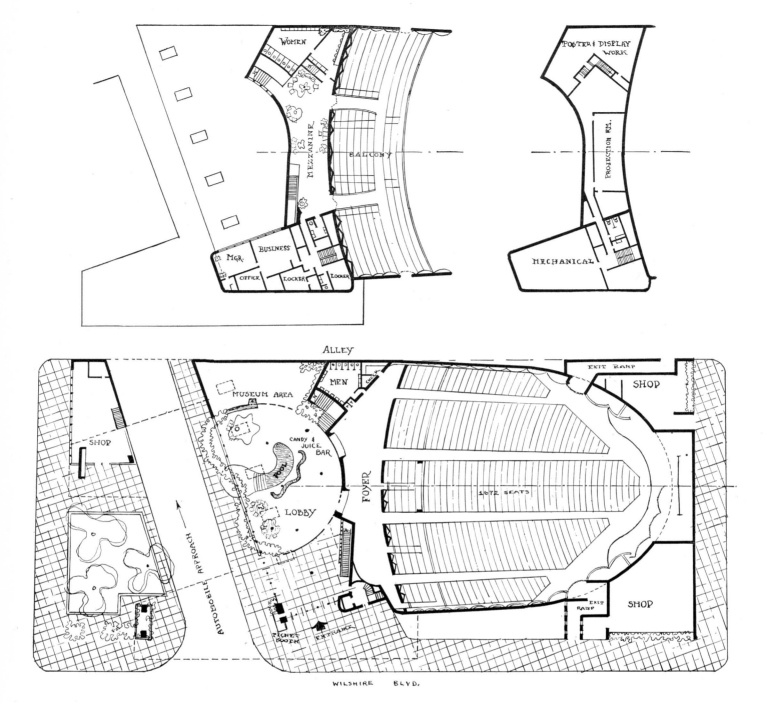

The following labels appear within the plans:

WOMEN

POSTER & DISPLAY WORK

MEZZANINE

BALCONY

PROJECTION RM.

MGR.

BUSINESS

OFFICE

LOCKER

LOCKER

MECHANICAL

ALLEY

EXIT RAMP

SHOP

MUSEUM AREA

MEN

CANDY & JUICE BAR

POOL

FOYER

1672 SEATS

SHOP

LOBBY

AUTOMOBILE APPROACH

EXIT RAMP

SHOP

TICKET BOOTH

ENTRANCE

WILSHIRE BLVD.

Precautions

The Beverly Paramount Theatre. All theatrical functions germane to presentation of motion pictures admirably accommodated. W. L. Pereira, architect.

Theatre planners appear to have been guilty of three erroneous practices in developing their basic plans:

1. Subservience to custom. There are numerous examples of duplication in existing theatre forms which appear to indicate the acceptance without question of existing forms as good.

2. Misplaced emphasis in the drawing up of programs, generally to the neglect of theatrical requirements.

3. Adoption of partly thought-out schemes involving changing the shape of the theatre. Often such schemes have the merit of well-founded dissatisfaction with existing forms but lack sufficient consideration of the practical aspects of realization. A simplified statement of the theatrical functions sometimes is accepted without expanding those functions to include their practical ramifications. Schemes for the elimination of the proscenium opening are based on the premise that total uniform theatrical effect can be achieved by emphasizing architecturally a unity of performance and audience.

Actually there is not and cannot be a unity of audience and performance. There is a basic duality in the theatre experience. The performance acts; the audience reacts. Both the performance and the audience need the recognition of this duality for the achievement of total uniform theatrical effect. A member of the audience, when called upon to participate in a performance, becomes aware of his existence as an individual and loses his wished-for submersion in the reacting, responding audience-as-a-whole. Similarly, when performers approach close to the audience or mingle with it, the assumed identity of the dramatic character falls away, the theatrical illusion is destroyed and the theatre experience is vitiated.

The size of the house does not guarantee the size of the audience, even where there is a large potential audience and a good show. The house must be well appointed and this item must be figured into the building costs. Moreover, good appointments often pay for themselves more rapidly than almost any other feature in theatre construction. The theatre at Amherst College has almost doubled its audience since it started to use its new and well appointed house. This is not a question of capacity since productions still do not play as many performances as they might. A luxurious community theatre within commuting distance of Times Square enjoys steady patronage despite distinctly Grade-B performances. This is largely because the house is one of the most attractive and comfortable in the country.

Attractiveness

This book is written at a time when it is particularly important to study the economic aspects of any theatrical enterprise before undertaking a building to house it. There is increasing competition for the entertainment dollar and the leisure hour, notably in the fields of spectator sports and radio, and television entertainment. To compete, the theatre, any type of theatre, has to furnish a good show for the money. Building costs are high; every part of a projected theatre must withstand careful examination and merit inclusion in the building on the basis of effectiveness.

Economics

The threatened cancellation of the 1948-49 Metropolitan Opera season illustrates the plight of theatres whose production facilities are obsolete, and whose operation is inefficient. To build a theatre building which cannot pay its own way is almost certain to limit the number and scope of theatrical performances for which there is an audience.

The success of any theatre may be measured in dollars, or in terms of artistic achievement. The same conditions make for success however measured, and there are almost no valid exceptions. Financial and artistic success are basically interdependent. The importance of the economic criterion in commercial production need only be acknowledged. Less obvious is the necessity for an economically sound school, college or community theatre. To attempt to teach the theatre in a plant incapable of commercial standard production, or capable of professional quality only at such cost in labor as to make a commercial production impossible is very bad pedagogy. The inefficient school theatre must perforce put on a low grade performance, or expend an unjustified amount of effort and money to get a passable show. Neither alternative is educationally warranted.

Operating Economy

The rapidity with which money can be lost in the theatre is proverbial. Not even a hit playing to full houses is sure to be profitable. A famous Broadway producer was often one show behind his bills, despite his spectacular string of highly successful shows. The Winthrop Ames Gilbert and Sullivan revivals, conceded to be the finest productions those operettas had ever had, played to large houses for several seasons, yet are reported to have been something less than a financial success. David Belasco's production of Molnar's MIMA cost so much to produce and so much to operate that it was mathematically impossible at prevailing prices for it ever to pay out. At least one prominent community theatre can operate only because its angel underwrites the annual deficit. The high operating cost of plays more than any other single phenomenon accounts for the reduction in the number of legitimate houses in New York and the virtual disappearance of the road. Nothing any theatre planner can design or build into a theatre can stop a producer from putting on a show with a basically unsound budget. The most the planner can do is to make the theatre efficient in its operation. This in itself will help to reduce the red figure.

While operating costs do not vary from production to production in the house presenting motion pictures only, the total operating cost is the largest single expense item. In the case of the motion picture theatre more than any other performance type, the audience patronizes the comfortable, well-appointed, well-maintained house, and will often choose such a house rather than seek a preferred picture.

Audience

The one and only irreplaceable element in the theatre is the audience, which wants entertainment and will pay for it. The actor-audience relationship to be most effective demands a certain scale. A small house invites a patronizing attitude and is by that fact defeatist. It also fails to take in enough money to put on a good show. For a theatre to be architecturally and economically sound, the dimensions of the house must be established by the limits of seeing and hearing required for the largest type of production for which the house is planned.

A concomitant of this principle is that the income producing capacity of the house limits the size of the production it should be designed to accommodate. For example, a house which can gross no more than $30,000.00 a week need not have a stage capable of mounting THE ETERNAL ROAD. Conversely, a stage on which grand opera can be produced demands a house which can get the show off a $50,000 nut with money to spare. In this connection it must be remembered that a big show is a specialized show. Many big houses spend too much of their careers dark, and a dark house costs money.

It follows then that any theatre must be so planned as to be able to pay its way whether or not that is requisite in the type of operation immediately envisioned. To pay its way, the theatre must amortize building cost, must amortize potential decline in ground value or must pay ground rent. It must pay taxes, production costs, and operating expenses. To be successful it must earn a profit on capital invested. During non-commercial operation, the theatre is usually relieved of one or more of the cost items. It sometimes needs to provide only for building maintenance and replacement. It is usually built on tax exempt land, the cost of which is seldom charged to the theatre as such. A non-commercial theatre often has to pay its own operation cost. Gifts and popular subscription of capital funds may pay for land and building. In an education institution, maintenance and some operating costs may be charged against the teaching function which has income from tuitions and possibly endowment. Profits, if any, may usually be allocated to the improvement of the plant, contingent reserve or an eleemosynary use.

An interesting fable concerning audience choice is the story of a large theatre which was owned by a motion picture exhibiting organization, as were also a large number of neighborhood houses in the area. This theatre always made money but when it was operating the neighborhood houses of the same chain had poor audiences. It was discovered that the chain made more money with the large theatre closed, than with it open. This situation was in part attributable to high costs of operation as contrasted with the neighborhood houses.

Just as there is an upper limit to capacity (about 2,000) beyond which operating costs increase very rapidly, so there is a lower limit below which operating costs do not drop appreciably. It takes the same number of people back stage (house crew) and only a few more ushers to staff the Shubert Theatre (capacity about 1400) as the Little Theatre (capacity 299). The implications as to economical size are obvious.

Stage

Much has already been made of the relation of the production facilities to audience size. There are economic limits to stage size also. An inadequate stage makes productions so poor that you can't give seats away, or so costly that you can't sell them. Conversely a production requiring an extraordinarily large and highly mechanized stage cannot be operated or amortized in a house whose potential gross is low. *The economic limit for stage size is the stage which will accommodate as elaborate a show as the house capacity can support.*

It may appear that the economies of having production complete within the plant, freedom from certain costs and taxes, and the availability of cheap or free labor, favor non-commercial operation. This notion has led to the feeling that lower operating costs could compensate for structural deficiencies. However, this is not the case. Under commercial operation working capital is at least adequate or there is no operation. The commercial theatre must, by its nature, appeal to as large an audience as possible. The best available personnel for planning, publicizing, preparing, operating and performing in a theatre are available to commercial productions because high rates of pay are possible, and the result is that the commercial standard of performance is substantially above that which the non-commercial theatre can achieve except at rare intervals. Low operating costs do not offset this combination of advantages. The theatre which expects to attract an audience, whether it be a summer theatre, a theatre in the high school, or an opera house in the metropolis, must be planned to the specifications adequate for successful commercial operation if it is to fulfill its purpose.

Labor Costs

Where operation of the theatre is simple, easy, and efficient, precision of operation is assured and there is economy of both time and effort. One man with a winch can get counterweights up to the loading gallery better and faster than five men with block and tackle. One man at a switch can shift a full stage setting mounted on a motor-driven stage wagon. As has been previously indicated, inefficiency which will break a commercial production can stultify the same production in a school or community theatre.

Despite this apparently obvious situation, many high school theatres built at costs sufficient for theatres in which practically anything could be presented, contain stages unsuited for mounting the simplest of plays. One college has a theatre which has some architectural virtues but it is on the top floor of a building. Scenery can be gotten to the stage only by being carried on the roof of an elevator to the floor below the theatre, thence up a flight of stairs and thence through the house to the stage. Some theatres into which it may be easy to take the show impose difficulties on the process of setting up the show, including the erection of temporary flying systems inside a permanent plaster dome or rebuilding all scenic units to stand vertical on a sloped floor.

Theatres without stage crossovers, with remote dressing rooms, with inadequate lavatories and showers, without traps, without intercommunication systems, render operation difficult. The sum of these disadvantages is to make a theatre which nobody wants. Although somebody may have to put up with it, it will be abandoned as soon as anything better is available. It cannot compete with a theatre which does not cost so much to operate either in dollars or in volunteer man hours.

To make a theatre economically sound it is necessary to spend enough on the plant to insure minimum production and operation costs. This principle, although it seems obvious, is sometimes very difficult to demonstrate to people who build theatres for others to operate. The theatre is probably the only place where the folly of inefficiency is not only condoned, but vigorously defended. Such defense does not mitigate the folly.

Storage

Perhaps only less fortunate than the show which is too expensive and elaborate for the theatre, is the show which, playing in repertory, has to be taken out and stored between performances. This is one of the major operating expenses of the Metropolitan Opera where shows are frequently hauled back and forth between the warehouse and the theatre. Even where ground space is at a premium, this situation can be somewhat mitigated where building codes provide, as does the current New York code, for the storage of scenery below stage in fire proof vaults to which access can be had by stage elevator. In the college or community theatre where sets are stored to be re-used, if only as material in new sets, the cost of productions, labor excluded, can often be 30 to 50% less than the cost of the same productions identically designed and built for combination production. The storage function is requisite if the theatre is ever to do repertory economically, and the theatre in which storage facilities permit parts of one show to be re-used for another will always have an economic advantage over the theatre in which the production is destroyed at the end of the run.

Other Sources of Income

Chapter 5 sets up the requisites for multiple uses for the lounge. The bar in the Metropolitan Opera House and the Ballroom in the Philadelphia Academy of Music may well have other uses than those connected immediately with the performance. The Free Synagogue uses Carnegie Hall. Town Hall was used for motion pictures during its first years of operation for the months between concert sessions.

It is often feasible to originate radio and television programs in theatres. It is axiomatic that the more continuous the operation of a theatre, the more money it can take in; the more types of activity it can house or types of production it can mount, the more certain it is that its operation will be financially successful.

The construction of *new code* theatres both in and out of New York awaits the realization by entrepreneurs and investors of the profit possibilities in theatres built into other types of buildings. Present theatres bring in no income when dark, but carrying charges, taxes and certain wages continue. These fixed charges in new code theatres may be absorbed or shared by the steady-income portion of the building, reducing the burden of the dark periods, and consequently reducing the theatre rent. This rent reduction may be expected to render the new-code theatre in New York more attractive than old code houses, and, in the case of the road theatre, to increase the income of the touring show.

Where the theatre function does not have to amortize the cost of the building, admission prices to legitimate productions may be reduced to the point where they can compete with motion pictures.

Even where multiple functions are not possible within the same building, it is possible for a number of buildings to share the cost of services, such as steam, electric power, and air conditioning; all of which can economically be distributed within the radius of a block or two. Building for other occupancies over lobbies and auditoriums of two or more theatres in the same building, now projected, promises to result in substantial economies for the theatres.

Cost often determines whether or not a theatre is to be built. The first rough estimate for theatres in which any type of production can be mounted may be derived from:

1. Local building costs per cubic foot for construction using similar materials to those planned for the theatre.

2. Audience size. A minimum house capacity which may be expected to be reasonably safe for commercial legitimate operation is in the neighborhood of 1000. Minimum cubage for a thousand seats is approximately 250,000.

3. The stage for economical legitimate operation will have at least the cubage of the house.

If the theatre builder has not sufficient funds to build for the cubage thus derived, he had better not build at all but look for a structure with walls and a roof which may be rebuilt for theatrical purposes.

Theatre buildings often cost more than those responsible for their construction at first envision. When a limited budget will not provide all that is desired, compromises are sought. The nature of these compromises often determines the immediate usefulness and ultimate fate of the theatre. It is therefore necessary to plan at the outset what will be built as a minimum, and the order in which compromises will be made, if necessary.

It is obvious that the first requisite is a building which can be operated efficiently. Therefore shape and size of house and stage cannot be limited below what was planned as an optimum. A shop connected with and opening onto the stage may be left for future con-

Sharing Expenses

Costs

Priorities

struction, but the principal stage area cannot be cut down, because increasing such area after the theatre is once built is much more expensive than building correctly in the first place. It is probably better to build another theatre than to try to improve one which is basically wrong. Public rooms, offices, etc., at the back of the house (the foyer and lobby) can be added after the building has been in operation for some seasons. Theatre builders do not generally like to change the portion of the building containing the public rooms, since it is the section usually first seen from the outside and presents the theatre's façade. However, if a temporary lobby is used for functions of lobby, lounge, and foyer, the audience will be no worse off than it is in the average commercial legitimate house now. Adequate facilities can be built when funds become available. Deferment of construction of portions of the front of the house as here indicated will in no way interfere with the efficiency of production, but will interfere with the comfort of the audience until the audience is in the house.

Much stage equipment is portable and may be acquired as funds are available provided the essential structural provisions are made in the original construction. If an adequate trap room is built in the original instance, elevators can be installed at any time. If an adequate gridiron is constructed, counterweight and line sets can be added as necessary. If an adequate lighting control system is planned, conduit

Photo, C. G. Rosenberg.

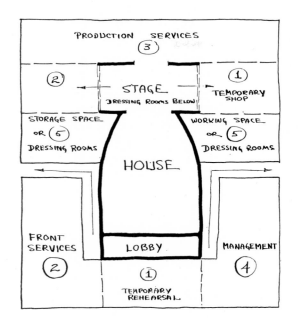

PRODUCTION SERVICES
(3)

(2)   STAGE   (1)
    DRESSING ROOMS BELOW   TEMPORARY
                            SHOP

STORAGE SPACE   WORKING SPACE
or (5)   or (5)
DRESSING ROOMS   DRESSING ROOMS

            HOUSE

FRONT
SERVICES   LOBBY   MANAGEMENT
(2)   (1)   (4)

            TEMPORARY
            REHEARSAL

Numerical order, based on importance of function, in which additions to the basic theatre block may be made.

and control room for it installed, lighting instruments, accessories and control units can be added as acquired. In fact, with the exception of the gridiron, the ventilation system and the seats, almost all items of theatre equipment can be added after the theatre is built. If a good theatre is to be achieved and funds do not permit its completion, it is a waste of the money to restrict the shape or size of house or stage. If these cannot be built to specifications which will make possible efficient operation and audience comfort, a theatre building project should not be undertaken.

This book has presented elements of good theatre planning, and has defended those elements on various grounds. It is perhaps not amiss to note that building a good theatre is smart economics. The Music Box in New York, one of the least inefficient and uncomfortable of existing legitimate houses, was, when it was built, so much better than the other houses in Longacre that it had its choice of shows and operated as one of the prize gold mines in that section for many years. It has seldom been dark. People associate its name with a good show.

Good theatres will compete successfully with inefficient ones. Current projects provide for the construction of numerous new theatres in New York within the next decade. This is a fortunate situation, for the economics of the existing structures are all against their survival for many seasons. Revival of the road is a logical sequel to the construction of new theatres which are attractive and comfortable for audiences, suitable to modern methods of play production, and, because of their inclusion in buildings for other uses, commercially profitable.

index